Ed Faulkner's Tennis

Ed Faulkner's

THE DIAL PRESS

NEW YORK 1970

HOW TO PLAY IT— —HOW TO TEACH IT

Edwin J. Faulkner
and
Frederick Weymuller

Preface by Arthur Ashe

Book Designed by George H. Buehler

Parts of this book first appeared in
World Tennis in slightly different form.

Library of Congress Catalog Card
Number: 70-76967

Printed in the United States of America

Fourth Printing, 1972

TABLE OF CONTENTS

Preface by Arthur Ashe ◆ 7

Co-Author's Note ◆ 9

Foreword ◆ 13

1 Beginning ◆ 19

2 Learning the Forehand ◆ 25

Beginner Drill 1: The Forehand ◆ 40

3 Teaching the Forehand ◆ 42

Teaching Hints 1: The Forehand ◆ 54

4 Forehand Trouble Spots ◆ 55

Forehand Trouble Spots (Chart) ◆ 84

5 Learning Control and Footwork on the Forehand ◆ 93

Beginner Drill 2: Control and Footwork ◆ 101

6 The Backhand ◆ 102

Beginner Drill 3: The Backhand ◆ 111

Beginner Drill 4: Switching Between Forehand and Backhand ◆ 112

Teaching Hints 2: The Backhand ◆ 113

7 Backhand Trouble Spots ◆ 114

Backhand Trouble Spots (Chart) ◆ 141

8 Rallying ◆ 146

9 The Serve ◆ 149

Beginner Drill 5: The Serve ◆ 168

Teaching Hints 3: The Serve ◆ 169

10 Service Trouble Spots ◆ 171

Service Trouble Spots (Chart) ◆ 198

11 The Volley ◆ 206

Beginner Drill 6: The Volley ◆ 218

Teaching Hints 4: The Volley ◆ 219

12 Volley Trouble Spots ◆ 220

Volley Trouble Spots (Chart) ◆ 227

13 Supplementary Strokes ◆ 230

Beginner Drill 7: The Lob ◆ 251

Lob Trouble Spots (Chart) ◆ 251

Beginner Drill 8: The Drop Shot ◆ 253

Drop Shot Trouble Spots (Chart) ◆ 253

Beginner Drill 9: The Overhead ◆ 254

Overhead Trouble Spots (Chart) ◆ 255

Beginner Drill 10: The Half Volley ◆ 256

Half-Volley Trouble Spots (Chart) ◆ 256

14 Tactics for Rallies ◆ 258

15 Tactics for Games, Sets, and Matches ◆ 269

16 Match-Play Strategy ◆ 274

17 Conclusion ◆ 278

Appendix ◆ 291

PREFACE

by Arthur Ashe

There is an old saying: "If at first you don't succeed, try following the directions." Learning tennis from scratch to the point where one becomes City Champion, State Champion, or Wimbledon Champion can be very frustrating. This book by Ed Faulkner and Fred Weymuller makes that road to the City Championship, even to Wimbledon, as simple and clear as possible. No detail is spared.

Ed Faulkner's Tennis stresses technique that lends itself to just about anybody's physical capabilities. It draws on years of observing and coaching great players, as well as players of all ages, and it is applicable whether you are short and stocky like Charles McKinley, tall and slender like Pancho Gonzales, or of medium build like Rodney Laver.

The emphasis is on individual progress at one's own pace, with progressively more difficult lessons presented in their proper order. Tennis, perhaps more than any other sport, requires attention to small details, especially in the formative stages of learning. If proper attention is not given to these details, further practice and play can actually impede one's progress.

Not everyone who wants to learn to play can avail himself of a qualified teaching professional. Realizing this, the authors have designed the book to take full advantage of a kind of "buddy system." By going along with him from lesson to lesson, the pupil-reader's wife, brother, mother, anyone, can serve as a critic; moreover, two beginners can teach each other, on their own or as a follow-up to group instruction where time and space are at a premium and individual attention is not possible.

The psychological requirements of developing a winning attitude are broad and have much to do with a player's approach to life. It is my firm belief that 70 percent of all tennis matches are won or lost before the players walk onto the court! On a world tour with the same group of, say, seventy-five players, I would predict that no more than eight or ten of those players would win *any* of the tournaments. If he wants to be one of those eight or ten players, or one of a corresponding group at a lower level of play, the reader must develop a sound winning attitude. To put it another way, he must develop the outlook of "playing to win" rather than "playing not to lose." *Ed Faulkner's Tennis,* with its attention to small details, goes a long way to developing such an attitude. The content of each lesson presents a new challenge; the challenges grow progressively more difficult with each stroke and as such add immensely to the player's confidence.

Learning to play tennis should also be pleasurable, as it will be with the successful completion of each step of this book. A sense of achievement and progress grows as each successive lesson is mastered, up to the ultimate pleasure of winning one's first real tennis match. At that moment, one's delight is usually cause for celebration.

A final word on strokes. The authors are aware that to make a complete tennis player, the complete assortment of strokes must be presented. The half-volley and the drop volley, to use two examples, can be vital weapons in a player's arsenal, and both are presented here, along with all the others, in the simplest possible terms.

Whether you are a teacher, tennis professional, beginner, advanced student, weekend player, or club player, there is something of value for you in this book.

CO-AUTHOR'S NOTE

The methods described in this book have grown out of the more than fifty-five years of Ed Faulkner's tennis-teaching experience. Ed's career began formally in 1915 when he took his first job as a tennis professional at Lake Placid, N. Y., as a fifteen-year-old (he had decided to become a tennis teacher when he was seven). He continued to take tennis jobs during the summer—with part of one summer off to play baseball in the International League as first-baseman with the Rochester ball club—through high school and college. He deliberately sought out a college curriculum that would meet his needs as potential full-time tennis teacher and for two years attended Springfield College in Massachusetts, famed for its physical education courses. He went on to Cornell University as a special student to have at least some exposure to the liberal arts.

After a short period of holding lesser jobs, he became in 1921 the professional of the Germantown Cricket Club, then the scene of many Davis Cup Challenge Rounds and the home club of all-time great, William T. "Big Bill" Tilden. These two studied tennis in all its aspects and learned from each other. In 1925 and 1926 Ed coached the U.S. Davis Cup team, and in 1927 the triumphant French Davis Cup team known as the Four Musketeers. He again coached the U.S. team in 1932 and in 1964, the latter year at the request of his good friend and pupil Vic Seixas.

In 1929 Ed started his illustrious career as the tennis coach at Swarthmore, a small, coeducational Quaker college in a pleasant Philadelphia suburb. Swarthmore does not seek out tennis players, nor any other kind of athlete. Since Ed's interest has always been in *all* tennis players, not only the proficient, students in Swarthmore's compulsory physical education classes and junior varsity players have found themselves getting as much attention as varsity players—more if they showed real interest and desire. Nevertheless, in his forty years there, Ed's teams have compiled a record of 370 wins vs. 127 losses, leading to his election as one of the first four tennis coaches in the Helms Foundation Hall of Fame for outstanding college coaches. Swarthmore has thought enough of him to make him a full professor, a distinction held by few coaches in liberal arts colleges not offering a degree in physical education.

For twenty-three of his Swarthmore summers Ed was the professional at the Inn's Tennis Club in Buck Hill Falls, Pa. There, in 1940, I took my first tennis lesson from him, at the age of eleven. I was a volunteer staff member three years later, and then a paid staffer for subsequent summers through college and graduate school. In 1956, while I was a reporter for the *Wall Street Journal,* Ed and I collaborated on the forerunner of this book, a series of articles which appeared in *World Tennis* in 1956 and 1957 under the title "Teaching the Beginner." After eleven years as a financial writer, I made my hobby my vocation and became the tennis and squash professional at the Heights Casino. For the past four summers Ed and I have been at the Chase Tennis Center in Westtown, Pennsylvania, where we worked at putting this book together.

Ed Faulkner's method of teaching tennis has evolved from careful observation of the best players. In addition to the Davis Cup teams he has coached, Ed has worked individually with many of the sport's finest. Notable among them are Vic Seixas, who took his first lessons from Ed; Pancho Segura, whose backhand Ed helped, plugging a weakness in a game that became one of the finest; and Charles Pasarell, whose strategy and tactics Ed helped develop.

There are comparatively few players whose game conforms in all details—even the good ones have their idiosyncrasies. One of Ed's quests has been to separate these idiosyncrasies from the points that really matter, such as the pattern of swing, the way the player positions himself for the ball, and his powers of concentration. Though Ed's method is elaborate, detailed and well dovetailed, he has always, till now, carried it around in his head and used whatever part of it seemed most applicable at a given moment.

One of his greatest fortes in teaching has been his ability to analyze a person's strokes. In this book he has set down the major problems that occur in all facets of the game, showing how to analyze these problems and what to tell a player to enable him to correct them.

In writing a book of this sort, the interdependence of the people involved is staggering. At every critical juncture someone came along with the needed advice or help. Eve Kraft of the Princeton Community Tennis Program, wanting a longer text than our brief brochure based on our *World Tennis* articles, bumped our heads together to get us going. John Fry of *Ski Magazine* put us in touch with The Dial Press, whose Donald Hutter and Polly Packard deserve great thanks. Neil Chase of Chase Tennis Center supported us every step of the way, taking pictures, lending us equipment and space for our work, inspiring the campers to help us as film subjects and in many other ways. Ronald Woods, a Chase counsellor and tennis coach at West Chester State College, helped with proofreading. Donald H. Byerly of the Westtown School gave photographic aid and advice. Thanks must be given to Robert T. H. Davidson for advice on making stills from movies, which cut our production costs considerably. Thomas Buechner III, Donald Congdon, Mrs. Thomas Damon, John Evans, Clayton Price, and Harold McDonald, and many other members of the Heights Casino in Brooklyn, gave aid and counsel at important times. Richard Kaiser is responsible for the diagrams. Thanks go to Bruce Daniels for modeling all photo sequences showing the correct way to hit each of the strokes, to George Duncan for feeding balls to be properly hit, and to Kim Massie for photographing them. But special acknowledgment must be made to the person who kept insisting on knowing when each successive step was going to be completed—Josephine Faulkner.

Fred Weymuller

FOREWORD

This is a book about how one learns tennis. It is written for everyone who has a vital part in the process, whether he is a learner or a teacher. Many books have dealt with learning tennis, and a few with teaching it; this book does both.

From this book, if you apply yourself, you can teach yourself tennis even though you have never played before. If you are more experienced, you may be able to clear up a difficulty that has plagued your game for years. This is a book that can be used by two people working as a team, even though they differ in age, coordination, or strength. Thus, father and son, mother and daughter, husband and wife, or any combination of siblings can learn the game together.

This is also a book for the teacher—the professional, the salaried coach, the volunteer. Its approach is intended to give you the analytical eye you must develop if you are going to make expert judgment on what is wrong with a stroke and how to improve it. To this end we have made liberal use of still-picture sequences taken from movie films. The first series shows the pupil making a stroking error; the second shows the pupil hitting the ball with that error eliminated, or much improved. The means of doing these before-and-after sequences have been available for many years, but no tennis book known to us (and few sports books) has used this method.

The problems illustrated in the film sequences were real ones confronting real campers at the Chase Tennis Center in Westtown, Pennsylvania, or at the Heights Casino, Brooklyn, New York. In each case, Ed Faulkner or Fred Weymuller—or both —worked with the pupil. In some cases, the problem was cleared up right away. In others, the "after" filming was not done until several weeks of hard, daily practice had been put in. The problems selected are those which a careful study of the movie films of the entire camp showed to be the most common. As a player, you will have to wrestle with some of these problems at the closest possible range. If you are a teacher, you will have to wrestle with all of them at one time or another.

For the most part, this book will be addressed directly to the individual who is teaching himself to play tennis. All the initial presentations of the various strokes will be addressed to him. Discussions of various problems will refer to the "player" rather than "you," since such problems will involve teachers as well. Teaching oneself tennis is hardly the easiest way to proceed, though it is the least expensive. Its greatest reward is the self-confidence it engenders if your results are good. An easier, more sociable way is to work with a relative or friend who is also eager to learn. You can take turns tossing or hitting balls to each other, checking up on one another to be sure you are following instructions.

A very important way to use this book, particularly if you run into problems, is to have films taken of your strokes. Do it on 8mm or Super 8 rather than 16mm (unless you already have a movie editor for 16mm) so that you can then examine the film on a hand-cranked viewer rather than on a projector. When filming, have your camera set to take its maximum number of frames per second. Buy or borrow a movie editor on which you can view your films. By using a movie editor or even less expensive viewer, you can advance the film at any speed you want. You can stop and look at a single frame, or run a particular sequence over and over. As you read the sections of this book that describe the things that can go wrong with a player's strokes, you will see that some of them will be picked up only by a second person—or a movie camera. Your job will be to have the films taken and then compare them with the discussion and the picture sequences in this book, which will call attention to those things on which the self-teacher must concentrate.

You will want to take films of your play from time to time to see how you are progressing. If you are an experienced player, the most important films you take

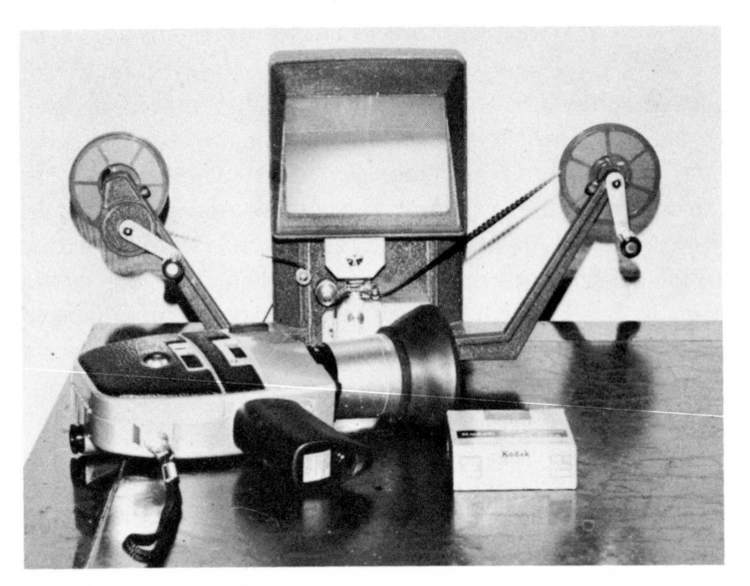

PLATE 1

FILM ANALYSIS TOOLS: *Movie camera, film editor, film cartridge.*

will be the first ones. You will need both a ball-tosser and a cameraman. The person tossing balls can stand on either side of the net, midway between the sidelines and about six feet back from the net. If he prefers, and is really accurate, he may hit the balls to you. The cameraman should stand on your side of the net, in the forecourt, and fairly close to the net. (Position will depend in part on the zoom capacity of the camera—get as close up as you safely can to take in the player and all his racket movement.) While taking pictures of the forehand and the serve, the camera should be on that side of the court. It should be moved to the right to take pictures of the backhand. (See diagram, p. 20.)

The cameraman should take three forehands, three backhands, three switches between forehand and backhand, and four serves. You will note we said "three switches between forehand and backhand." By this we mean the tosser should feed you a forehand and then, in the same amount of time it would take an opponent to return that shot, feed you another ball to the backhand. The cameraman should keep the camera running on you throughout the stroke sequence, as on pages 138 and 139.

For the experienced player who is using this book to diagnose errors and improve his strokes, this particular sequence should be examined first. It may bring to light the problem of whether you use the same face of the racket for both forehand and backhand. This issue is discussed from the player's point of view on page 137, and from the teacher's on page 46. Look at both treatments. If you do not have this particular problem, then look over the rest of your film and read carefully in the various sections on stroking "trouble spots."

This book is also for the coach or professional, and several chapters and sections are directed to him. While our descriptions of the basic strokes and much of the balance of this book are addressed to the player, the teacher should be prepared to adapt this material to his own uses.

We are assuming that the principal reader of this book is an outright beginner. If you are an experienced player with a specific stroking problem, we suggest that you look through the section on "trouble spots" concerning the particular stroke that is bothering you. Read it, have films taken, compare them with the photographs in the book, and follow the recommended remedies.

The main sections of this book are the four basic strokes, supplementary strokes, tactics, and strategy. Throughout the book we will explain how something is done, how to teach it to yourself or someone else, and finally, how to cope with the difficulties likely to arise. In all cases we will give reasons for the grips, swings, and teaching methods we advocate.

Before we begin, we must explain a convention we will follow in this book to simplify instructions: All directions are given on the assumption that the player is a right-handed male. To the left-handers and the girls—and particularly to the left-handed girls—we convey our apologies, and our hope that you will not have too much difficulty in translating as you read along.

Ed Faulkner's Tennis

1
Beginning

If you are a complete beginner, you need first a good, general idea of how tennis is played. You have undoubtedly seen the game, perhaps even seen it played well. Occasionally, you may have seen tournament matches on television. The first thing you must realize (and most people instinctively grasp it) is that a player is trying to hit the ball over the net and into the court in such a way that his opponent cannot return it.

Everything about the game flows from this one central idea. Tennis is a civilized form of hand-to-hand combat. It is a battle of coordination and strength and endurance. In these respects it is similar to a boxing match, except that ability to withstand physical battering is a small factor. It is a battle of will and strategy. In these respects it is similar to a chess match, except that it requires physical as well as mental effort.

The Game of Tennis

First, you should purchase a copy of the rules and read them over from beginning to end; then reread them at least twice during your first year of tennis and annually thereafter.

The Tennis Court

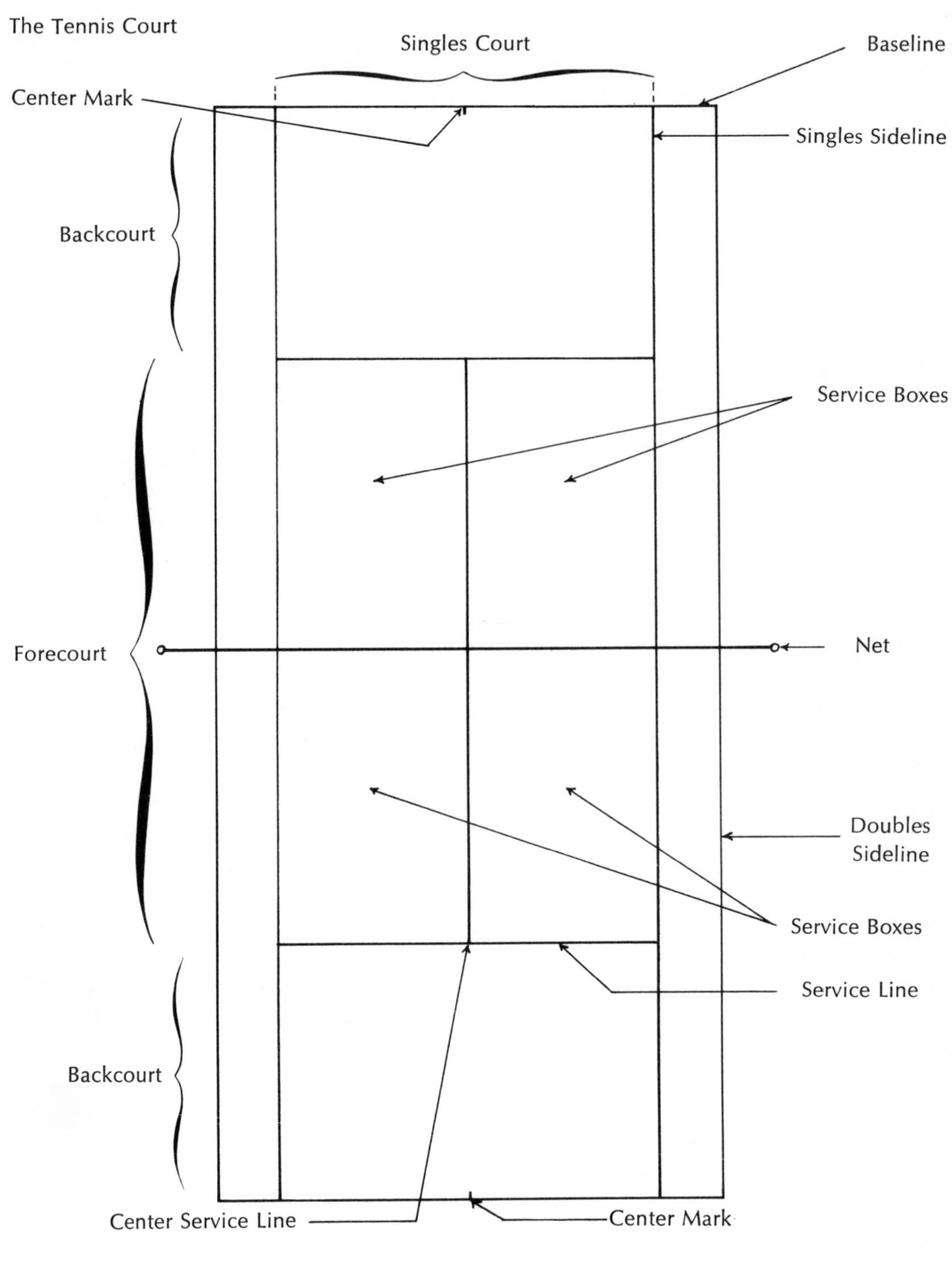

DIAGRAM 1

The tennis yearbook, containing much else of interest as well as rules, is obtainable through the U.S. Lawn Tennis Association, 51 East 42nd St., New York, New York 10017. Membership in the USLTA—highly recommended—brings a discount price for the yearbook.

Tennis matches are either singles (two players) or doubles (four players). The court on which a match is played is a rectangle, 78 feet by 36 feet for doubles and 78 × 27 for singles. It is divided in half by a net along its short axis. The net, strung between two metal posts, is 3 feet high at the center and 3½ feet at the net posts, which are 3 feet outside the sidelines. The lines denoting the end of each court are called the baselines, connected to each other by a pair of sidelines, the inner one for singles, the outer one for doubles. The narrow strips, 4½ feet wide, between each pair of sidelines are called the alleys. Parallel to the net and 21 feet on each side of it are the service lines. Each of these is bisected by a line that runs under the net and perpendicular to it, thus dividing each forward part of the court or forecourt, into two boxes. It is into these boxes that the server—the person putting the ball into play—must serve alternately. The remainder of each court, the area from the service line to the baseline, is called the backcourt. A line called the center mark, a few inches long, divides each baseline. The server must stand to the right of it if he is serving into the left-hand service box. He stands to the left if serving to the right-hand service box.

A match is usually the best two out of three sets, that is, the first player or doubles team to win two sets wins the match. If one player wins one set and the other player wins the second set, then a third set must be played to determine the winner of the match. Women's matches are always the best two out of three sets, but men's matches in topflight tournament play often require three out of five sets to win.

The first player to win six games wins a set, unless the score is tied at five games each, in which case the player must win by a two-game margin. Thus a set may be 7-5, 8-6, 9-7, and so on (and we really mean "and so on," since some sets have recorded as high as 49-47). Normally, six games is sufficient and the score can be 6-0, 6-1, 6-2, 6-3, or 6-4. A set, thus, is a series of games wherein one player has won at least six and in any case has won two more than his opponent.

The first player to win four exchanges of shots wins a game, unless the score is tied at three exchanges each, in which case he must win by a margin of two exchanges. It may seem an oddity of the game that rather than getting one point for winning an exchange, your score rises in multiples of five. For winning the first point you get 15; for another point, 30; at your third point, it goes up to 40; the fourth exchange that you win (provided your opponent has less than 40), is simply called "game" and isn't even given a numerical value. If you each have 40, the score is called "deuce," because you must get two points in a row to win (and deuce, you may remember from card games, means two). The first point after deuce is called "advantage" and a player will simply call out "my advantage" or "your advantage," or some such abbreviated version as "my ad" or "your ad," or "ad in" and "ad out." If the advantage holder wins the next point, he wins the game. If he loses it, the score goes back to deuce—and of course the score can seesaw between deuce and advantage indefinitely.

The reason high numbers are used in scoring a game is to distinguish it from the score of the set, that is, the number of games each player has.

When announcing the score in a game, the server's score is always given first, even if his score is lower than his opponent's. Thus, if the server has one point and his opponent has three, the score is 15-40. If a player has no points (or games) at all, his score is said to be "love." This seems to distress a lot of people, but as it is a part of the history of racket games and still the standard English-language term, you might as well use it if you expect to be understood by people who play tennis. According to the *Oxford English Dictionary,* its origin, like that of deuce, is in gambling, especially in cards, as in: "Shall we play for love or money?" It is interesting that no one has been able to come up with a really adequate substitute word of one syllable that can be clearly heard from one end of a court to the other. "Zero," "nothing," "naught," "null," "oh," and so forth either take too long to say or just don't register clearly.

To start a match it is customary first to warm up, by exchanging shots with your opponent from the rear of the court; then with first one and then the other player at the net (where they should practice overhead shots as well as volleys); and then by each player practicing serves. When both players feel ready, one of them spins his racket and lets it fall so that the trimming at the top or bottom of his strings shows either its rough or smooth side. At it is spun, the other player calls out "rough" or "smooth." The winner of the toss may elect either to serve or receive, or to choose which end of the court he wishes to start on. He may have only one of these choices —the opponent gets the other—but he may, instead, require his opponent to make the choice first.

To start play, the server stands behind the baseline to the right of the center mark and serves into the service box diagonally opposite. He is allowed two attempts to do this, but if he misses both he loses the point. If his serve is in (goes into the correct box), his opponent must return it over the net and anywhere in the server's half of the court, that is, within the area bounded by the singles sidelines and the baseline. The players exchange shots in this manner until one of them can't return the ball. The one who hits the last good shot wins the point.

Play continues until either the server or his opponent has won enough points to end the first game. The players then change courts with each other, proceeding to do so after every other game, or when the score in the set adds up to an odd number, as in 1-0, 2-5, 7-6, etc. This procedure, changing on the odd game, is used to prevent one player from having to look into the sun or hit into the wind throughout a match, should such conditions prevail.

If you want to win points you have to be able to hit the ball accurately, be able to hit it both hard and soft, and manage to keep returning it until the other fellow makes a mistake. An opponent can be overpowered, outwitted, or worn down —or any combination of the three. Your game should have as much power, quick-wittedness, and endurance as you can possibly manage.

Equipment and Practice

In choosing a racket it is vital that any person whose hand and arm are not strong (this could apply to any youngster, most grown women, and men who are out of practice) has a racket that is not too heavy. In the case of young children it should also be sufficiently small. Many stroking problems have their start because the player's first racket was too heavy. In general, most women and girls, and most boys aged twelve through sixteen, should be using a racket with a handle that is $4\frac{1}{2}$ inches around, weighing about 13 to $13\frac{1}{2}$ ounces. Grown women who are quite small should use a full-length racket but with a $4\frac{3}{8}$-inch handle. Smaller boys and girls should use a racket scaled down in length as well as in weight and handle size. With a very small child, the standard junior racket simply is not small enough. Remove the leather grip, cut off one inch, sand down the wood, and replace the leather. A few women, some older boys, and most grown men will use a racket with a $4\frac{5}{8}$-inch handle weighing $13\frac{1}{2}$ to 14 ounces. Larger, stronger men will use a $4\frac{3}{4}$-inch or even larger handle, and the weight will get up around $14\frac{1}{4}$ or $14\frac{1}{2}$ ounces. Few players, if any, use larger rackets than that nowadays.

It is not too vital at first that the quality of the racket be unusually high, as long as the weight and handle size are correct. Nylon strings will do. Later on, good quality and gut strings will be important.

The next step is to get a minimum of a dozen balls to practice with. Used balls, provided they still have some life in them, are perfectly acceptable. If you push your thumb into a ball and it resists firmly, it still has adequate spring, but it should also have some nap on its cover.

Finally, you need a place to play. A tennis court? Yes, if it's handy, but it is far from being an absolute necessity until you've learned the basic strokes and are ready to play. A playground or a gymnasium will do or, for that matter, any enclosed space where you don't have to worry about damaging the fixtures. If you're working alone, you will need a practice wall to hit against, or a rebound net, or at the very least a curtain or fence.

We would also like to make two suggestions about practice. First, it is better to practice often for short periods than occasionally for long ones. You'll find many basics of tennis to work on in the next few pages which do not require a trip to the courts or practice area. They can be done at home. Do them for awhile, go on to something else, and then come back to them—repeatedly. The other suggestion is an extension of the first: If you do not immediately succeed in accomplishing what you set out to do, go on to something else; then come back to the task you got blocked on, and keep coming back. Have confidence that you will get it, even if at first it seems not only difficult but impossible. Keep in mind the fact that plenty of people with serious handicaps have learned how to play an enjoyable game of tennis.

2
Learning the Forehand

The easiest stroke with which to begin learning tennis is the forehand. Any stroke that you use to play a ball on your right-hand side is a forehand. If you have to reach across your body to play a ball that is on your left side, that stroke is a backhand.

The Forehand Grip

The first matter to be settled is your grip. To begin, take the throat of the racket in your left hand, holding it so that the racket face is perpendicular to the ground. Now look carefully at the handle: It is an eight-sided solid. The flat plane on the top we will simply call the top. The slanted plane to its right is the right bevel, and that to its left, naturally, the left bevel. To the right of the right bevel is the right vertical panel. To the left of the left bevel is the left vertical panel. The others, which are less important, are the right under bevel, the left under bevel, and the bottom of the handle. These terms apply whether you are talking about forehands or backhands.

In finding a grip the most important part of your hand to position correctly is the heel, by which we mean the lower left hand corner of your hand (see picture). For the forehand, place the heel of your right hand on the right bevel (exactly on it) and your thumb on the left vertical panel. Close your fingers around the handle,

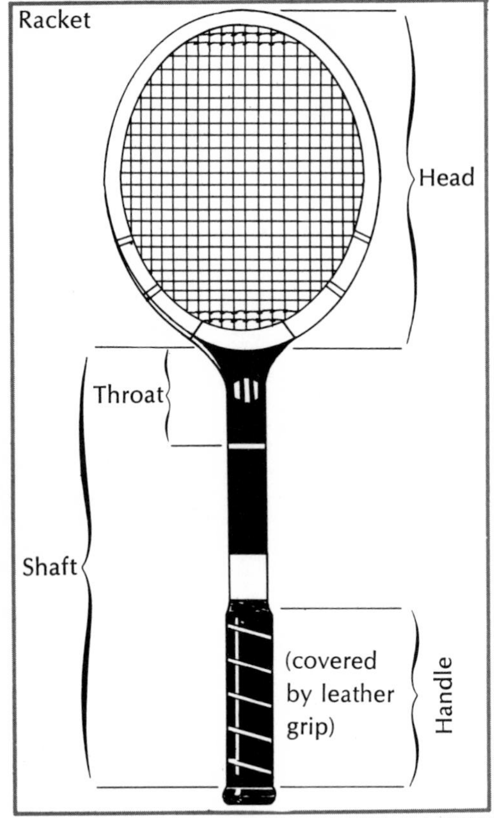

DIAGRAM 2 **PARTS OF THE RACKET**

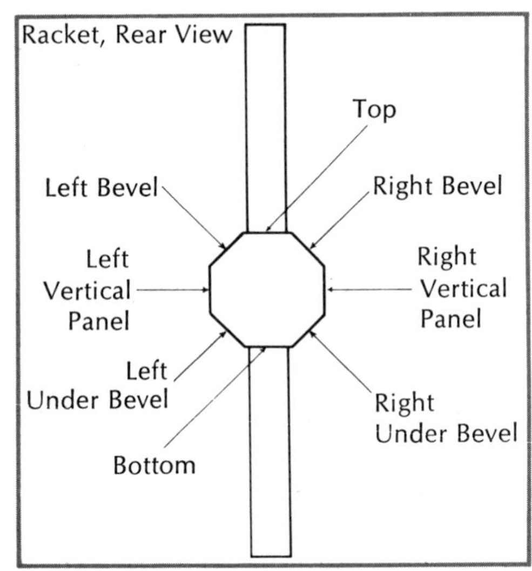

DIAGRAM 3 *Planes of the handle seen from butt of racket.*

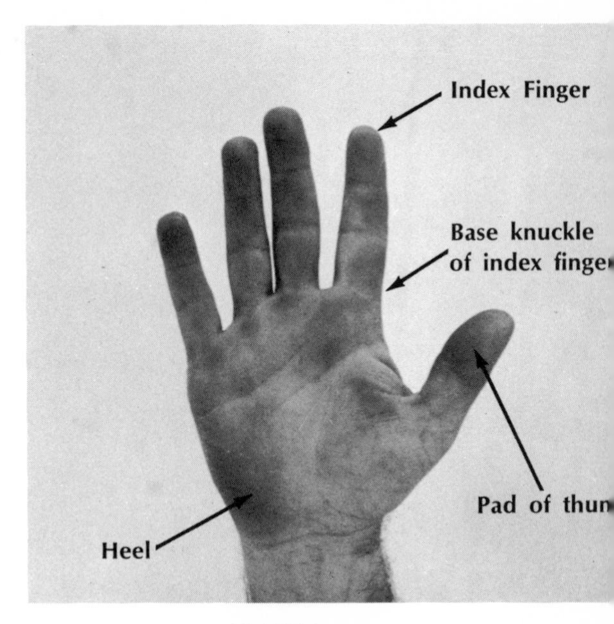

PLATE 2

PARTS OF THE HAND *which must be placed correctly on the handle to arrive at correct grips.*

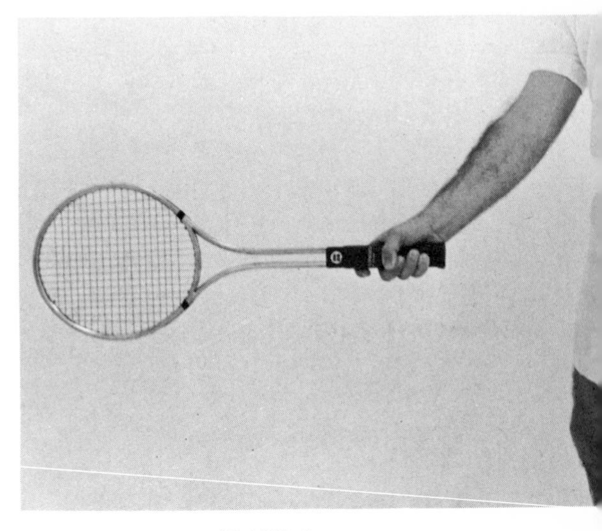

PLATE 3

EASTERN FOREHAND GRIP *showing heel on right bevel, thumb on left vertical panel.*

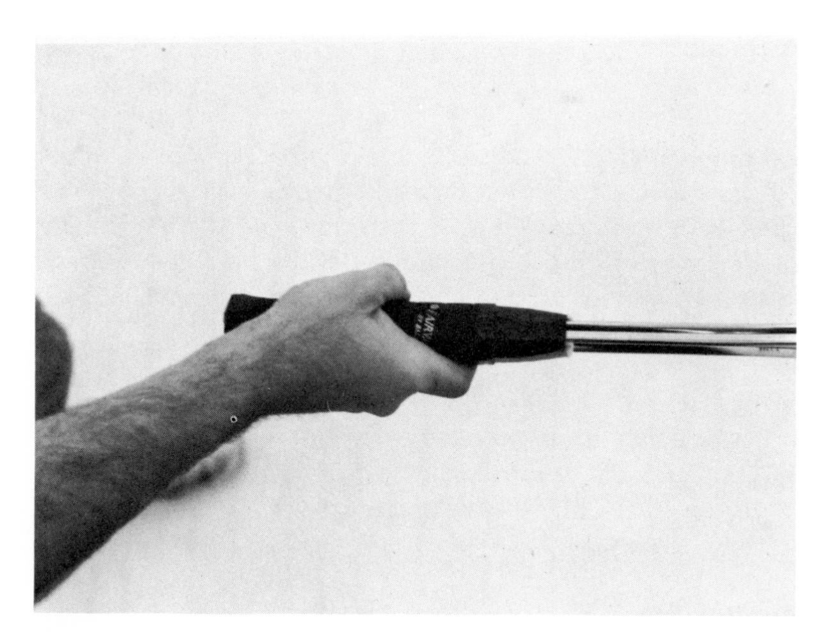

PLATE 4

TOP VIEW *of Eastern forehand grip.*

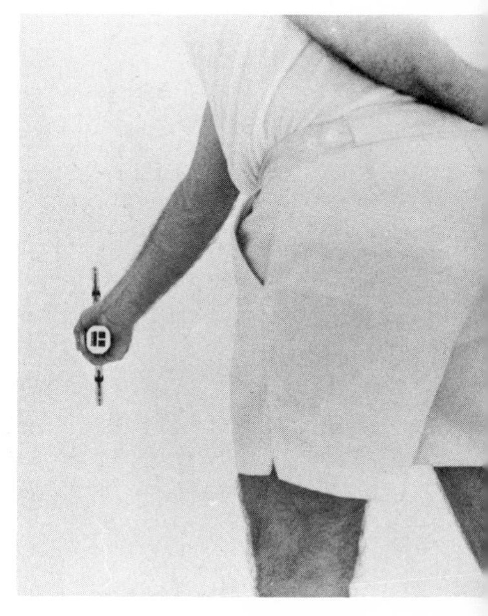

PLATE 5

REAR VIEW *of Eastern forehand grip.*

spreading the index finger slightly up from the others beyond the thumb. The inside base knuckle of your index finger should be on the right vertical panel, close to the edge it shares with the right bevel. This is the Eastern forehand grip.

You will find that this grip will be just right for a ball that bounces around waist high, and that it will adapt easily to lower or higher balls. It got its name because the clay courts that are common in the Eastern part of the United States produce that type of bounce. There are two other grips named after regions, the Continental and the Western.

The Continental, which requires the heel of the hand to be on top of the handle, tilts the racket face back. It is good for handling low balls, all right for waist-high ones, but very weak for high-bouncing balls. It got its name from the continent of Europe, specifically France, where the soft dirt courts produce a low bounce.

The Western, which requires the heel of the hand to be on the right vertical panel or even the right under bevel, tilts the racket face forward. This gives strength on high-bouncing balls but not on low ones. Its name originated on the hard cement courts of California.

To be one hundred per cent sure you can find your grip, take a piece of colored tape (a letter "F" for forehand stamped out on a plastic labeler is a good trick) and stick it on the right bevel. Put it above the grip so that your hand will not cover it, but where it will remind you on which plane you should put the heel of your hand. See the pictures and be sure you know exactly where we mean and which part of your hand we term the heel.

Practice locating this grip until you can do it with your eyes closed, for you won't be able to check it while you're playing. Keep the tape on the handle until you have learned the backhand grip and can make the change from forehand to backhand, and back, without looking. That will be some time off.

The Forehand Waiting Position

After the grip comes the correct waiting position, that is, the way you should be standing as the ball starts toward you. It is very important to get the waiting position right in all its details since good habits established early can make the rest of the job much easier. Spread your feet comfortably apart, about the width of your shoulders, with your knees slightly bent and your heels just off the ground. Your right hand

PLATE 6

WAITING POSITION: *Feet spread, weight forward, knees slightly bent, racket head opposite left shoulder, left hand at throat of racket.*

holds the racket with the Eastern forehand grip and your left hand cradles the throat of the racket, taking care to see that the racket face is perpendicular. The right hand is opposite the middle of the body a little above waist height, with the wrist bent back just slightly. The left hand is a few inches higher and extended about a forearm's length out from the body. The result is that the racket head is about opposite your left shoulder.

Try to be alert and attentive without feeling strained. Perhaps the two most important details are keeping the heels slightly off the ground and the wrist slightly laid back. With the first, you'll get a faster start and a cleaner pivot; with the second, you'll have the right wrist position from the beginning and not need to adjust it during the swing.

Furthermore, with the racket head at shoulder height, it is in an ideal position to start its backswing for a waist-high ball. The ideal swing is continuous, with the backswing at shoulder height and the forward swing at waist height, for a waist-high ball. Naturally, for a ball that is above or below waist height, backswing and forward swing should be lowered or raised accordingly, though the distance between them should be kept constant.

Also important is the position of the racket head opposite the left shoulder (instead of the middle of the body, as one might think), for it gives you a slight head start toward the backhand, which has to be met earlier than the forehand.

Before you read ahead to find out about the forehand swing, practice the waiting position and the grip. Check over all the details: feet spread, weight forward, heels just off the ground, knees slightly bent, forehand grip correct, wrist slightly laid back, left hand at the throat of the racket, racket head opposite your left shoulder. If someone is working with you, have him check you on these points. Run over them enough times so you can assume the correct position without thinking about it.

The Forehand Swing

The elements of any tennis stroke include: the waiting position, the grip, the use of the left hand, the pattern of the swing (backswing, swing, follow-through), the angle of the racket face (particularly as influenced by elbow and wrist), the use of the feet, and the transfer of weight. The forehand (and for that matter, the backhand) can be learned in two stages: the footwork and the swing. It is our experience that it is easier to get the footwork right first and then learn the swing. Trying to learn both at the same time is extremely difficult, since it is very hard to correct a footwork and a

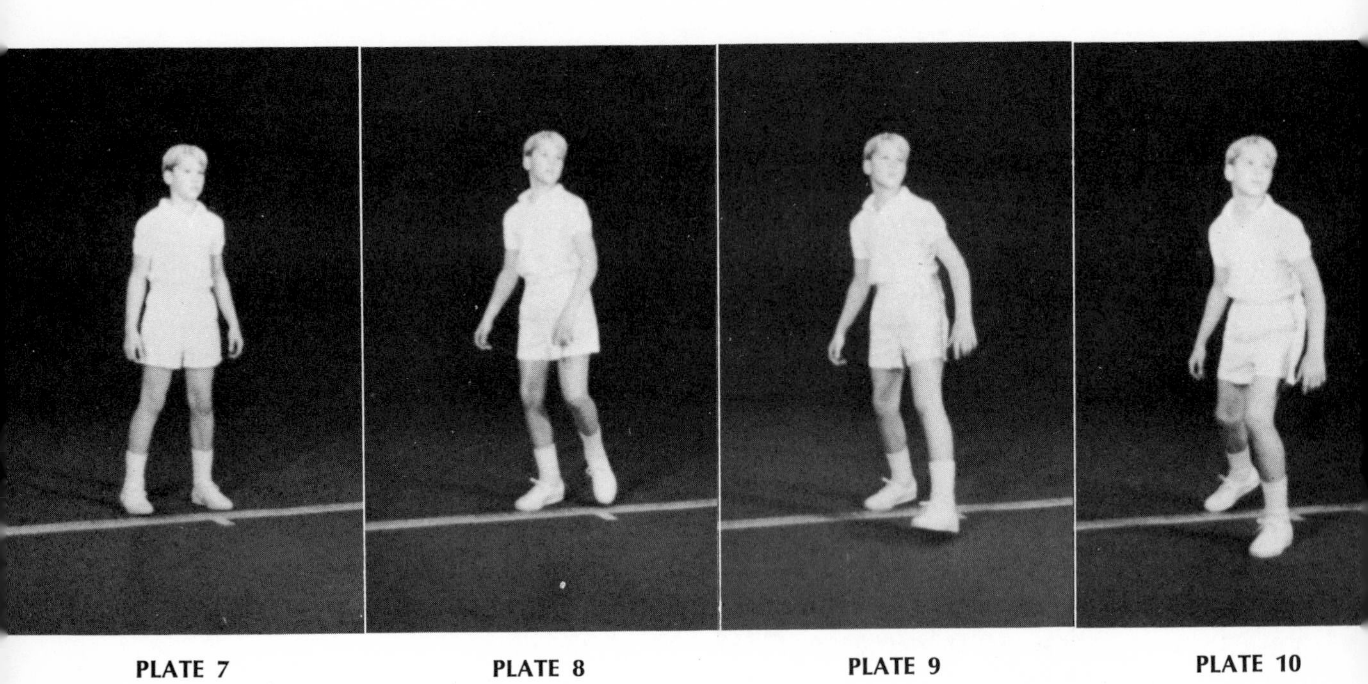

PLATE 7 **PLATE 8** **PLATE 9** **PLATE 10**

PIVOT AND STEP *should be learned first; swing can then be timed to steps with comparative ease.*

PLATE 11 **PLATE 12** **PLATE 13** **PLATE 14**

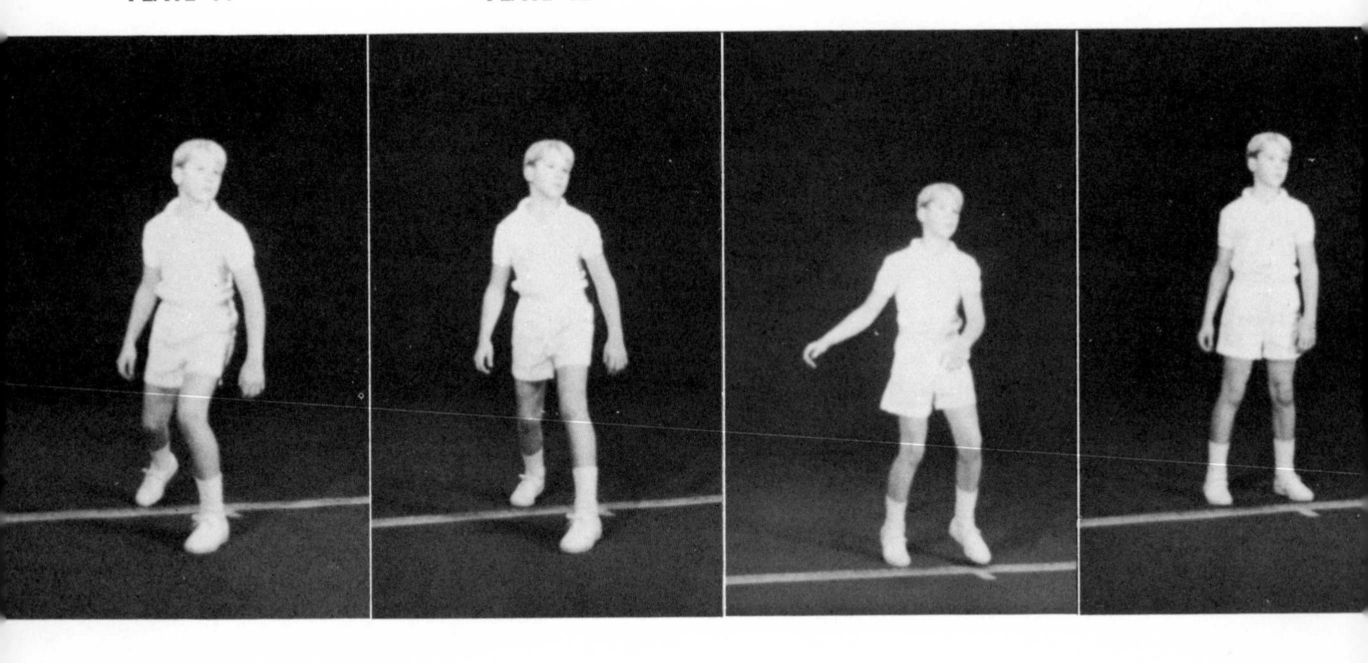

swinging error at the same time, and errors have a way of cropping up in both departments simultaneously.

It is very important to work on the footwork long enough and repeatedly enough to be sure you have it right before moving on to the swing. Take the waiting position (remember, your heels are off the ground), pivot clockwise on the ball of your right foot, and step toward the net with your left foot. Your left foot should be set down at an angle of 45° and about on a line with your right foot. This stance will place you squarely sideways to the net. There are two very common errors to be avoided here: to step too far toward the right with your left foot, and to set it down parallel to the net. Both of these misdeeds make it difficult to transfer your weight forward into the ball. With the left foot angled at 45° it will be possible to send your weight forward so that the left knee is out over the left foot.

Now, practice the pivot and step with the left foot, transfer your weight forward as if you were swinging, and then bring the left foot back to starting position. Try it with your eyes closed. Do it again and again till it's comfortable and natural.

Now you are ready to learn the swing. As the ball comes across the net toward you, start to turn your shoulders to the right. As you do so, your arms naturally turn with you and the backswing is underway. By now, your left hand can start guiding the racket farther back, leaving your right hand to take over by itself once the racket is opposite the right shoulder. On back it goes, still at shoulder height, until it reaches the full extent of the backswing. It now descends to waist height and as it starts forward, you move your left foot over so that it is ahead of the right. Your body weight is still on your right foot for the moment, but as the racket picks up speed in its path toward the ball, your weight is transferred from the back foot to the forward foot.

To hit the ball straight ahead, meet it at waist height opposite your left foot (not opposite the middle of your body since the weight is being transferred past that point). At the moment of contact with the ball, the racket, if viewed from directly overhead, should be exactly parallel to the net with its face absolutely flat (neither opened nor closed). The racket then follows through on the level of the ball until it comes up naturally because of the attachment of the arm to the shoulder. This upward motion, some of which is made while the racket is still in contact with the ball, imparts topspin, helping to keep it in the court. The finish is about head-high or higher, on waist-high bounces.

A word must be said about the timing of the motion. The turn of the shoulders and the backswing begin as soon as the ball crosses the net, proceeding as quickly or as slowly as the speed of the ball dictates.

As noted earlier, this swing is continuous because the racket goes back at shoulder height and keeps on moving as it comes down to waist height and starts its motion forward. A straight backswing, on the other hand, which comes to a stop at the back of the swing, may cause two undesirable results: The wrist often bends too far back, causing loss of control of the racket face; and, the racket may stop and have to be started again, sacrificing accumulated momentum. With a continuous swing there is gradual acceleration. The swing is at its fastest just as contact is made so that you experience the very brief but perceptible feeling of having the ball squash into the center of the racket and spring out. You should feel as though you are hitting not one ball but a row of ten or more, magically suspended in the air. It is during this "perceptible period," incidentally, that the slight upward motion of the racket imparts topspin to the ball. (Topspin is a most important type of spin. More accurately called forward spin, it causes the ball to curve downward. It acquired its name from billiards where the cue must hit the top of the ball to make it spin forward.)

You are now ready to try the forehand swing without a ball. Be sure your grip and waiting position are correct. Go through the pivot and step (without the swing) a few times to be sure they are firmly in mind. Then, as you start your pivot, guide the racket back with your left hand at its throat until the racket head is opposite your right shoulder; let go with your left hand, keep taking the racket back with your right hand until the racket is pointing directly behind you, put your left foot into position, lower the racket to waist height, bring it forward into the ball, transfer your weight forward and finish with the racket head high and pointing straight ahead of you. Look at the pictures showing the forehand on pages 33 and 34, and also the "after" pictures in the "Forehand Trouble Spots" chapter.

At this critical juncture it would be very valuable to have a full-length mirror or at least some semi-distinct reflecting surface (metal or glass) to practice in front of. Take a few swings, then look again at the pictures and keep comparing your own efforts. When you have the feeling that you can make the swing without having to think of each little detail in words, you are ready to start hitting a ball.

PLATES 15 through 38, opposite and page 34

FOREHAND SWING *begins as player pivots on right foot and simultaneously starts racket back at shoulder height by pushing with left hand; as player positions left foot, he lets go of racket with left hand. Racket continues back and is lowered to waist height, pointing to opposite backstop. Racket face has remained perpendicular to ground throughout.*

PLATE 15
PLATE 16
PLATE 17
PLATE 18
PLATE 19
PLATE 20
PLATE 21
PLATE 22
PLATE 23
PLATE 24
PLATE 25
PLATE 26
PLATE 27
PLATE 28
PLATE 29
PLATE 30

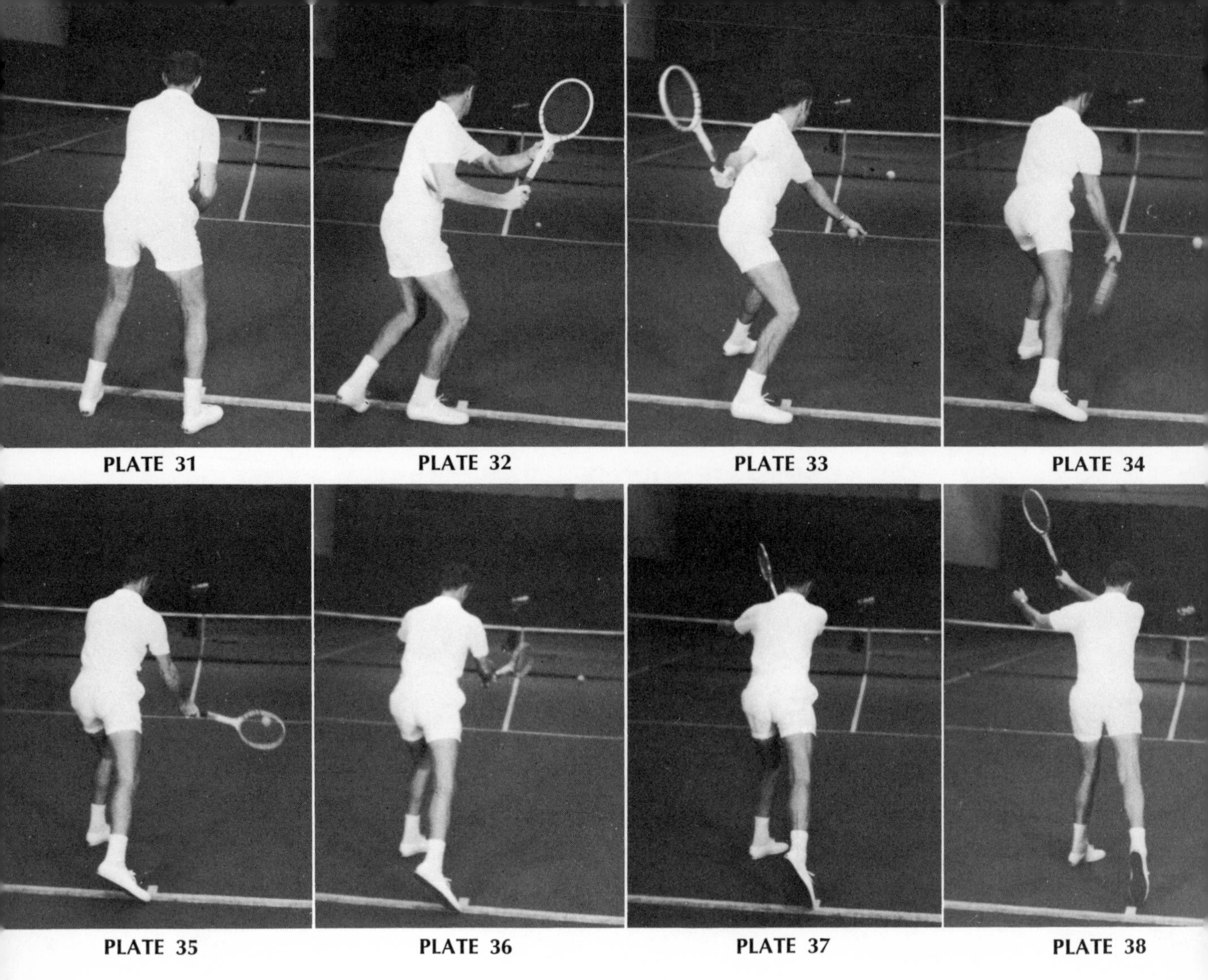
PLATE 31 PLATE 32 PLATE 33 PLATE 34
PLATE 35 PLATE 36 PLATE 37 PLATE 38

Learning to Hit the Forehand

Your first attempts at hitting the forehand will be greatly eased if you can get a friend to toss balls to you. If you are teamed up together to teach each other tennis, so much the better. Let's assume for the moment that you have a court to practice on.

Your friend should stand on your side of the net, two or three feet in front of it, in the middle of the court. This puts him just about astride the center service line. You should stand about midway between the sidelines at the back of the court. If you sense that you may at first have some trouble hitting the ball over the net, stand inside the baseline. With some kind of marking device (chalk on a hard court, a stick on a clay court), mark where you are going to stand and where your friend is going to stand. His objective is to toss the balls to you on a perfect bounce, approximately ten feet in front of you and three feet to your right. This causes the ball to be just about waist high and one step to your right at the moment you hit it. To give you the easiest possi-

PLATE 39

TOSSER, *well supplied with balls, provides underhand waist-high tosses to hitter for practice at controlled speeds.*

Best Camera Positions

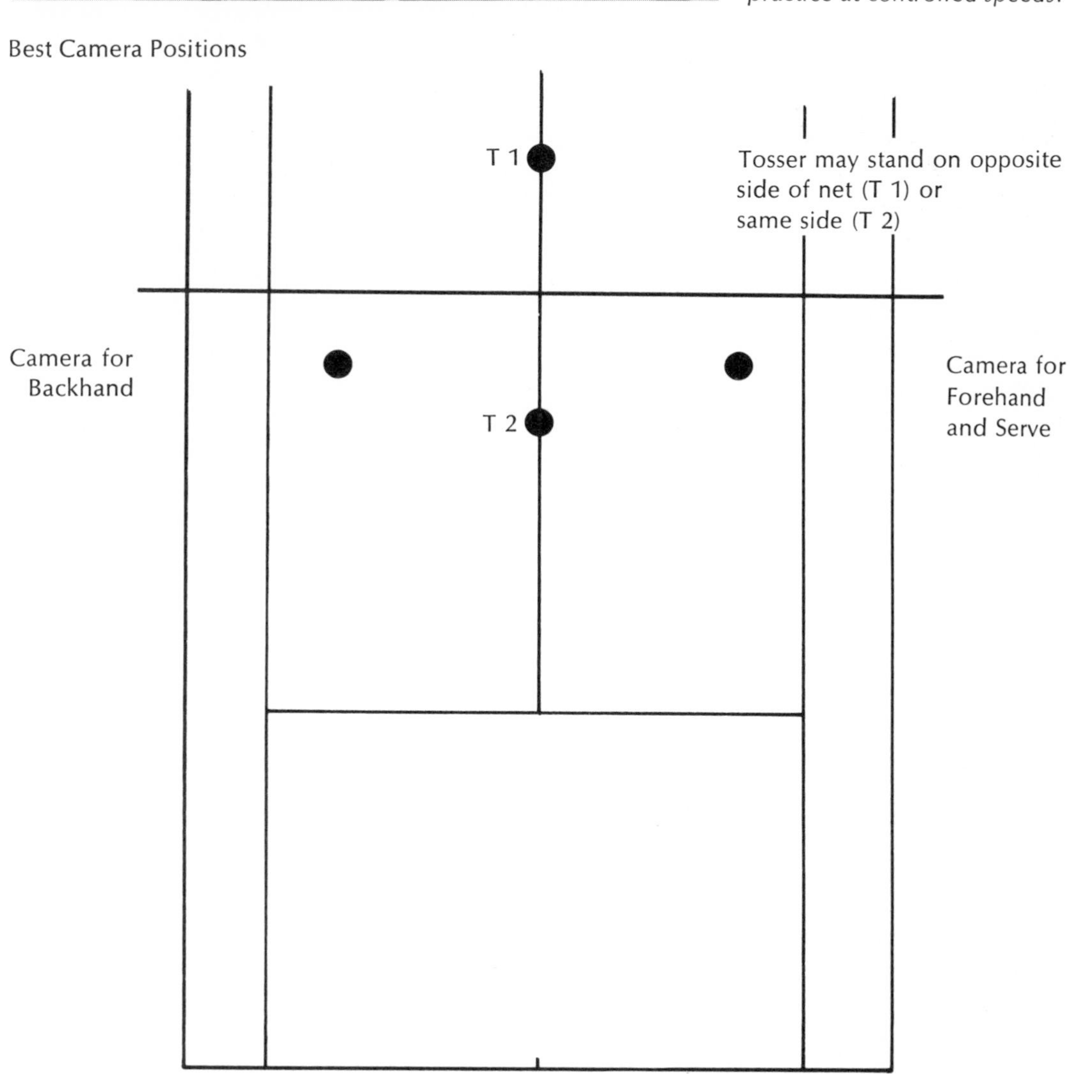

DIAGRAM 4

ble ball to hit, he should toss underhand. Overhand may seem more comfortable and even more accurate at first, but the ball is usually too tough for the hitter to handle.

Your friend has other jobs more demanding than tossing. He must be sure you are completely ready before he tosses. He must be ready to tell you whether you are standing correctly. If he has been reading this book with you, learning along with you, he should be able to give you considerable help on what you are doing wrong. Naturally, you must be as well prepared as he so that you can help him when it's his turn.

Your first effort will be simply to hit the ball over the net into the court. For some, this will happen right away. For others, it will be difficult even to make contact with the ball. The oldest and truest piece of advice in the game is to watch the ball, but that is only part of the battle. You must know where your racket is as well as where the ball is, and since you can't look at them both at the same time, you have to feel where your racket is. A good way to get over this early stumbling block is to have your friend stand near you and hold out a ball so that when you take a very gentle swing at it (his fingers should be well away from the side of the ball exposed to your racket), you feel the pressure of the ball against the middle of your racket. Another method is to practice your swing gently against a doorknob, being careful not to damage either your racket strings or the door. After a few practice swings at the stationary target, resume trying to hit tosses, then alternate these procedures until you are making contact.

Once you are hitting the ball with some regularity, keep careful track of how many balls out of 20 tosses you can hit into the court. When your score gets to 16 or 17, start narrowing down the target area. See how many you can hit past the opposite service line but short of the baseline. Then limit your shot to an even smaller area.

If you are working by yourself, your task will be a little more difficult. You will need a practice wall you can hit a ball against. To set the ball up you will have to toss it with your left hand while you are taking your swing. And to get any good

PLATE 40

HAND-HELD BALL *is good target for practice swing while trying new grip and learning "feel" for center of racket face.*

practice against the wall, you will have to regulate your shots so that the ball will come back within hitting range.

In tossing the ball to yourself and hitting it, you must try your hardest to stick to the swing and footwork we have already outlined. Stand facing the wall you are going to hit against, about thirty feet away from it if the ball will rebound strongly, closer if you are hitting against a fence or net. With chalk or a stick, mark where your right foot is going to be at the start of each rally. Now pivot, take your step with your left foot, and make a mark at the tip of your left shoe. Mark a small circle two feet to the right of that and parallel to the net. In that circle is where you will drop the ball when you make your toss.

SELF-TOSS *is made with hand palm-up as player pivots from waiting position. Racket is brought back with same continuous motion recommended for all forehand swings. Player's feet are in position and weight is transferred into ball.*

PLATE 41 **PLATE 42** **PLATE 43** **PLATE 44**

PLATE 45 **PLATE 46** **PLATE 47** **PLATE 48**

Now, take your waiting position. Your left hand holds a ball against the throat of the racket. Start your pivot and bring your racket back, letting go with the left hand and tossing the ball up about six inches, so that it will fall into the little circle you have drawn. Continue your swing, hit the ball as it reaches waist height on its bounce, and follow through. By tossing the ball up you will have enough time so that you won't have to rush your swing. Merely dropping the ball gives you just barely enough time—too little when you're learning. Do not, under any circumstances, throw the ball downward with any added force, for you won't stand a chance of hitting it properly.

Practice bouncing the ball and hitting it from the self-toss, over and over. At first, watch the ball carefully and just try to meet it in the center of the racket. If you have trouble, hold the ball in your left hand and tap it with the middle of your racket face so that you get the feeling of proper contact (or try the doorknob method again).

As you begin to feel you are acquiring some accuracy, pick out an area on the surface you are hitting against and aim at it. This area should be between three to six feet above the ground (the proper height for your shots to clear the net on a court) and can be fairly wide at first—ten or twelve feet. Narrow it down gradually. Mark an area on the ground or floor where you want the rebound to come so that it will give you enough room to prepare your stroke. Probably six to eight feet in front of you, and two or three feet to your right as you face the wall, will be adequate. Concentrate on using the correct form as it's very easy to pick up bad habits now that will betray you later on.

You are now ready to see how many times in a row you can keep the ball going against the wall. If the ball comes to your backhand side, do not play it and do not run around it to play a forehand. Run as hard as necessary for any ball on your forehand side. Play every ball on the first bounce. Any ball hit on the second bounce breaks your string of good shots, just as it ends the point against you in an actual game.

Your progress on the number of consecutive shots you can get in the target area will probably be quite uneven. To get up to three in a row is probably the most difficult step of all. From three, you will get up to seven or eight fairly quickly, and your average will stay there for awhile; but do not be surprised if you drop back to less than three from time to time. Your next breakthrough should be a fairly good-sized one. Work hard on getting accuracy and regulating the speed of your shots. Above all, be sure you are following directions with regard to swing and footwork.

Be sure your swing is continuous and your pivot correct. From time to time, review your swing opposite a full-length mirror.

If you hit the wall target on 17 out of 20 self-tosses, or if you keep up a rally of ten good forehands against the wall, you are ready to take your forehand on the court and to start learning the backhand. The next two chapters of the book are addressed to teachers and cover the things that can go wrong with the forehand. The latter chapter takes up difficulties in the order of their occurrence in the swing, so if you have an idea of what your own problem may be, leaf through the forehand trouble spots and find it. And as a double check, it wouldn't hurt to read through the entire section.

Beginner Drill 1

The Forehand

Grip

1. Identify the three main parts of hand: heel, pad of thumb, index finger, and keep them in mind.
2. Locate top, right, and left bevels and right and left vertical panels of handle, being sure racket face is perpendicular to the ground (picture, p. 26).
3. Take forehand grip—heel on right bevel, thumb on left vertical panel, index finger spread slightly up handle.
4. Put piece of tape on right bevel as reminder of where heel goes.
5. Practice finding grip with eyes closed.
6. Have friend hand you racket while your eyes are closed—find grip. Try this ten times, checking against pictures, pp. 26 & 27.

Waiting Position, Pivot, and Swing

1. Take correct waiting position and have friend (or full-length mirror) check you for the following:
    a. Feet spread comfortably.
    b. Heels just off ground.
    c. Eastern forehand grip.
    d. Left hand at throat of racket.
    e. Racket head opposite left shoulder.
    f. Racket face perpendicular.
    g. Wrist bent back just slightly, but *not* cocked.
2. Study pivot on pp. 30-31 and do it twenty times.
3. Do swing and pivot together, checking against description on p. 31 and accompanying pictures. Have mirror or friend check you, too. Do twenty swings three different times with great care and attention to detail.

Preliminary Practice

1. Take friends and some dozen tennis balls to a court, playground, or gym; stand about thirty-five feet apart and practice tossing balls underhand on one bounce to each other.
2. Mark a spot on ground (or use towel or hula hoop) where tossed ball will bounce waist-high to your partner. See if you each can hit it seventeen out of twenty times.
3. Have friend hold out ball. Take twenty gentle practice swings against it. Start from waiting position and do full pivot each time.

Hitting Practice

1. Take positions, friend tossing, you hitting; hit at least twenty before switching. Aim shot straight ahead, high enough to clear net, and past service line if possible.
2. If tosser is backed against wall or fence, mark net height and target

area on wall. See how often you can hit target.

Review

1. Review grip. Do twenty correct finds with eyes closed, partner handing you racket any which way.
2. Review pivot. Do twenty in a row.
3. Review full swing and pivot without ball, doing twenty in a row three separate times.

Self-Toss and Hit

1. Learn how to bounce and hit a self-toss (see description and pictures, p. 37).
2. If on a court, bounce and hit the ball over the net into the singles court. Do twenty, keeping track of number of good hits, three separate times.
3. If hitting against wall, mark off generous target area and proceed as above.
4. If wall rebounds well, hit ball so it returns about ten feet short of you and three or four feet to your right. When you can get one out of three balls to do this, try to keep a rally going.
5. Using forehands only, try sustaining a rally. Play balls on one bounce only and try for every ball. Start twenty rallies, noting which was the longest.

Tests

1. Hit seventeen out of twenty tosses over the net and into court three different times.
2. Hit ten shots in a row three different times against a wall.
3. Review this entire section two more times before going on.

3
Teaching the Forehand

The Teacher's Role

Though the first chapters of this book have been addressed to the player (and, for the most part, to a player who is teaching himself or working with another inexperienced player), you as a teacher should be able to take charge of the activities described, prescribe additional exercises, and provide both timely encouragement and criticism. If you have had considerable experience teaching, you will be able to head your pupil away from trouble before it starts.

Our emphasis in this book is on individual teaching. The group situation is excellent for the initial presentation of a tennis stroke and for drilling the stroke. It does, however, become awkward when the teacher sees something requiring individual attention which can only be corrected at the expense of the rest of the group. In practice, the instructor can spend only short periods of time with any one person; usually, he must tactfully point out the person's difficulty to the rest of the group so that they can cope with the same problem should they encounter it. By noticing frequent recurrences and reminding the offender, the group instructor can get many pupils through minor adjustments. But there is no escaping the fact that major errors have to be handled through individual correction; such attention should be paid immediately if the player is to progress smoothly.

In the past decade, group techniques for teaching tennis have become increasingly widespread and sophisticated. Rarely today do we see twenty children lined up on a club court to hit two forehands at a time, fed to them by a member volunteer, then go around to get in line again. The practice now is to keep each child busy the entire time by having small groups work simultaneously on several different drills, according to their ability levels. A particularly outstanding job is being done in Princeton, New Jersey, by Eve Kraft. Her Princeton Community Tennis Program has engaged nearly every man, woman, and child in the area in group tennis at one time or another in its fifteen years of existence. One of the great strengths of the program has been the pooling of knowledge of tennis pros and physical education teachers in the area. The former provide the ideas to be taught, while the latter supply the knack for handling large groups in a limited space.

Other outstanding work has been done by professionals Judy Barta and the late Cap Leighton who have spread the gospel of group teaching to tennis teachers in widely separated areas of the country. Many of their alumni run programs of their own.

We wish, therefore, to leave to such outstanding people the business of describing group techniques. We will concentrate instead on *what* the teacher should teach, whether it be to groups or to individuals, what to look for in the way of mechanical difficulties, and what to prescribe to remedy them. Consequently, from here on we will assume that the teacher is teaching the individual and that he will make his own adaptations for the group lesson.

First, a general caution. Try to find the correct balance between instruction and drill. Too much instruction (explaining how to make a stroke) will confuse even the best pupil, while mere drill (practicing the stroke) without adequate explanation means you are wasting time and, more seriously, your pupil's money. So give him as much instruction as he can reasonably absorb, drill as much as the remaining time allows, then sum up the lesson and give the pupil enough to work on for four or five practice sessions.

Sizing Up the Pupil

When beginning with a new pupil, find out what sort of a person you are dealing with and try to establish friendly contact. You can gain both his confidence and some useful information by asking well-chosen questions and making astute observations. First, you want to know what the pupil's experience with tennis has been. Has he played before? Has he had any instruction? What is his experience in other sports? Has he played on teams or just in informal games? Does he like the other sports he has played? By the range of his experience with sports you will find out whether he enjoys athletics and will likely have a good attitude toward tennis, and whether he is capable right away of fairly complex physical actions. You may also find out if he has habits from other sports that will help or hinder what you will be teaching.

If he is a young pupil who has been enrolled by his parents, is it their idea or his that he should take the lesson? If it is theirs, is he willing and interested? If the pupil is an older person, whose motivation and pocketbook are his own, the chances that he will be willing to work are much better of course. You should note whether the pupil is lazy or active, fat or thin, well-built or somewhat ungainly. These physical factors may indicate in advance the speed at which you will be able to teach. The intelligent instructor will keep registering such impressions for future reference.

If the pupil is shy and self-conscious, you will have to put him at ease. Conversely, if the pupil knows it all, seems almost as though he were trying to give you the lesson, some quiet deflation is required. The opportunity is sure to come soon enough. A good gambit is to ask some technical questions, such as how to control depth, height, and direction of the ball (page 93) under heading "Control and Footwork on the Forehand"). It is surprising how many people cannot explain these points, only to find them ridiculously obvious when explained.

Most teachers of tennis, professional or amateur, have a mixed clientele that includes beginners, intermediate and advanced players, some who have started with him, others who have had instruction elsewhere, and still others who have played a great deal but have had no instruction. When starting with a pupil who has had previous instruction or is experienced but untaught, it is necessary to find out how well the person plays, how many lessons he feels inclined to take, and what his objectives are. The whole idea of the individual lesson is to tailor the instruction to the pupil. You don't start in with the forehand if the pupil tells you he is having trouble getting his second serve in. On the other hand, if the pupil is young and has a wild forehand with a Western grip and a lot of wrist, it is your duty to show him that his results will always be limited by his stroke, that he must change it if he wants to improve. You will likely have to cite specific reasons and even take statistics of his errors in play to show him how much weaker that stroke is than the rest of his game.

When working with older pupils whose habits are solidified, you will find it much more difficult to get them to make radical changes in their games. But you will also find it very rewarding, since they will concentrate, understand what you tell them, and apply themselves thoroughly.

Preliminary Activities on the Court

If there is any doubt about a very young pupil's readiness to start tennis, or if you'd like a definite line on how well-coordinated he is, simply take a tennis ball and have a catch with him. See if he can catch and throw easy tosses; then throw grounders as well as hard liners, making the pupil run a bit to field the ball. If he moves well, makes few errors except on difficult chances, and throws overhand with a good elbow bend at the back of his windup, you can be sure he is not only ready but will develop quickly.

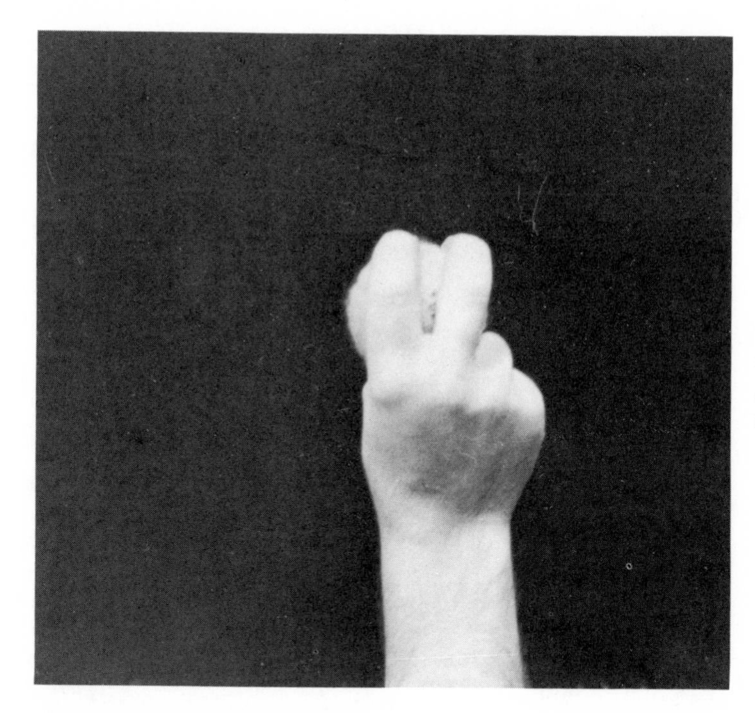

PLATE 49

BASEBALL GRIP *helps pupil's overhand throw, is also right grip for tossing hand on serve.*

If he cannot catch easy balls or throw overhand at all, or if he is undecided about which arm to use, progress is almost certain to be slow; a recommendation to wait a year or more may even be in order. This is only a rough test, but it is much safer than to say arbitrarily that a child should begin "as early as possible," or at the specific age of six, ten, twelve, or whatever.

The "size up" test can be skipped if the teacher is fairly well assured that the pupil is ready. The next procedure will indicate much of the same information anyhow. Have the pupil take his racket, tell him where to stand in the court (if he is a complete beginner), and then see how he hits the ball without any instruction at all. *(In teaching any stroke see what your pupil does naturally before you proceed with your instruction.)* Hit first to the forehand and then to the backhand. Hit separate shots, for there is no need to try to keep a rally going. You will be able to tell from the way the pupil moves and swings whether he has good potential. What you are actually looking for is to see whether or not the pupil uses the same face of the racket for both forehand and backhand. Here we have one of the most fundamental of tennis faults, one that escapes the notice of many tennis teachers and can handicap an otherwise good player very severely. Quite a few beginners slip into this habit (provided you give them no warning clue) and the time to stamp it out is right at the start.

Let us look more closely at this fault. It is most likely to be committed by a pupil who naturally picks up the racket with a Western grip.

The result of this grip is that on both forehand and backhand the player swings with the racket face tilted forward, or covering the ball, instead of perpendicular to the ground or flat into the ball. He thus has trouble controlling the height of his shot,

PLATE 50

WESTERN GRIP: *Heel of hand is on right under bevel, base knuckle of index finger on right-hand edge of bottom of handle, thumb on top.*

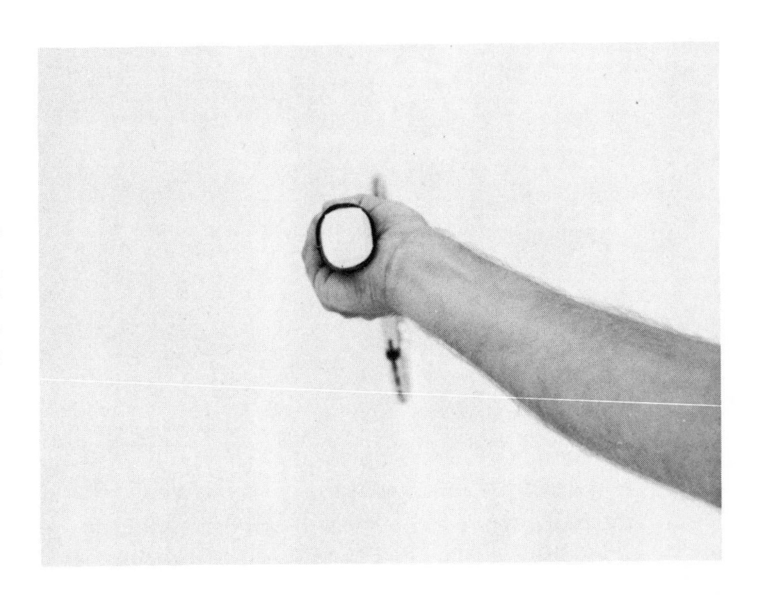

PLATE 51

WESTERN FOREHAND *forces player to turn hand up to counteract natural forward tilt of racket face.*

PLATE 52

WESTERN BACKHAND, *old style, calls for turning hand upside down, hitting with same face of racket as forehand. Some grip change customary, but some old-timers still do it without any.*

and often compensates by resorting to awkward wrist motions. Here is how it looks: He will hit a forehand and follow through with the racket face almost horizontal, a full 90° beyond the perpendicular. Then, with almost no change in grip, he will turn the racket another 90° farther, using the same face to hit the backhand. When another shot is hit to his forehand, he reverses the process, turning back a full 180°.

These are the most obvious symptoms of "same siders," but many teachers will miss other, more subtle versions. In the Western type, there is little or no change of grip; the pupil swings through with his arm upside down on the backhand, and the awkwardness is readily apparent. But suppose the pupil uses an Eastern grip. While he hits a fairly clean forehand without much turnover of the racket face, and seems to use the same grip on the backhand, he has great trouble getting from one to the other. Probably, instead of pulling the right hand back one-quarter turn in changing grips, the pupil flips the top of the racket toward him, causing the handle to make a three-quarter turn in his hand until he winds up with something approaching the backhand grip. He may then return to the forehand in the correct manner (with the one-quarter turn), or he may use the three-quarter flip.

BEFORE

FLIPOVER *of racket occurs just after completion of stroke. Note that in Plate 58 outline of racket head is in light and that in Plate 59 it is in shadow, indicating racket face has been turned over while player kept his hand still. Same face will be used for backhand as for forehand.*

PLATE 53 **PLATE 54** **PLATE 55** **PLATE 56**

PLATE 57 **PLATE 58** **PLATE 59** **PLATE 60**

PLATE 61 **PLATE 62** **PLATE 63** **PLATE 64**

PLATE 65 **PLATE 66** **PLATE 67** **PLATE 68**

AFTER

NO FLIPOVER *occurs here as player keeps racket face vertical and moves hand from forehand to backhand grip and prepares to hit ball with opposite face of racket.*

In any case, when first hitting the ball with the pupil, pay close attention to his racket face between strokes to see if it turns all the way over. By correcting the same-sider early, you will save him a lot of anguish.

Many a same-sider is unaware of what he is doing, and, if directly accused, would deny it. Here is an infallible method of convincing him. Point out some distinctive feature on the shaft of his racket just above the handle ("Made in U.S.A.," 4½ L" or some such mark always appears on one plane of every racket shaft) and tell him to keep that mark up as the top for all his shots. Now hit some balls to him, alternating between his forehand and backhand. Sooner or later he will switch grips in his old way and you'll see the racket face flip over. When it does, stop immediately and ask him where the printing is. "Hmm, it's down."

"Why, so it is. How do you think it got there?"

"I don't know. I guess I must have turned it."

Follow up this advantage by explaining the correct grips (p. 26, forehand, p. 103, backhand) and the method for changing from one to the other (p. 138); then have the pupil drill intensively, always keeping that distinctive mark up, until the habit is well fixed. The correction is easy to make with younger same-siders, much more difficult with older ones. With the latter you must weigh the results they get against the difficulty the change presents for them, the time available for practice, and their desire to improve.

Why the Forehand First

Once you have determined how interested and well-coordinated a pupil you have and what his natural tendencies are in the handling of the racket, you are ready to get down to the serious business of laying the foundation of his game—teaching the ground strokes. However, if your pupil is not a beginner, start where you and he agree you should. Observe carefully what his specific problems are and do your best to improve his results by changing his strokes only so far as is manageable in conforming with what we advocate.

Why begin with the ground strokes? Why not begin with the serve? Because it is important that the pupil get some satisfaction from his very first lesson. Ground strokes are considerably easier to learn than the serve because the swing is much less elaborate and does not involve difficult coordination between the hands. Consequently, the visceral satisfaction of making solid contact with the ball is apt to come much sooner. The more sophisticated satisfaction of keeping the ball in play will follow soon, and then will come the subtle satisfaction of maneuvering one's opponent around the court and finally putting the ball away. After some solid confidence and proficiency have been built up, the pupil will be much more willing to tackle the job of learning the serve. Furthermore, as he will have obtained valuable familiarity with the racket, the ball, and court, his task will be lightened considerably.

Teaching the Forehand

With the complete beginner, the first step is to illustrate and explain the waiting position. Be sure the pupil understands the reference points on the court (the two sidelines and the baseline) so he will know both where to stand and where to move to hit the ball. Explain that the position midway between the sidelines will allow him to get to shots on either side of the court and that he must get back to the middle after each shot.

Once the pupil realizes that any ball that comes to him on his right-hand side is a forehand, demonstrate an actual forehand shot by dropping the ball and hitting it over the net. Always demonstrate first. With an unusually good athlete you may not have to do any more than that.

Next, explain to your pupil that the swing consists of two main parts: footwork and swing. Teach the footwork first so as to get him used to the pivot and the proper placement of the left foot. He must get the footwork down pat, for later on he will be too busy trying to watch the ball and control his racket arm.

To spell out exactly what you mean by footwork, use the same method we have already recommended to self-teaching readers of this book (p. 30). Using chalk or some other marking device, outline the fronts of the pupil's shoes as he stands in waiting position. Then make a mark showing where his left foot should go, making sure that it extends no closer to the right sideline than his right foot. Be sure also that it shows the left foot angled at 45°. See plate 10 on page 30.

Now, have the player take the waiting position, with his heels just off the ground. Then have him pivot, put his left foot on the mark, and transfer his weight forward onto the toes of that foot as if he were swinging. Have him do it at least ten times before going on to explain the swing. Later in the lesson, have him do another ten of these without swinging; return to this brief drill from time to time when it seems as if he is forgetting.

Your pupil should now be able to attempt the swing. Explain it to him step by step: Start the racket back at shoulder height, pivot the shoulders and turn on the ball of the right foot; let go with the left hand as the racket passes the right shoulder; continue the backswing at shoulder height until the racket is all the way back; lower the racket to waist level; start it forward into the ball while putting the left foot into position (on mark); swing the racket into the ball while transferring weight from the rear foot to the forward foot; then follow through with the racket head moving up to head height and the arm fully extended.

Stress that the motion of the racket must be continuous, in order to avoid looseness of the wrist and loss of momentum. A diagram, such as the one below can be drawn with pad and pencil (or traced on the court) to show the path of the racket. This continuous motion resembles a flattened circle, which, loosely speaking, is an ellipse; so, for want of a better term, let us call the swing elliptical.

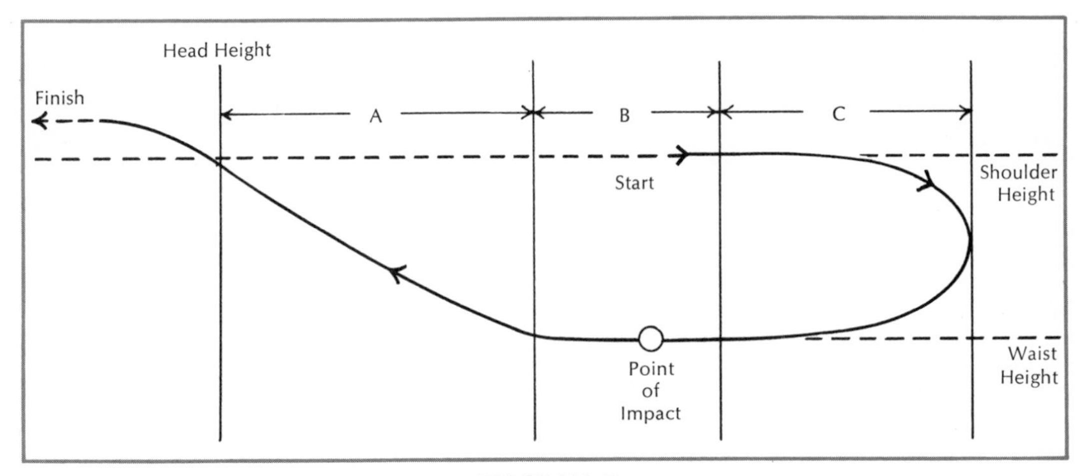

DIAGRAM 5

RACKET STARTS *back at shoulder height and picks up power during "C." As it moves into ball and carries it, depth is obtained during "B." The ball is still in contact as the racket starts to come up naturally during the early part of "A." Topspin for control of length is obtained by the upward follow-through to head height.*

Now is a good time to familiarize your pupil with the essentials of spin. As a prop, you need only a wheel that spins on an axle, such as a detached bicycle wheel, baby carriage wheel, or anything else that is convenient. (A small one is good for individual lessons, a large one for groups.) Demonstrate the principle of spin by moving your hand first up, then down the back of the wheel. It thus spins forward or backward, just as the ball will if it is hit in the same manner. Have the pupil try the upward brushing so that he can see how to fit the idea of topspin into his motion. (We will go into the backspin stroke at a later juncture.) Keep the wheel handy for use when explaining the serve and volley, as well as a reminder for those who have difficulty achieving topspin because they do not get their racket head low enough.

After demonstrating the swing a few more times, let the pupil try it without the ball, just imitating. The next teaching maneuver can be very helpful if your own coordination is up to it. Stand behind the pupil, gripping his racket with your hand just above his; then, drop a ball with your other hand and guide his racket through the stroke. As the ball whizzes into the opposite court, say "Nice shot!" to your pupil. This will give him a much more complete idea of how it feels to hit the ball than he might otherwise get. Another way to accomplish the same end is to let him take a gentle swing against a hand-held ball.

Your pupil should now be ready to try to hit a few balls. Have him take his waiting position midway between the sidelines—at the baseline if he is good-sized, farther in, if smaller. Even a small child should be no closer to the net than three feet from the service line. Check to see that his grip is correct and that his left hand cradles the racket throat—in fact, check these points every time your pupil gets ready to hit a shot, and do not proceed until they're right. Now, take up your position, on his side of the net at the start, then move to the other side once he is returning the ball with some assurance.

You are now ready to toss or hit the ball to your pupil. Tossing is recommended with young and small beginners, and with the older, larger pupil who you sense may have difficulty making contact with the ball. Your own accuracy has a great deal to do with how quickly the pupil learns to make solid contact with the ball, so try hard to deliver tosses that will take long, lazy, waist-high bounces requiring no more from the player than a single step forward. Ball-tossing machines, though a great aid to the teacher, are usually premature at this stage, since even their softest setting may be too hard for the beginner. Also, the machine must be turned off and on for each shot or the pupil will soon be overcome by the relentless barrage of balls. Tossing is nearly as accurate and can be timed to suit your pupil's pace.

Don't try to keep up a rally at this stage. Set up each ball as perfectly as you can, and once the pupil begins to hit with some consistency, feed him a ball that will require taking a few steps. Be sure that he gets back to the middle each time after hitting it. Keep stressing the necessity of correct footwork and swing mechanics; in particular, be certain that the pupil keeps the racket face perpendicular throughout his swing.

Let your pupil know each time he has hit the ball correctly. Don't stop to correct every little fault. Keep to two or three major ones, in clear sequence, and always add "Watch the ball." For example: "Set your racket opposite your left shoulder, not your waist. Start it back early and *watch the ball.*" Remember, too, that for each point of theory you introduce, you must give your pupil the technical reason for it.

Teaching Hints 1

The Forehand

1. Be sure pupil understands object of game, knows where to stand, and such elementary terms as forehand, backhand, etc.
2. Show and explain Eastern forehand grip (p. 26). Pupil should know grip by name, by sight, and, with eyes closed, by feel.
3. Demonstrate correct waiting position, emphasizing heels off ground, racket head opposite left shoulder, etc. (p. 28).
4. Demonstrate entire forehand swing motion.
5. Demonstrate footwork of stroke without swinging, emphasizing proper placement of feet (p. 30).
6. Have pupil do footwork without swinging. Repeat ten times.
7. Demonstrate and explain actual swing with racket (pp. 34-35).
9. Guide pupil through stroke. Draw diagram of pattern of motion.
10. Have pupil try swing without ball. Do five times, make corrections, then another five and correct, etc., till twenty have been done.
11. Explain importance of continuous motion (p. 52).
12. Demonstrate and explain topspin (p. 52).
13. Hold ball in your hand for pupil to swing against (p. 36).
14. Toss or hit balls to pupil. Be sure ball bounces waist-high, one step to his right, and slow enough for pupil to manage. Be accurate.
15. Praise good shots, don't quibble over small faults. Concentrate mainly on grip, pattern of motion, and attention to ball. Whenever necessary, review.
16. Give pupil a goal (scaled to his age and coordination). A commendable first-time performance would be seventeen out of twenty shots (on easy tosses) hit over the net, into court, using correct form. If this is unrealistic, scale it down—or up.
17. Acquaint pupil with dimensions of the court, rules, and scoring of tennis.

4
Forehand Trouble Spots

Whether you are a teacher working with a pupil or a player trying to improve your own game, you can help your progress tremendously by using films. For the player working alone, film is almost a necessity—there is no other way he can see himself. For the teacher, film is a great help because it bears out what the teacher has been telling the pupil all along. Either way, film provides the player with just the right amount of dissatisfaction with his game to make him want to improve it.

It is important to film every facet of one's game in order to uncover trouble spots, and we will start here with a number of problems which occur on the forehand. Some are pretty much confined to beginners, but many pester even experienced and very proficient players. We will analyze them in order of their occurrence during the stroke, which order, incidentally, is excellent for a teacher or player to follow until he acquires the skill of penetrating to the heart of the problem quickly. There is an added value in proceeding in this way: many mistakes begin at the start of the swing. The grip particularly affects one's swing. The Western grip is often seen in conjunction with a high backswing, excess topspin, and a rolling over of the racket face on the finish. The Continental grip often results in too much use of backspin.

Waiting Position

The error most commonly found in the waiting position is to have the racket head at waist height rather than opposite the left shoulder. This often results in too straight a backswing, that is, a backswing made at the same height as the forward swing, and has three undesirable effects: a stop at the back of the backswing and therefore a loss of momentum; an opportunity for excess wrist movement to creep in; and, the swing can develop into a slap so that if the follow-through continues on the same plane, it will be difficult to obtain topspin. Each of these problems is dealt with in greater detail later in this section.

Another common error in the waiting position is to hold the racket straight out from the midline of the body. This position is likely to produce a strained attitude with the player's arms out too far. Some think of it as halfway between the forehand and backhand, but the trouble with this is that while your right arm is behind your body for the forehand after you pivot, it is ahead of your body for the backhand—which must be met sooner. Consequently, on the backhand, your backswing has farther to travel (the width of your shoulders) than it has on your forehand backswing. (Compare plate 178 with plate 217.) The waiting position we recommend takes this into account by stationing the racket head opposite the left shoulder, that is, closer to the backhand than the forehand.

PLATE 69

RACKET HEAD *parallel to midline leaves racket too far from backhand position.*

Another waiting position error that can easily pass unnoticed is standing with the racket face horizontal, or nearly so. This almost certainly happens because the player uses a semi-Western or Western grip, which turns the forehand face of the racket down. When a player adopts the Eastern grip, he should get into the habit of holding the racket face perpendicular between strokes; this will greatly improve his chances of keeping it that way throughout each stroke. Check on this regularly and do not proceed until it is right.

Some players wait for the ball with their hands apart, that is, without supporting the throat of the racket with the left hand. This places an extra burden on the right hand since it must grip tightly at all times. One often hears such a player complain that he can't hold on to his racket handle because it gets too sweaty. Furthermore, without that left hand he will undoubtedly find it awkward to change grips from forehand to backhand.

Other trouble spots in waiting position include a stiff-kneed stance. Unless the player has his knees slightly flexed, he won't be able to push off quickly. Holding the arms too far out from the body or jutting out the elbows adds strain, which can tell over a long match. Some players wait with one foot ahead of the other, opening to one side, which invariably makes it difficult to handle shots on the opposite side of the body.

PLATE 70

HANDS APART: *position shown puts strain on racket hand between shots, complicates grip change and prevents guidance from other hand.*

PLATE 71

HORIZONTAL *racket face is sign of Western grip, possible use of same face of racket.*

Grip

Undoubtedly, for tennis teachers and pupils alike, more problems revolve around the grip than around any other aspect of the stroke. As we said before, the grip adopted can determine the nature of the entire stroke. Some beginners will be able to adopt the Eastern forehand grip right away and never resort to any other. This is particularly true of athletic boys, especially if they are not weighted down by too heavy a tennis racket. Girls, and boys with limited athletic ability or with too heavy a racket, are quite likely to slip toward the Western grip if left to their own devices. Actually, the grip they tend to settle on is the semi-Western. The part of the hand which is farther up the handle—the index finger—is the same as in the Eastern grip; the heel of the hand, however, is allowed to slip down off the right bevel to the right vertical panel. This lowers the racket head in relation to the forearm and tilts the racket face forward. A player adopting the semi-Western grip too frequently uses a straight backswing with an excessively laid-back wrist, often resulting in a stopping of the upper arm as the racket is brought forward so that the stroke lacks follow-through.

One possible explanation of the semi-Western grip—worth an actual statistical study—is that its use stems simply from lack of strength. By the time a child has acquired the strength to hold a racket, the pattern can become too well-fixed to change. For this reason, we believe the beginner should make sure his racket is light enough (and, if necessary, short enough) to allow him to swing comfortably without resorting to the semi-Western grip. Secondly, the player should take steps to build up the strength of his grip by swinging the racket with its press on, both before and after each practice session or lesson—even if the player's racket does not require a press.

There are several gripping errors which, though common, are minor. These include choking up on the racket, holding the racket too close to the end of the handle, putting the index finger up the handle, holding the fingers too close together in a hatchet-like grip, putting the thumb up the handle, and so forth. Players can often correct these faults with very little difficulty.

PLATE 72

SEMI-WESTERN GRIP *puts heel of hand and base knuckle of index finger on right vertical panel, thumb on left bevel.*

PLATE 75

EXTENDED FINGER *prevents player from taking Eastern forehand grip, forcing semi-Western instead.*

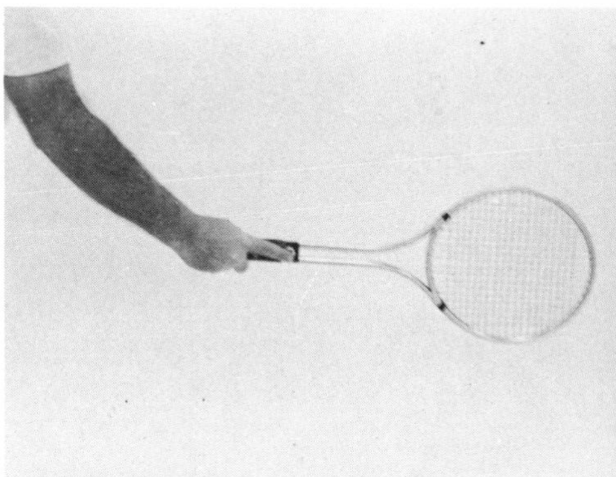

PLATE 73

CHOKING UP *racket shortens arc of swing, often leads to wristy slap. Often a sign of inadequate hand strength for weight of racket.*

PLATE 76

HATCHET GRIP *with fingers close together amounts to Continental grip, leads to wristy play.*

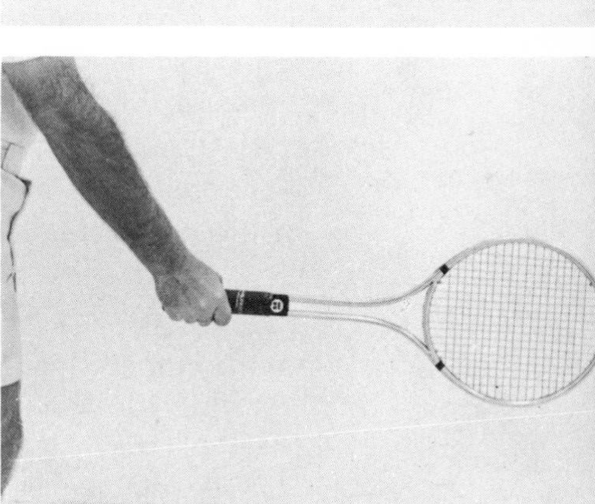

PLATE 74

LONG GRIP *with heel of hand off handle results in infirm grip.*

PLATE 77

THUMB UP *handle gives insecure grip, makes racket more likely to turn in hand if ball is hit off center.*

PLATE 78

FINGERS OPEN *as player brings racket back, changing grip from new to old; sense of racket face angle is confused by this maneuver.*

Basically, though, most grip problems involve rotating the hand too far around the handle in one direction or the other, toward the Continental or the semi-Western and Western. When a player who has been using one of those grips first attempts the Eastern, he will frequently shift back to his old grip at some stage during the swing. To detect the error takes careful observation by a teacher, standing close to the pupil. The self-taught player can discover his own problems by having film close-ups taken of his racket hand during the swing.

With some players, the change is fairly obvious, since the fingers open during the backswing. This is quite a serious fault as the player is not likely to have good control of the racket at the time of impact. With others, the movement of the grip almost approaches legerdemain. The player will inch the heel of his hand off the right bevel as the racket moves back, hit the ball with his old grip, and then resume the new one just as he is coming back to waiting position.

In either case, the player should grip tightly during the backswing and feel the pressure of his fingers on the racket handle. Teachers dealing with this problem must monitor the pupil constantly, telling him when the grip is right and when it is wrong.

With players who use grips other than the Eastern, it is first necessary to decide whether a change should be made. If the player is young, has time to practice, is ambitious and willing to work, then there should be no problem. If he is older, has little time to practice, and is satisfied with his present level of stroke production, then he shouldn't bother. The plain fact is that it may take a thousand or more practice shots before the new grip is going to feel really comfortable. In the meantime, he can expect it to feel not merely awkward but perhaps even painful. Why is it worthwhile to persevere? Because the Eastern grip provides more power in all forehand shots, as well as the best way to vary spin from heavy top- to heavy backspin. The Continental is fine for low balls and backspin shots, but a real handicap on high balls and topspin. Just the reverse can be said of the semi-Western or Western.

In some cases of faulty grip, it may be more practical for the player to change his swing first, as, for instance, with someone who has difficulty translating ideas into physical action. A continuous swing can be made with any of the grips mentioned above. The correct waiting position can be learned, as can the correct footwork. The whole stage can be so set that all that remains is to change the grip; the change will then fit in naturally. Occasionally, a player may be able to change in five minutes a grip he has used all his life; more often, it takes quite a time.

The player should get the details clear (see page 26) and use colored tape on the bevel to remind him of his changed grip. When he first tries it out, he is very likely to hit much too low if his normal grip was Continental, much too high if his normal grip was semi-Western or Western. He should realize beforehand that this is likely to happen, since the Continental grip naturally opens the face of the racket and till now the player has always closed it. If he did not tilt the racket face forward, he would never be able to hit the ball. Conversely, if he used the semi-Western or Western he always had to open the face somewhat, in order to hit the ball high enough to clear the net. If he makes the same corrections while using the Eastern grip, the racket face angle will still be incorrect since the Eastern keeps the racket face perpendicular to the ground. If he is hitting too high, he should aim at the bottom of the net. If he is hitting too low, he should aim six feet over the net. He should experiment with wrist angle until he finds which is best and then stick to it. Once he has the general altitude of his shots under control, he should drill and drill until he gets accustomed to, and happy with, the new grip. Anyone working with such a player should drill him from easy to progressively more difficult changes until he can make the new grip hold up under tougher circumstances than his old one would have.

Use of the Left Hand

The left hand is important for five basic reasons. It bears most of the weight of the racket between strokes, thus giving the right hand an opportunity to relax. It holds the racket while the right hand changes grips. It helps turn the shoulder sideways for the swing. It starts the racket on its backswing, assuring that the backswing will be in the correct pattern. It also helps to keep the face of the racket perpendicular during the early part of the swing.

The most frequent bad habits are not using the left hand at all, holding it too far down the handle or sliding it down, and taking it off the racket too early in the backswing. Occasionally, bizarre uses of the left hand crop up, such as turning it completely around, gripping the tip of the racket, or spreading it against the racket face. All of these habits are comparatively easy to correct if teacher and pupil are willing to persist. A teacher must remember that to overlook these points, which may seem small, can contribute to more serious problems, such as excess wrist. If a player develops tidy left-hand habits in changing from forehand to backhand, he will be able to stand up to heavy bombardment from the other side of the net.

To repeat, the player must see to it that he uses the left hand to bear most of the weight of the racket between strokes, to steady the racket while the correct grip is obtained early in the backswing, and to start the racket back in the correct pattern. He should make practice swings—in front of a mirror if possible—attending carefully to these points on each swing. As he gets further along, he can alternate forehands and backhands and do the accompanying footwork as well. This, of course, is one of the favorite exercises in group classes, but it can work just as well with individual instruction. These habits are too important and too easy to acquire to be left to chance, so the player should drill, drill, drill.

Backswing

The path that a racket traces during backswing and forward swing can be varied in a number of ways. We believe maximum effectiveness comes from the backswing we advocated earlier. The next best thing is to bring the racket back from waist height, raise it to shoulder height during the backswing, lower it to waist height again, and bring it forward up the back of the ball. The only disadvantage of this swing (which is, in fact, used by many of the top players who say they use a straight backswing) is that it wastes motion: Since the racket usually finishes at head height, there is no advantage in lowering it to waist height in waiting position only to raise it again as soon as the next shot comes along.

There are two other types of backswing which are basically acceptable but could be improved. The first brings the racket back too high. We most certainly do not advocate a "circular" swing, nor do we use that expression—except to describe a backswing that is excessive. By bringing the racket back over his head, a player uses up too much time and has to move the racket too far to get it down for a waist-high ball. A related problem, sometimes simultaneous, is to bring the racket back too close to the body, but otherwise in the proper path. This can result in a shorter swing than is desirable and a loss of power.

The most common incorrect backswing is the straight one, though players carefully following the methods advocated here are not too likely to use it. Quite a few players with other experience will use it, mainly because it is widely taught. While it may be simple to tell a pupil to pull the racket straight back and bring it forward on the same plane, it can instill bad habits that will be hard to overcome. In the first place, there is almost certain to be a stop in the backswing. All of the momentum of the backswing is thus lost and none of it can go into the forward swing. Along with this, the wrist may be laid back so that the swing becomes a slap. When a player uses a straight backswing he frequently carries the racket at waist height in waiting position, often as not complicating it with a semi-Western grip; girls, particularly, do this.

In another recurrent backswing variation, the racket is brought back well below ball height. The player then lifts it up, bringing it forward in an upside-down continuous motion that cannot produce any power. Still another oddity is the straight backswing with a lift at the back of the swing, as if the person wanted to cock the racket over his head for an overhead smash. This will almost certainly make the player hit down on the ball and get backspin whether he intends it or not.

All of these problems plus most other variations can be avoided with the continuous swing. Failing that, we recommend a basic remedy. First, the player must be convinced that his present swing could be improved. The prospect of added power and a smoother swing should encourage him. The fact that he may have a stop in the backswing, use too much wrist, or have control problems should cause some

PLATES 79 through 94 on page 64

STRAIGHT BACKSWING: *Player changes from straight backswing (shown in BEFORE sequence, Plates 79–86) to continuous swing (shown in AFTER sequence, Plates 87–94).*

PLATES 95 through 110 on page 65

UPSIDE DOWN *swing pattern (Plates 95 to 102): racket is lowered to knee height on backswing (Plate 96), raised above ball height, meeting ball late and carving it slightly; upper arm motion is somewhat restricted. In AFTER sequence (Plates 103 to 110), backswing is just about as high as it was low in BEFORE series. Racket is now lowered at back of swing and brought forward and up to impart topspin.*

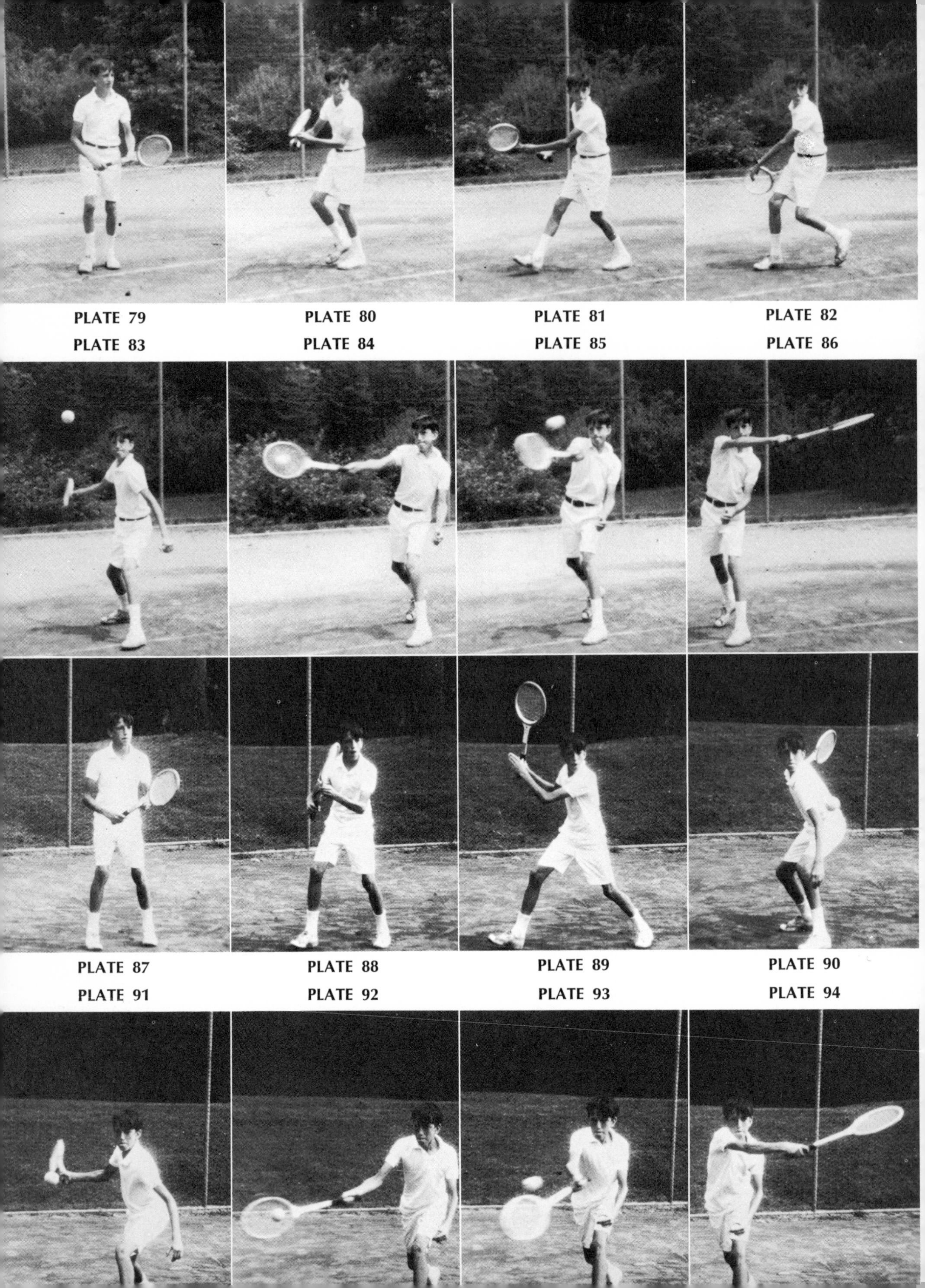

PLATE 79 PLATE 80 PLATE 81 PLATE 82

PLATE 83 PLATE 84 PLATE 85 PLATE 86

PLATE 87 PLATE 88 PLATE 89 PLATE 90

PLATE 91 PLATE 92 PLATE 93 PLATE 94

PLATE 95 PLATE 96 PLATE 97 PLATE 98

PLATE 99 PLATE 100 PLATE 101 PLATE 102

PLATE 103 PLATE 104 PLATE 105 PLATE 106

PLATE 107 PLATE 108 PLATE 109 PLATE 110

dissatisfaction with his present results. On the other hand, he may set great store by an earlier coach who taught him the straight swing—from which he gets fairly good results. The best way to attack the problem is to film the player's swing and compare it with the photographs both in this book and in other tennis books.

If the player is willing to change, he should review or learn the correct continuous motion (see page 32), making sure he understands the importance of waiting with the racket head opposite the left shoulder. Then he should act out the steps, comparing the path of his old swing with the new one, preferably practicing in front of a mirror. Next, balls should be tossed or hit to him, one by one, with plenty of thinking time between shots. Gradually step up the difficulty of the feeds so that the new swing is tested by progressively tougher shots.

At first, a player learning the continuous motion frequently gets into difficulty by bringing his racket back too high. Finding that time is fleeting and he still has not

PLATE 111 **PLATE 112** **PLATE 113** **PLATE 114**

PLATE 119 **PLATE 120** **PLATE 121** **PLATE 122**

completed his backswing, he takes a shortcut and carves down into the ball, putting backspin on it. This, of course, loses the whole advantage the continuous motion is intended to gain. To remedy this, the player should keep his forearm parallel to the ground during his backswing, then make a special effort to lower it at the back of his backswing. In this fashion, he can get his racket head below the level at which he will meet the ball, automatically brushing up the back of it and giving it the desired topspin.

INADVERTENT SLICE *(Plates 111 to 118): Player learning continuous motion swing pattern takes racket back too high, hurries and shortens arc by carving ball from above. Told to start backswing earlier and lower forearm before swing, player, in AFTER sequence (Plates 119 to 126), puts topspin on drive even though backswing remains too high.*

PLATE 115 **PLATE 116** **PLATE 117** **PLATE 118**

PLATE 123 **PLATE 124** **PLATE 125** **PLATE 126**

There is one other backswing problem that must be considered. Some players, out of excessive caution, will take too short a backswing. This is desirable on an exceptionally fast surface or against a hard-hitting opponent, but few beginners face such situations. The player should check—or have someone check him—to see if his backswing is too short; if so, he must get an early start on it and take a fuller swing.

Racket Face Angle

A player should keep his racket face perpendicular to the ground throughout the swing. He can only determine this through the eye of the camera or teacher—if he shows any irregularities, there is work to be done.

First, he should establish clearly in his mind just what the racket face is doing. If it opens on the backswing, it may stay open, in which case the player will get backspin or slice. At the other extreme, it may roll forward or even roll completely over. If the racket face closes on the backswing, it may remain at that angle, imparting topspin. Or, it may correct itself, and even open too much as the racket comes through, finishing face up. Another even more bizarre pattern is for the racket face to close at the start of the backswing, open as it starts forward, and roll over as it meets the ball. A relatively simple variation finds the racket face perpendicular during the backswing, but rolling forward or else tilting back and scooping under the ball during contact.

The next thing to determine is whether the racket face problem is a fairly simple, isolated one, or whether it stems from a questionable grip and/or a poorly conceived or executed pattern of motion. If the player uses the Eastern grip, has a continuous motion, and usually obtains topspin, he can attack his problem head on. The films will show him what he is doing with the racket face during the swing, that not keeping it perpendicular complicates his control of ball height.

Some players roll the racket forward in what is otherwise a good swing. This may be an accident, or it may occur because the player has been taught to roll it forward. The teacher must determine if the player is doing it intentionally or accidentally, in either case persuading him that the racket face must be kept perpendicular but brushed up the the back of the ball to obtain topspin. Any tilting of the face should be employed only to regulate how high the ball flies through the air.

If a player obtains rollover accidentally, he may also scoop under accidentally. Sometimes this can be a quite serious problem. The player makes what looks like a generally good swing but hits the ball way off center, without control. In this case, it may help to emphasize the importance of concentrating on having the racket face perpendicular on the finish, for then he may have it perpendicular at the moment of contact, as well. The balls should be tossed to him with an extra moment or two between shots to allow him time to check his stroke. After feeling the impact of the ball against the perpendicular racket a few times, he will be able to meet the ball with the center of the racket face more easily and consistently.

Since many racket face problems are tied in with faulty grips and swings, it is necessary to decide what to deal with first. Proceed one step at a time, not adding anything new until there is measurable improvement. Pick first that aspect of the problem which will show the most rapid improvement, to encourage the player and give him a sense of accomplishment. Then sail into the tougher part of the problem.

Players who turn the racket face down on the backswing usually use a semi-Western or Western grip, often with a straight backswing and a waiting position with

SEMI-WESTERN GRIP *and typical swing pattern (Plates 127 to 134): low waiting position, racket face down (Plate 128), extreme layback of wrist, lowered racket head at contact, follow-through around neck, are features. In AFTER sequence (Plates 135 to 142 on Page 70), waiting position is higher, racket head higher on backswing, face perpendicular at end of backswing, level at impact, well extended on follow-through.*

PLATE 127 **PLATE 128** **PLATE 129** **PLATE 130**

PLATE 131 PLATE 132 PLATE 133 PLATE 134

PLATE 135 PLATE 136 PLATE 137 PLATE 138

PLATE 139 PLATE 140 PLATE 141 PLATE 142

the racket held too low in. For some, changing their grip and swing may eliminate the downward turn of the racket face, particularly if the perpendicular face on the finish is stressed. If a player encounters difficulty with the grip change or the new swing pattern, he should first attend to the angle of the racket face, since better control and more solid contact will result even if both his grip and swing are wrong. This approach is equally helpful if the player closes the racket face, opens, and then closes it again. On the other hand, if the player has a semi-Western grip that allows him a continuous swing but turns the face down on the backswing, the grip change and concentration on keeping the racket face perpendicular may do the job.

Closing of the racket face on the backswing may also occur with any grip if the player lifts his elbow on the backswing. This is a different problem altogether and requires a different approach. In this case, the player should keep his elbow down and let the tip of his racket lead the way back, making certain that his elbow is not tucked in too close to his body since this will cramp the swing.

Opening the racket face on the backswing is quite commonly associated with the Continental grip, which men and boys are far more likely to use than are women or girls. Here, too, an effort to keep the racket face perpendicular on the finish will result in short-term improvement, so that the more fundamental problems of grip and swing pattern can then be attacked.

Elbow and Upper Arm

Besides leading the backswing, as mentioned above, the elbow can cause additional trouble if it remains bent throughout the entire swing. When the racket is brought back, there is a point during the swing—just at the start of the forward swing—when the arm should be almost fully extended. If a player's arm remains bent at this point, he should straighten it out so that it will not be cramped at the time of contact. Relaxation is the key, here, for it will allow the player to swing in a wider arc and thus get up more speed. This problem is more common in girls than boys, and again may be traced to using too heavy a racket.

OVERLEAF

OPEN RACKET FACE *on backswing (Plates 143 to 150): Starting from low waiting position, player brings racket back with face open, elbow cramped. On finish, racket is wrapped around neck. In AFTER sequence (Plates 151 to 158), player starts in higher waiting position, keeps racket face perpendicular, hits farther away from body and finishes out ahead. Hint of cramped elbow still present.*

PLATE 143 PLATE 144 PLATE 145 PLATE 146

PLATE 151 PLATE 152 PLATE 153 PLATE 154

One cause of elbow misuse during the backswing and at the time of contact is that the player has gotten too close to the ball. Crowding results in a cramped elbow. (This problem will be taken up more fully under footwork.) Suffice it to say that the player should give his arm full swinging room, by moving back from a ball that is coming towards him and not crowding a ball he must run for.

PLATE 147 PLATE 148 PLATE 149 PLATE 150

PLATE 155 PLATE 156 PLATE 157 PLATE 158

While it is possible to keep the elbow too bent, it is equally wrong to keep it too stiff. A stiff elbow keeps the player too far from the ball and detracts from the leverage he gets by bringing his arm back with the elbow slightly bent and then extending the arm during the forward swing. To overcome this problem, the player should examine the photographs of the forehand on pages 33–34 to see exactly how the forearm is supposed to work during the swing. If it is parallel to the ground during the backswing and extends downward at the end of the backswing, the player will be forced to make proper use of his elbow.

UPPER ARM MOVEMENT *restricted (Plates 159 to 166): Pattern starts at good height, racket is lowered adequately at back of swing. Eyes, however, are straight ahead, ball is met late—opposite right leg—and upper arm stops, showing no progress from Plate 162 through 165, moving in 166 long after ball is gone. Player was told to move upper arm forward on follow-through. In AFTER (Plates 167 to 174), note longer follow-through, steady progress of upper arm. Contact is opposite left leg. Concentration on ball, however, is still not adequate.*

PLATE 159 **PLATE 160** **PLATE 161** **PLATE 162**

PLATE 167 **PLATE 168** **PLATE 169** **PLATE 170**

By far the most common difficulty with most girls' forehands (and many boys' as well) is the failure to get the upper part of the arm through on the finish. This can occur with or without a cramping of the elbow on the backswing or at the time of contact. A player's follow-through should be checked to see whether his upper arm remains alongside his body or if it has moved forward across his chest. If it has not moved forward, the teacher should simply take hold of the racket handle along with the pupil and carry it through to a good, full finish to show where this places the upper arm. The self-taught player can spot this trouble on film and clear it up by moving his upper arm forward as in plates 173–174. This adds to the finish of the stroke and makes the racket stay on the ball longer, giving added power and better control of depth. Most pupils can clear up this problem quickly, though they will need frequent reminders.

PLATE 163 **PLATE 164** **PLATE 165** **PLATE 166**

PLATE 171 **PLATE 172** **PLATE 173** **PLATE 174**

PLATE 175

CORRECT WRIST ANGLE *places forearm at approximately 45° angle to line of racket.*

PLATE 176

WRIST ANGLE *in waiting position shows racket head neither cocked nor sagging; wrist is partly laid back.*

Wrist

Certainly one of the major trouble spots in the strokes of most beginners and intermediate players is the wrist. And, to make matters a little more complicated for teachers, there are many outstanding players who make extraordinarily good use of the wrist. Should the teacher, therefore, be lenient about it? Emphatically no! Only the player who is way ahead of his contemporaries in ball sense, stroke production, and plain good judgment should be given liberty in this matter. A Rod Laver, Chuck McKinley, or Rosie Casals—a player with a willingness to try anything and some hope of bringing it off—can be encouraged. Most ordinary mortals, and this includes other ranking players, should not meddle with the wrist in the course of a stroke.

The best use of the wrist is to set it correctly during the waiting position and keep it that way throughout the swing. The most common and least harmful type of wrist motion is to lay the wrist back, as, for instance, in the Eastern forehand grip where the wrist *is* laid back slightly. It should result in the line of the forearm being off the line of the racket as viewed from above at the moment the player hits the ball (see picture).

Unfortunately, many players lay the wrist back farther than is desirable. They then have to meet the ball too far ahead and are apt to cramp their swing. They are

PLATE 177

WRIST CURLED *forward: most common waiting position error among girls.*

PLATE 178

CORRECT WRIST ANGLE *at contact with ball is same as in waiting position—about a 45° angle of forearm to racket shaft.*

PLATE 179

EXCESSIVE LAYBACK *of wrist makes timing difficult.*

also likely, when they find their racket moving along behind schedule, to whip the head through, slapping the ball and losing control. Some players lay the racket head back so far it becomes almost impossible for them to time their swing. If racket and arm remain in the proper position, the player has only to time his arm, not the racket. He will know that if his arm is in the right place, the racket will be, too. When the timing of the arm and racket becomes separated, all kinds of computing problems befuddle the brain.

With some wrist faults, the player leaves the racket head in the waiting position and leads the backswing with his wrist. The racket head has to come along after a bit, but the wrist is ahead all the way to the end of the backswing. The racket head whips on past the wrist as the wrist starts forward and trails until just about time to meet the ball. Then the racket head speeds up and passes the wrist, flailing the ball to some unknown portion of the opposite court, net, or fence. If a player is thoroughly double-jointed, he can even do this with the elbow, imparting a roll to the arm, as well. There is really no limit to the rolls, pitches, and yaws a person can inflict on his arm while swinging a tennis racket—a fact that has provided much activity for the medical profession. A word should be inserted here that while there are as many varieties of "tennis elbow" or "tennis wrist" as there are valid medical theories on treating the injury, a much neglected remedy is simply to avoid joint strain by doing something about the player's grip and swing. Players using sound form rarely suffer chronic joint trouble of tennis origin. Occasional trouble, yes, for anyone can hit a single ball badly or play before he is properly warmed up. But his average stroke, executed correctly, will not irritate the troubled spot.

One fault seen fairly often is a slight limpness of the wrist. Any unorthodox wrist movement can be severely limited by gripping tightly, and this should be a teacher's principal admonition to those having this problem. He can easily demonstrate it by taking hold of the pupil's racket just above the handle. He then wiggles the racket head, at the same time challenging the pupil to stop it. Immediately, the pupil will clamp such a grip on the racket handle that the teacher will have difficulty moving it, thus proving his point that the tighter the grip, the more restricted the wrist movement.

A common and fairly subtle wrist error is having the wrist cocked. It often occurs in waiting position or in pushing the racket head up at the start of the backswing. The result is that the racket does not get far enough and comes off the ball too soon on the follow-through. Much more important, it makes it very difficult to get the racket down below ball height at the back of the backswing so as to impart topspin. A player can avoid wrist cock at any stage during the swing if he sets his wrist at the proper angle at the start of the swing and maintains it throughout.

The same prescription applies to the player who allows the racket head to sag. That is, he should keep the racket shaft parallel to the ground when he meets the ball, which, incidentally, will also help him bend his knees for a low ball.

The worst wrist problem of all—rolling the wrist over during the swing—has been covered in the section on the racket face angle. When the wrist is the principal offender in the rollover, emphasis should be laid on tight gripping, as well as ensuring that the racket face finishes the stroke perpendicular to the ground.

Follow-through

Anything that breaks contact prematurely between racket and ball can be considered bad. The best evidence that this is happening, of course, is that the ball doesn't go where the player wants it to, or gets there too slowly. One of the best ways for the teacher or self-taught player to decide what to do about it, is to focus on the follow-through. Often, though not always, it gives evidence of what went wrong during contact.

We have already discussed three major types of poor follow-through: with the racket face closed; with it open; and with the upper arm stopped. Finishing below the ball indicates that the player has chopped or sliced. Finishing way above the head (rather than about at head height) indicates the player has obtained excess topspin—bad against a backcourt opponent, good against a lagging net rusher.

More serious, because they do almost no good under any circumstances, are follow-throughs that wrap the racket around a player's neck or body. The player should try to have his racket moving on an imaginary plane parallel to the sidelines or the center service line. It obviously can't stay there indefinitely, but it can and should travel through this plane several feet. Many players, for a variety of reasons, pull their racket in off this plane, or force it out beyond it and spoil the finish of their stroke. (The effect of these unnecessary steps can be seen on plates 180–182 on page 80.)

A teacher working on this problem should explain to his pupil how pulling the racket off the plane detracts from his finish. Add, "Of course, you don't really have excessive finish, do you?" He will almost certainly agree. Then stand to his left and have him hit a forehand. Put your own racket at his left shoulder and about head high. As he finishes the stroke and wraps his racket around his neck it will clash fearfully with yours, suggesting that perhaps his finish is a little excessive.

PLATE 180

RACKET FOLLOWS THROUGH *over straight line if player retains his foot position through stroke.*

PLATE 181

PULLING BACK *left foot results in pulling racket inside main line of stroke.*

PLATE 182

STEPPING BEYOND *line forces racket past ball, throwing stroke off line.*

Sometimes this follow-through is accompanied by, or even caused by, extreme opening of the shoulders. The arm must not be allowed to drag too far behind the shoulders or a great flailing stroke, very difficult to time, will result. The simplest remedy for excessive follow-through is to have the racket point to the opposite backstop on the finish. If this does not work, the player should put out his left hand and catch the racket as it comes forward. This same trick can help overcome excessively high finishes.

PLATE 183

EXCESSIVE FOLLOW-THROUGH: *Idea registers clearly if teacher holds own racket behind player so player's racket hits his.*

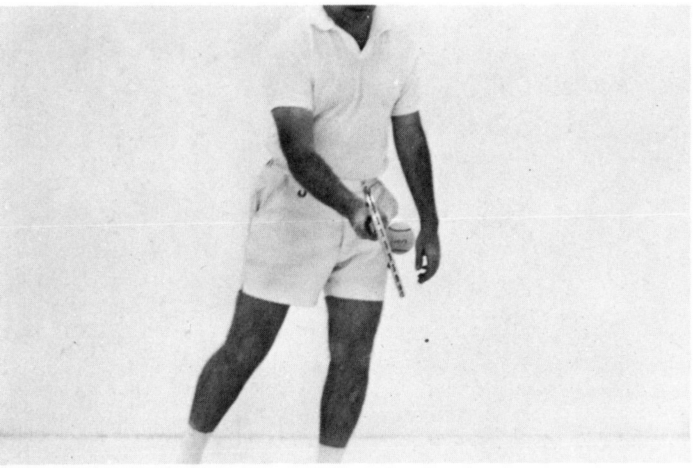

PLATE 184

OPEN RACKET FACE *will send ball up.*

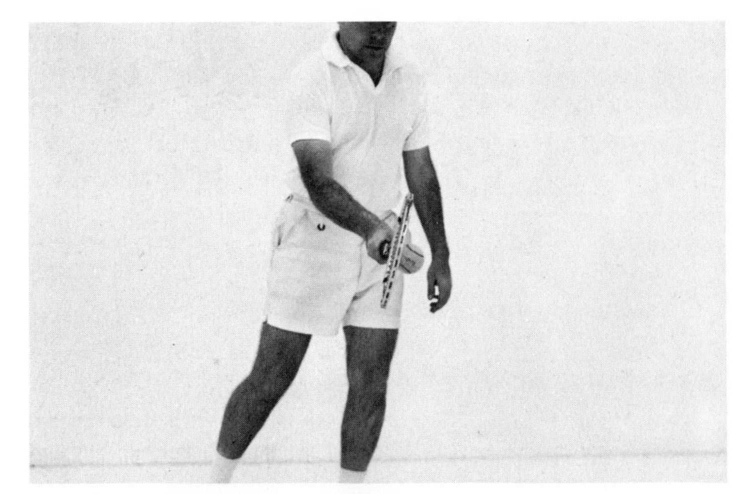

PLATE 185

CLOSED RACKET FACE *will send ball down.*

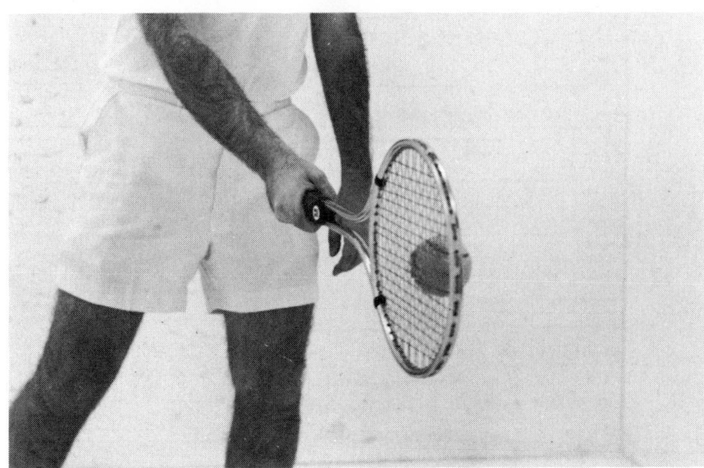

PLATE 186

BALL MET EARLY *goes toward opponent's forehand corner.*

PLATE 187

BALL MET LATE *goes toward opponent's backhand corner.*

Timing and Concentration

Poor timing of racket face to ball can be manifested in many ways. One common fault with beginners is to swing at a uniform and very cautious speed throughout. The result is a mushy stroke or dainty poke. The player should speed up the finish of the swing so that its fastest part comes at the moment of contact. Timid beginners will quickly find that they can hit a firm, solid ball, just like more experienced players.

Another result of bad timing is to slug the ball when the player doesn't really want to. Often, his swing may be accompanied by a lifting of the elbow or a whipping of the wrist so as to speed up the movement of the racket head. The reason almost certainly is that the player has delayed his backswing too long, suddenly finds the ball upon him, and with a violent lurch tries to make up for lost time. He may catch up so fast he actually hits the ball too soon. The remedy is to start the racket back as soon as the player knows whether the ball is coming to his forehand or backhand, time his backswing to the speed of the ball, and then accelerate the swing as the ball gets closer. The player working on this needs someone experienced to call out to him at the start of each stroke, "Racket back, racket back, racket back." He may be relieved to know that timing is also a problem with experienced players who are out of practice, or playing on a faster surface than they are accustomed to.

Another sign of poor timing is when shots fly high and out even though the player seems to have a sound grip and pattern of motion. If so, instead of hitting hardest when it will do the most good, the player is, in fact, pulling his punch. Some people grasp instinctively how to deliver a blow or make an impact—most others can learn.

A player with this sort of wildness should make a special effort to watch the ball and make his racket speed up to its fastest just before and during impact. In addition, it is a good idea for the player to have a specific place picked out for each ball to go. By aiming each ball and realizing that there is plenty he can do to make it get there, the player will see it better and improve his timing. Timing, as we will see in the next chapter, permits the lateral control of shots which are essential to a successful tennis game.

Forehand Trouble Spots

NOTE: In this section you will frequently find page references given in lieu of longer explanations. "Ditto" means "the same as immediately above"; "see left" means "the same as in the adjoining column to the left," but wording should be revised to apply to a player rather than a teacher.

Problem	Why it is a problem	What teacher should do	What player should do
Waiting position			
1. Racket head opposite waist instead of left shoulder.	Leads to straight backswing (with stop action, wrist slap) and wastes motion and effort.	Explain how higher position fits better into continuous swing, helps player be ready. Drill the correct way.	Understand why it is helpful and drill. See p. 54.
2. Racket head opposite midline of body.	Is too far away from backhand. See p. 54	Ditto.	Ditto.
3. Racket face horizontal instead of perpendicular.	Probably a sign of Western or semi-Western grip; adds to difficulty in controlling height of ball.	If grip is Western or semi-Western and player is willing to change it, proceed to do so, and at the same time, correct the waiting position.	Check your grip against description and pictures of Western grip (p. 27) and semi-Western (p. 58) as well as Eastern (p. 26). Review section under "Grip" for best way to learn new grip. No point in changing waiting position unless you change the grip too.
4. Left hand off the racket throat.	Puts entire burden on right hand, leading to fatigue and slippery grip; makes player switch grips by flipping handle, weakening control of racket.	Explain job of left hand in steadying racket during grip switch, allowing right hand to rest, helping with backswing. Drill alternate forehand and backhand swings without ball till letter-perfect. Then try them on the court with tossed or hit balls.	Drill swings, then use left hand properly while balls are tossed to you.
5. Standing stiff-kneed.	Too much strain, leads to slow start.	Tell player to bend knee of forward leg as he transfers weight in to ball.	See left.

Problem	Why it is a problem	What teacher should do	What player should do
6. Arms stiff (elbows out, or in some strained position).	Uncomfortable. It's good to be alert but you don't have to be miserable.		
Grip			
1. Semi-Western.	Tends to tilt racket face forward during contact—player compensates by turning wrist back, so racket comes off ball early. Is all right for high bouncing ball, not so sound for low balls.	Explain how racket face angle is distorted and how wrist must compensate. Show how new grip will keep face perpendicular and work better at all heights, not just on high balls. Warn player if he turns wrist back with new grip, his shots will go high. Hold ball out for him to swing against, then try easy tosses.	Check your grip against description and pictures of semi-Western (p. 58) and Eastern (p. 26). Be sure heel of hand is on right bevel and fingers spread. Be warned that new grip will tend to send your shots high, so aim lower than usual. Swing with new grip against a ball held by someone, then against tossed balls. Check your grip after every shot, be patient, and keep drilling till it is comfortable.
2. Western.	Same as semi-Western only more so. Often produces excess topspin as well.	Same procedure, but it may be necessary to change to semi-Western first, then progress to Eastern.	Same procedure as with semi-Western. If transition is difficult, try semi-Western till it is comfortable, then move over to Eastern.
3. Continental.	Tends to tilt racket face backward on contact. Player compensates by turning wrist forward, complicating control of height. Some help on low balls, weak on high ones.	Explain how racket face angle is distorted and how wrist must compensate. Show how new grip will keep face perpendicular and work better at all heights, not just on low balls. Warn player if he turns wrist forward with new grip, his shots will go down. Hold ball out for him to hit against, then try easy tosses.	Check your grip against description and pictures of Continental grip (plate 76) and Eastern (p. 26). Be sure heel of hand is on right bevel and fingers spread. Be warned that new grip will tend to send the ball down, so aim higher than usual. Swing with new grip against a ball held by someone, then against tossed balls. Check your grip after each shot, be patient, and keep drilling till comfortable.
4. Changing grip during swing.	Causes uncertainty in control of racket face.	See what change takes place, when, and why. Usually it is from Eastern to semi-Western	See from films (or have someone observe you) if you open fingers at any time during

Problem	Why it is a problem	What teacher should do	What player should do
		(or from new grip back to old). Show exactly what grip should be, then have player keep that grip throughout swing.	swing. Take Eastern forehand grip and swing against hand-held ball till comfortable. Then try against tossed balls. Re-film and see if you still do it. Note: to see this properly on film, film from behind and do close-up of the hand.
5. Hammer grip.	Puts racket head above wrist level, shortening arc, making it difficult to get racket down on backswing to achieve topspin. May also lead to excess wrist movement.	Have player put fingers at angle to handle, spreading them out. Often this is enough to change a Continental to an Eastern.	See left.
6. Thumb up handle.	Insecure grip.	Tell player not to and check it regularly. Most get over this quite quickly.	Don't.
7. Finger up handle.	Ditto.	Ditto.	Ditto.
8. Choking up on racket.	Racket too heavy and hard to handle.	Suggest player hold racket down at end. If he can't, suggest he try a lighter racket.	See left.
9. Hand too far down, heel off handle.	Causes excess wrist movement.	Move hand up handle and be sure heel is on right bevel. If this amounts to a change from semi-Western to Eastern, see problem #1, this section.	See left.
Use of the left hand			
1. Not using the left hand at all. 2. Holding left hand too close to handle.	Poor control of racket, greater likelihood of wrist wobble, greater burden on right hand, poor or inaccurate grip change.	Show player function of left hand—to bear weight of racket, resting right hand between shots, steadying racket for grip change, guiding racket during early part of backswing. Drill repeatedly without ball, then with tossed ones.	See left. Use left hand on throat of racket to guide it back, letting go when racket head is opposite your right shoulder. Drill many times without ball, then on tossed ones.

Problem	Why it is a problem	What teacher should do	What player should do
3. Starting with left hand at throat of racket and sliding it down. 4. Taking left hand off too soon.	Poor control of racket, greater likelihood of wrist wobble, greater burden on right hand, poor or inaccurate grip change.	Show player function of left hand—to bear weight of racket, resting right hand between shots, steadying racket for grip change, guiding racket during early part of backswing. Drill repeatedly without ball, then with tossed ones.	See left. Use left hand on throat of racket to guide it back, letting go when racket head is opposite your right shoulder. Drill many times without ball, then on tossed ones.
Backswing			
1. Racket back from waist height but swing is continuous.	Extra work and slight lack of readiness.	Drill on starting at shoulder height.	See left.
2. Racket back too high.	Uses up too much time, swing distance too great to get down to a low ball.	Explain how excess height of swing eats up time. Show proper swing, with racket head coming back no more than head-high.	Practice swings opposite mirror and keep racket head below head height during backswing. Do enough to be able to feel the difference, then try on court with tosses.
3. Racket back too close to body.	Restricts length of backswing and follow-through, thus limiting power and depth.	Have player take racket back farther away from body and stay farther away from ball.	See left.
4. Straight backswing.	Classic problem; often accompanied by semi-Western grip. Causes loss of momentum and excess wrist movement. Often occurs with waist-high waiting position.	Show player correct pattern of motion from waiting position through follow-through. If grip is also at fault, decide whether to change it too, and if so, which to do first.	Check film to see if this is a problem for you. Perfect correct waiting position and continuous swing in front of mirror, then try with tosses and in play. If grip change is involved, see "Grips" in this section.
5. Upside-down backswing.	Racket goes back knee-high, comes forward waist-high. Power thus difficult to obtain.	Explain and show correct pattern, have player try it. Resulting improvement in power will help reinforce idea.	Examine own films, practice correct pattern before mirror till you can *feel* you are doing it right. Then try it on court with tosses.

Problem	Why it is a problem	What teacher should do	What player should do
6. Straight backswing with a lift at the back of the swing as if cocking racket for overhead.	Wastes time, contributes nothing to swing, often forces player to chop since there is not time to get the racket down.	Same as above, but stress importance of getting forearm down before forward swing begins.	See left and above.
7. High backswing followed by carving down back of ball.	Deprives player of topspin drive; often occurs as player tries to learn continuous motion.	Stress importance of getting forearm down before racket starts forward; also, be sure backswing starts promptly and is not too high.	See left.
8. Short back- and forward swing.	Often done by beginner afraid to swing at the ball. Result may be just what player is trying to avoid—hitting too far.	Have player start backswing earlier and make it longer, being sure to follow pattern for continuous motion. Good follow-through should be stressed also, even when swinging at slow speed.	See left.
Racket-face angle			
1. Opening racket face on backswing.	Leads to slicing or rolling forward on forward swing. Often linked with use of Continental grip.	Have player try to keep racket face perpendicular throughout swing. Emphasize checking it at finish of each stroke. If grip is at fault, correct it too. See problem #3 under "Grip," this section.	See left.
2. Closing racket face on backswing.	Can lead to excess topspin or scooping, that is, opening racket face on finish. Often linked with semi-Western grip.	Same as above except see problem #1 under "Grip."	See left.
3. Closing on backswing, opening just before forward swing and rolling forward as racket meets ball.	Can lead to serious trouble in controlling height of shots. Semi-Western grip most often seen with this problem.	Same as above. See problem #1 under "Grip."	See left.

Problem	Why it is a problem	What teacher should do	What player should do
Elbow and upper arm			
1. Leading the backswing with the elbow.	Tends to turn racket face down, complicating control, and to delay racket head's progress.	Stress importance of leading the backswing with the tip of the racket by keeping the elbow down.	Get clear understanding from pictures of the correct action of elbow and racket in swing. Practice before mirror, then with tosses.
2. Elbow remains bent throughout swing.	Swing is cramped and arm's resistance to impact of ball is less solid than if arm is more extended. Quite common with girls and often occurs with low waiting position, semi-Western grip, straight backswing.	Stress importance of letting arm relax and not lock at impact. Show player exact moment during swing where arm is extended. See plates 18, 26, and 34. Check if heavy racket is cause. Be sure player stays far enough away from ball.	Check films and see left.
3. Elbow too stiff.	Leads to rolling racket forward with loss of control of racket-face angle. Player is usually too far away from ball.	Show player how forearm should move during swing, starting out parallel, rising during backswing, then lowered before being brought forward. Show him how stiffened arm impedes control of racket face. Have him practice correct swing and play a little closer to ball.	See left.
4. Upper arm stops on forward swing.	Racket stops too, losing power and depth control.	Show player how stopping of upper arm stops racket. See pictures on pp. 74-75. Have player follow through with entire arm.	See left.
Wrist			
1. Excessive layback of wrist.	Some is desirable (about 45° angle between forearm and racket shaft as viewed from above), but excessive layback results in meeting ball too early and too briefly.	Have player set wrist at correct angle at start of swing and maintain it throughout swing.	See left.
2. Loose wrist.	Racket head flies about so that control is sacrificed.	Have player grip firmly at start of backswing and continue throughout. Show him how firm grip limits wrist waggling.	See left.

Problem	Why it is a problem	What teacher should do	What player should do
3. Whipping the wrist.	Player leads backswing with wrist; racket follows, but always out of rhythm with the hand, making racket head impossible to control.	Have player set wrist angle correctly and grip firmly throughout swing.	See left.
4. Wrist cocked.	Often interferes with getting racket down enough during backswing to allow hitting up the back of the ball for topspin. May also allow excess wrist movement and restrict follow-through.	Have player start with racket angle lower at waiting position and maintain it throughout swing.	See left.
5. Wrist droops.	Racket head drops, complicating control of racket-face angle and therefore height of shot.	Have player try to keep shaft of racket parallel to ground.	See left.
6. Wrist rolls forward	See problem #3 under "Racket-face angle."	See left.	See left.
Follow-through			
1. Excessive finish, around the neck or body.	Racket comes off ball too soon, losing control of depth.	Hold your racket behind player's head so he follows through against it. Explain how this detracts from his stroke. Have his racket finish head-high, pointing to opposite backstop, caught by left hand, if necessary.	See left.
2. Excessive rotation of shoulders.	Stroke is more difficult to time since shoulder moves forward well ahead of racket. Best shots always go cross-court.	Have player get shoulders sideways and keep them that way until racket arm pulls them around. Sometimes a bad pivot keeps player from getting shoulders sideways, so have him practice pivot.	See left.
3. Pulling racket in from line of ball.	Racket comes off ball too soon, causing loss of power and adding unwanted sidespin.	Have player swing along a line perpendicular to the net (see plate 180).	See left.

Problem	Why it is a problem	What teacher should do	What player should do
Timing and concentration			
1. Swinging at uniform, cautious speed.	No oomph on stroke. Grip and swing pattern may be excellent but ball goes nowhere.	Have player speed up finish of stroke with gradual acceleration. Explain lateral control to player and have him hit to definite parts of the court. This will aid more solid contact.	See left.
2. Slugging without meaning to.	Causes errors galore. Backswing is started too late, player hurries, swings too fast and hard, thus out of control.	Have player start backswing earlier.	See left.
Footwork problems			
1. Stepping across too far with forward foot.	Sends player's weight towards sideline instead of towards net and into the ball.	Show player correct step, compare it with wrong step; show how former allows weight transfer into shot. Have player drill correct step many times with front foot at 45°.	See left.
2. Setting front foot down parallel to baseline.	Prevents knee from absorbing weight transfer. Result is either no transfer at all or resistance from knee at key moment.	Show player how correct foot angle allows smooth weight transfer forward. Have him practice correct pivot and step repeatedly.	See left.
3. Stiffening of forward leg as weight is transferred.	Resists forward weight transfer.	Show player how knee should bend. Correct as in #1 and 2, with repeated practice.	See left.
4. Striding forward with rear foot in the middle of the shot.	Pushes racket out beyond the ball, sends weight sideways, rather than forward.	Have player leave rear foot in position and transfer weight onto forward foot. Have him practice pivot repeatedly without ball, then on wide tosses.	See left.

Problem	Why it is a problem	What teacher should do	What player should do
5. Sliding rear foot under forward leg.	Forward leg resists weight transfer, reducing to practically zero.	Show player how forward leg blocks weight transfer of rear leg. Show correct move and drill without ball, then with tosses.	See left.
6. Putting foot over and yanking it back before completing swing.	Cancels any weight transfer. Usually happens because player is too close to ball.	Show correct method and have player try to stay farther away from the ball.	See left.
7. Hitting off wrong foot.	Maximum weight transfer not possible, sacrificing power and control.	Explain how short steps or skip steps will make feet arrive in correct position. Have pupil practice running to swing at hand-held ball. Hold ball different distances from player. Then have him practice against varied tosses.	See left.

5

Learning Control and Footwork on the Forehand

By now, as a self-taught beginner or one who is working with a partner, you should be able to hit 17 out of 20 balls tossed to you and get them into the court. It is now time to work on the three aspects of control: height, width, and length; or to use the tennis terms, height, lateral control, and depth.

The simplest of these to control is height, for it is simply a matter of tilting the racket face forward or back. In the early stages of learning the player must keep his shots well above the net. Later on, as he is able to combine control and power, he may bring them down somewhat, but he should never flirt with the top of the net if his opponent is in the backcourt. Only if his opponent is at the net and causing serious trouble should the player make a definite effort to keep his shots (other than lobs over the net man's head) close to the net.

Naturally, if a player finds it necessary to lob (a soft shot hit from underneath that balloons high and deep over an opponent at the net), he will tilt his racket face back considerably. Experimentation and experience will tell him how much is necessary.

If a player has a high-bouncing shot to play, well forward in the court, he has to tilt his racket forward to bring the ball down into the other court. Similarly, if he plays any shot before it reaches the top of its bounce he has to tilt the racket forward, otherwise the ball will bounce up his racket face and go higher than he means it to. If the ball is played almost immediately after its bounce—on the half volley, as it's called—then still more forward tilt of the racket is required, less if it is played on the rise but not yet at the top of its bounce.

Now, stop and think a minute about what you have to do to get the ball to go to one side or the other of your opponent's court. The sound way to hit one shot to your opponent's forehand corner, for instance, and the next to his backhand corner, is to time the ball correctly, to meet it first a little early and then a little late. Some of the wrong ways are to change your stance, rotate your shoulders, or twist your wrist. These movements either tip off what you are doing or complicate your control. It is much sounder to swing the same way every time, varying only the moment of contact.

Try to hit the ball cross court, that is, to an opponent's forehand corner, using your forehand and a self-toss. The way to do it is to bounce the ball slightly farther ahead of your left foot than you normally would to hit the ball straight ahead. Now try to hit the ball to an opponent's backhand corner, bouncing it a little behind its usual spot.

If you are working alone, repeat the same procedure on a practice wall, hitting the ball gently to make it come back on an easy bounce; then try a cross-court shot. Don't try to return that ball, just retrieve it and set up another. When the shot begins to be controllable, try one to the opposite side. Next, move to the court with balls tossed to you by a friend. Try a number of cross courts and then try an equal number to the backhand corner. Gradually, you will gain a sense of how soon or how late you must hit the ball to make it go to a specific lateral spot.

A third aspect of control is depth. This is the most difficult to achieve consistently—and the most valuable tactically. The best way to get depth is to keep the racket in contact with the ball as long as possible, principally by moving one's weight into the ball. The weight should be transferred forward, from the back foot to the front foot, on every possible shot. Early arrival at the spot where you are going to hit the ball is essential. Putting the forward foot at a 45° angle will help greatly since it allows the knee to bend to absorb the weight. A good weight transfer makes the ball go deep; well-applied topspin helps make it come down in front of the baseline.

There are some important Don'ts: Don't stride through with your rear foot or pull your forward foot back as you hit the ball. Don't stop your swing abruptly, or yank the racket up, or jab it down suddenly during the forward swing. If you think of trying to hit a whole row of ten balls instead of just one, you're likely to get the idea.

These three types of control—lateral, height, and depth—are the most important weapons in your armory. The better you understand them and use them, the more versatile will be your game. They offer you the means to hit the ball where your opponent cannot get it or will return it weakly.

In addition to learning to hit the ball to various parts of your opponent's court, you must now learn to play the ball back from various parts of your own court. Good habits of footwork are essential. If you have a partner in tennis progress, he should now start varying his tosses to you, systematically, at first. He should put a chalk mark on the court indicating where the ball will bounce for you to hit a forehand after taking three steps *(left, right, left)*. Practice this a number of times, making sure that you get back to the middle and start from the same place. Next, work on taking the same number of steps forward and then the same number backward. In each case, you want to be sideways to the net soon enough to be able to transfer your weight into the ball.

It is very important, when running for a ball you can barely reach, that you do not overrun it. You must put on the brakes early and control your weight or you will not be able to get back soon enough to play the next shot, and indeed may spoil the one you're working on.

Your friend should now vary the toss so that it does not work out to an exact number of steps. While you may find that your feet do not always wind up in the right position, you may also find that you have hit on the right answer for coping with this, namely, the skip-step. This involves bringing your trailing foot up to the forward foot, changing weight for an instant, then moving the forward foot ahead again. This step assures that you cover the last few feet of ground with your feet in the right position: with the left foot slightly ahead at the right.

Getting out of the way of the ball is another difficult problem. Any ball approaching closer than three feet to a player requires moving back, not stepping toward it. The poor player or the beginner will move back only if the ball comes right at him; indeed, he will try to put his foot over to hit a ball that is two feet from him, with the result that he crowds it and loses control. Instead, he should put his right foot back, pivoting on the front of the left foot and then stepping forward with the left as he transfers his weight into the ball.

The forward skip-step is only one of four possible adjustment steps to space a player correctly in relation to the ball (once his feet have reached the proper align-

TO GET CLEAR *of ball coming at him, player pivots on left foot and pulls right foot back. Plates 192 through 195 show return to waiting position.*

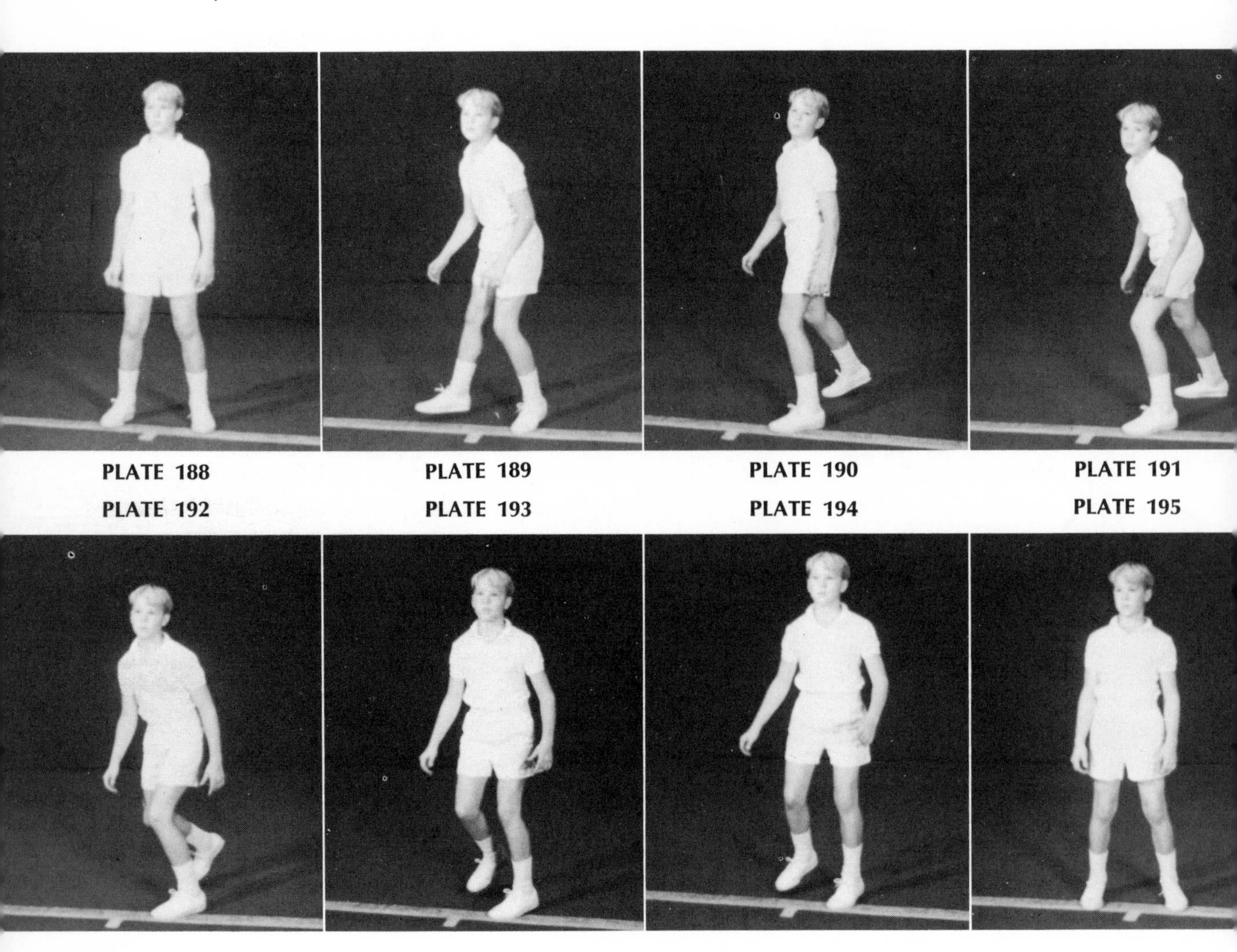

PLATE 188 PLATE 189 PLATE 190 PLATE 191

PLATE 192 PLATE 193 PLATE 194 PLATE 195

ment). Assuming he is already sideways for a forehand, he can skip step once to his left if he finds the ball falls shorter than he originally expected it to. To do this, he moves his right foot toward the net behind his left leg and then moves the left closer to the net. If he finds the ball comes deeper than he expected, he can move his left foot back and then follow suit with his right. Finally, in pulling away from a ball that is coming too close to him, he may find that one step with his right foot is not enough to clear him from the ball. In that case, he may try a backward skip-step. These little adjustments are practiced by experienced players, both the lightning-fast ones and the old-timers who look as if they never move.

In all footwork it is important to move on the toes and balls of one's feet and not to drag the heels. For those people whose physical training and footwork habits are a little subpar, some serious efforts at jogging and rope-skipping can be helpful. Simply jumping in place without a rope is one of the easiest of all exercises—a few hundred jumps can be done in next to no time—and doing it regularly a few minutes a day will help the somewhat overweight, out-of-shape, or would-be athlete *feel* like moving when he gets on a tennis court. While telling tennis players where they should put their feet can get a bit complex, one major point is easy to get across: Don't let your heels touch the ground while the ball is in play.

Footwork Problems

There are several highly recurrent footwork errors which mess up otherwise well-executed strokes in a most pernicious way. The first is stepping across too far with the forward foot. This tends to send the player's weight toward the sideline instead of toward the net and into the ball. Unfortunately, many teachers allow this step and some even actively advocate it, probably thus giving birth to the face-the-net-when-you-hit-the-ball school of tennis teaching. We firmly advocate getting the shoulders sideways on all strokes and taking approximately a square stance whenever time permits. If time doesn't permit, however, we certainly do not expect a player to stand on ceremony. He should hit the ball as well as he can whatever way he is standing at the moment.

PLATE 196

STEPPING ACROSS TOO FAR *makes a barrier of the left side of the body. Parallel front foot impedes weight transfer from right foot to left.*

Coupled with the giant cross step, and sometimes independent of it, is the next most frequent error, that of planting the forward foot parallel to the baseline. If the foot is parallel to the baseline and the player goes all out in transferring his weight into the ball (i.e., toward the net), he will either swing way around, wrench his knee, or fall flat on his face. With the foot parallel to the baseline, the weight can only be transferred straight ahead, because the knee bends only the way the foot is pointing. The answer, of course, is to angle the foot at about 45° so that it points toward the net post. In that way, enough weight can be sent forward to help propel the ball, the knee can absorb the weight, and the player will remain upright after swinging.

One other error often coupled with the parallel front foot is the tendency of the forward leg to stiffen as the weight is moved forward. This stiffening resists weight and tends to prevent it from getting into the shot. If the knee of the forward leg is allowed to bend, it will absorb the weight and pull it into the shot.

There are several other important footwork errors, such as striding forward with the rear foot in the middle of the shot, thus pushing the racket out past that imaginary parallel plane. This botches up a follow-through every bit as much as stopping the racket abruptly, or pulling it up or down too soon. The player must hold still at least for a moment when hitting a ball (except perhaps when moving forward, and even then, he must time his stride with the utmost care).

PLATE 197

STIFF FRONT LEG *prevents complete weight transfer.*

PLATES 198 through 213

RACKET FACE CLOSED *(Plates 198 to 205): From adequate start, racket face is turned down (Plate 200), then brought forward head down, meets ball too far ahead with player striding through with right foot before stroke is finished. In AFTER sequence (Plates 206 to 213, taken from different angle), player controls racket face angle, keeps right foot back, nevertheless transfers weight forward.*

PLATE 198 PLATE 199 PLATE 200 PLATE 201

PLATE 202 PLATE 203 PLATE 204 PLATE 205

PLATE 206 PLATE 207 PLATE 208 PLATE 209

PLATE 210 PLATE 211 PLATE 212 PLATE 213

Another error is to slide the rear foot under the forward leg as a substitute for a genuine weight transfer. Once again, the front foot planted parallel to the baseline may be the culprit. A backhand version of this problem may be seen on p. 131.

Finally, the player may put his front foot across and find the position so uncomfortable that he yanks it back before he has completed his swing. At its worst, this maneuver looks as if the subject has stepped barefoot on a hot plate. He has probably picked out the wrong destination for his foot and figures, quite rightly, that it will be uncomfortable. If he decides to step toward the net instead of the sideline, and at a 45° angle instead of parallel to the net, he will probably find the foot position a good deal more congenial. In fact, he will be apt to leave it there long enough to transfer his weight into the stroke.

These footwork errors bear close study, and a player who is working on them by himself will have to have movies taken of him in actual play to see how he moves for the ball. He must pick out which of the above-mentioned errors he is committing and have someone toss balls to him until he consistently practices the right footwork.

Beginner Drill 2
Control and Footwork

Height

1. Using self-toss and hit, or balls tossed by friend, hit five balls high over net; try to feel how far back you tilted racket face to do so.
2. Hit five just over the net: Feel difference in angle of racket face.
3. Deliberately hit five into the net, noting how much you had to turn your racket face forward to do so.

Side-to-Side Control

1. With a friend tossing, hit as many shots out of twenty as you can cross-court—towards opponent's forehand corner.
2. Hit twenty straight ahead.
3. Hit twenty down the line to backhand corner.
4. Hit twenty shots alternating to forehand and backhand corners.
5. Check with explanation on p. 94 to see that you are directing the ball by correct timing rather than stance, body or wrist rotation.

Depth

1. Hit twenty tosses straight ahead, as deep into opposite court as possible. Lean into the ball as you hit, transfer weight to forward foot, keep follow-through at ball level as long as possible before rising.

Combinations of All Three

1. Imagine opponent's court divided into four parts; two service boxes and backcourt areas divided by imaginary center service line extending to baseline. Hit twenty tosses in turn into each of the four areas.

Footwork

1. Review pivot and step, twenty times without swinging, twenty with.
2. Have friend hold out ball exactly three steps away (left, right, left). Keep heels off ground when moving. Run over and take practice swing, starting swing and pivot at the same time, twenty times.
3. Have friend toss twenty to you requiring the same number of steps.
4. Have friend vary twenty tosses so steps do not work out evenly. Take shorter steps or skip steps so feet arrive in correct position.
5. Practice reverse pivot twenty times, pulling right foot back and stepping forward with left (see explanation and pictures, p. 96).
6. Have friend hold ball so close to you you must step away to swing. Do twenty such.
7. Have friend toss twenty on one bounce directly at you. Move away from ball, step into it, and hit.
8. Have friend toss twenty short balls, requiring you to move forward.
9. Have friend toss you twenty deep balls, requiring you to move back.

Combinations of Footwork and Placement

1. Have friend toss you wide balls. (Return to middle of baseline after each shot.) Hit twenty to each quarter of the court.
2. Have friend toss balls right at you and follow same routine as above.
3. Have friend toss short balls, following same routine.
4. Follow same routine with deep balls.

6
The Backhand

Ready for the Backhand?

If you have pursued your studies diligently to date and can now return 17 of 20 forehands tossed to you so that you have to move around the court, you are certainly ready for the backhand. If your forehand has been disappointing but you have made all the progress you can for the time being, it's a good idea to move on, if only for variety. It is much more important to get the fundamentals of all strokes, so you can start playing, than it is to work on one till it is nearly perfect.

Your self-instruction on the forehand has probably taken quite a few short sessions of combined study and practice. While with a professional you might cover the same ground in one or two lessons, you will still need just as much drilling as the self-taught player who is carefully following this book. Players learning from a professional must realize—and the professional must hammer the point home—that it is necessary to clock quite a few hours of practice between lessons, since it would be prohibitively expensive to do so during lesson time.

If you are working alone, you should never let more than ten days elapse between practice sessions, or you will have to spend a good deal of time reviewing. This rule of thumb should be followed until the player has learned the forehand, backhand, serve, and volley. There is plenty to learn after that, but playing experience and practice on your own will take on more importance.

The Backhand Grip

In learning the forehand, you also learned a great deal about the backhand. The waiting position, the pattern of motion of the swing, and the difficulties that arise are all quite similar, but there are certain important differences. The greatest of these is the grip. For the backhand, attach a piece of colored tape (or the letter "B" stamped out on a plastic label) near the left-hand edge of the top of the handle, extending it far enough so you can see it above your hand. Take the racket at the throat with your left hand just as you would in waiting position, only without the right hand on the racket. Then, place the heel of your right hand on the edge indicated by the piece of tape, your thumb diagonally across the left vertical panel, and your index finger as far up the handle as the thumb. This gives you the backhand grip.

You are about to learn how to make a topspin backhand. One of the most astonishing things in all tennis is how few people can hit a topspin backhand. And yet, when great backhands are mentioned, the natural topspinners get a disproportionate share of the honors, such as Tilden, Budge, Savitt, and Trabert. Only Rosewall and Parker managed to overcome the mechanical limitations of their stroke to achieve a great backspin backhand.

In our opinion, this is almost entirely a matter of grip—specifically the location of the heel of the hand. Those who slice their backhand generally have the heel of the hand too far to the right of the top of the handle or even on the right bevel. Those

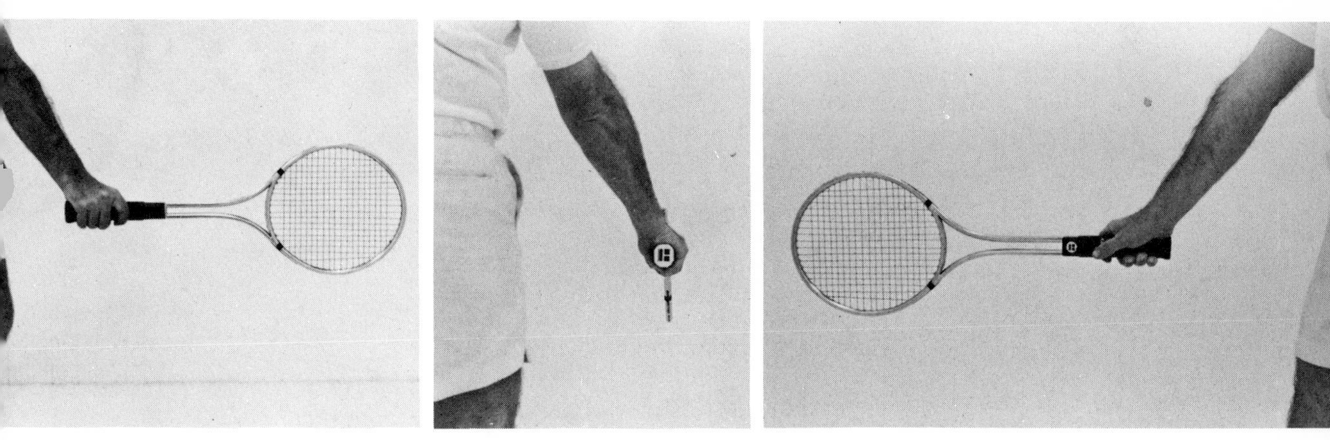

PLATE 214 **PLATE 215** **PLATE 216**

BACKHAND GRIP: *Heel of hand on left-hand edge of top of handle, thumb diagonally across left vertical panel, index finger separated slightly, up handle same distance as thumb.*

who get topspin regularly, comfortably, and effortlessly have the heel of the hand farther to the left, where it accomplishes several things: The thumb can act as a diagonal brace across the left vertical panel; it puts another solid hunk of flesh on top of the racket, namely, the heel; most important, it lines up the bones of the forearm right behind the heel so that the whole arm can act as a brace against the impact of the ball. Moreover, and essential to the success of the stroke, the Eastern backhand grip sets the racket face perpendicular at the moment of impact.

Learning the Backhand Swing

For the backhand, the waiting position is identical to the forehand except for the grip. From now on, you may await the first shot of a rally or a serve with the backhand grip—for two practical reasons: To hit a ball that comes to your backhand requires an earlier start, hence you will be readier for it; and, the backhand rather than the forehand should be used to play a ball coming right at you.

The principle of the footwork for the backhand is the same as for the forehand. Only the feet have been changed. (See pictures.)

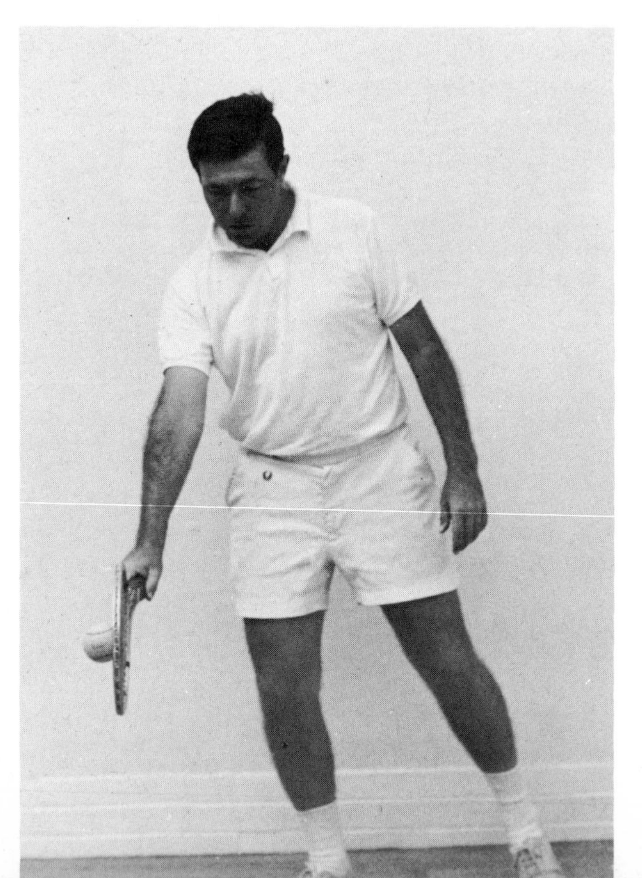

PLATE 217

ARM POSITION *on backhand is ahead of body, on forehand behind it; backhand must be started, met earlier.*

PLATES 218 through 233

BACKHAND FOOTWORK *drill (Plates 218 to 225) requires step with right foot, angling it forward at 45°. In AFTER sequence (Plates 226 to 233), for ball coming right at player, left foot is pulled back and pivot is made on right foot.*

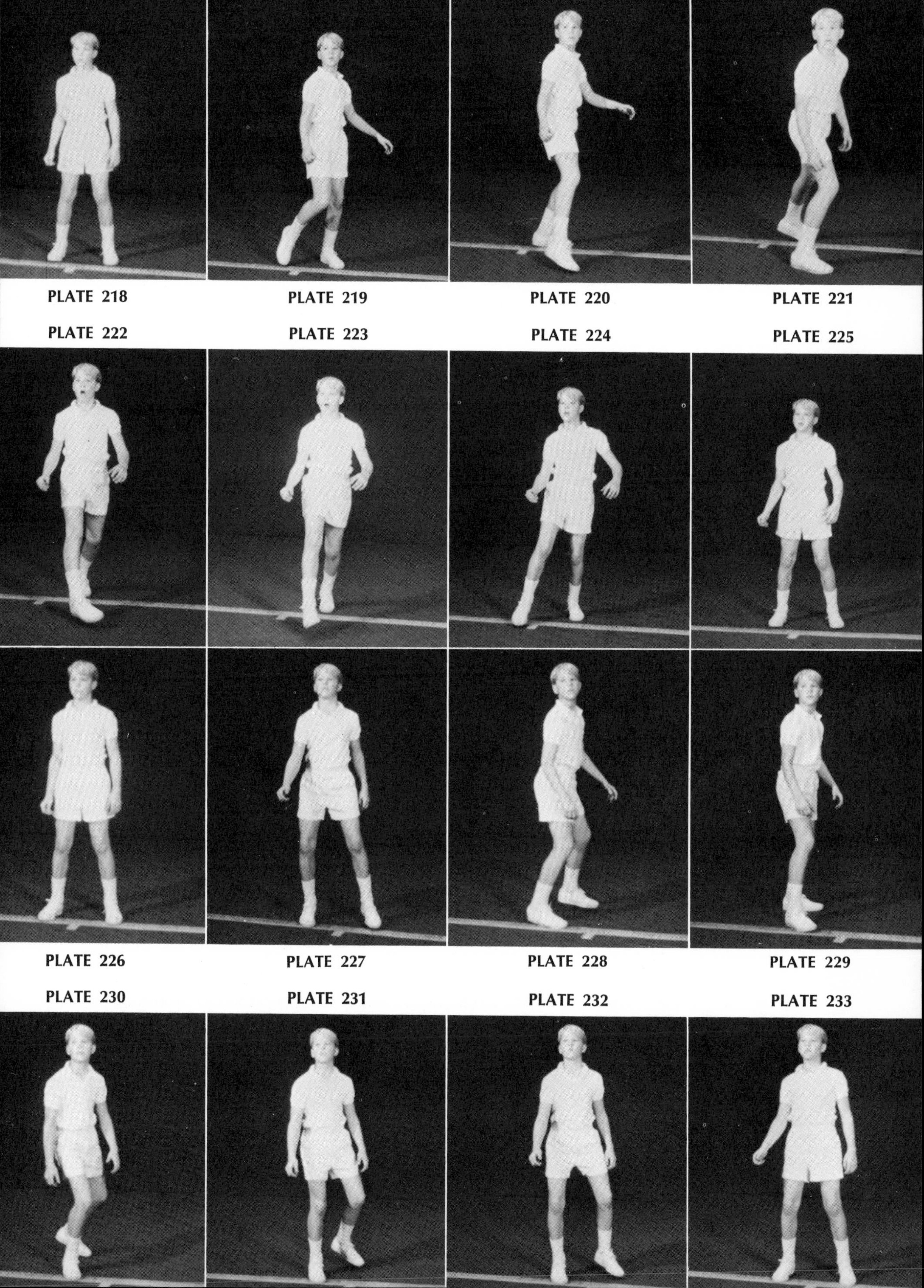

PLATE 218 PLATE 219 PLATE 220 PLATE 221

PLATE 222 PLATE 223 PLATE 224 PLATE 225

PLATE 226 PLATE 227 PLATE 228 PLATE 229

PLATE 230 PLATE 231 PLATE 232 PLATE 233

The backhand, in one of its important differences from the forehand, requires an earlier start because, as you pivot, your right arm is nearer the net by the width of your shoulders, thus has that much farther to travel on the backswing. To start the backhand, turn your shoulders sideways, pivot on the ball of your left foot, and pull the racket back at shoulder height with your left hand, keeping it in contact with the racket. At the full extent of the backswing, lower the racket with the aid of your left hand to waist level. It is only at this point that you let go of the racket with your left hand.

Care should be taken to see that the shaft of the racket is parallel to the ground at this stage of the backswing. This has the effect of getting the racket head low enough so that it will be able to brush up the back of the ball and apply topspin. On the forward swing, the ball is met well ahead of the right foot which is angled at 45° toward the net. The weight transfer is identical: back foot to front foot. The follow-through should find the racket at head height, fully extended from the body, with the racket face still perpendicular to the ground (as it should be throughout the swing). The shoulders, which turned away from the net on the backswing, are now only slightly opened.

Take some practice swings in front of a full-length mirror, comparing your swing with those depicted in the book. Concentrate on making the racket move upward slightly at the same time as it moves forward into the ball. Only in this way will you be able to get the topspin that allows you to hit hard, yet keep the ball in the court. A player who slices his backhand nearly always has to hit with less power.

To work on your backhand, proceed exactly as you did on the forehand. If you are working alone against a wall or a fence, you will now have to learn to make the self-toss on the backhand. It is not as hard as it might look. Face the wall at a distance of about thirty feet. Hold your racket with the backhand grip, the racket head

PLATES 234 through 257, opposite and page 108

BACKHAND SWING *begins as player pivots on left and simultaneously pulls racket back with left hand, adjusting grip to backhand, if not already there. As player positions right foot he lowers racket to waist height, then lets go with left hand. Forward swing and weight transfer are simultaneous. Ball is met six inches to a foot ahead of right leg. Racket finishes at head height, pointing to opposite backstop. Racket face has remained perpendicular to ground throughout.*

PLATE 234 PLATE 235 PLATE 236 PLATE 237

PLATE 238 PLATE 239 PLATE 240 PLATE 241

PLATE 242 PLATE 243 PLATE 244 PLATE 245

PLATE 246 PLATE 247 PLATE 248 PLATE 249

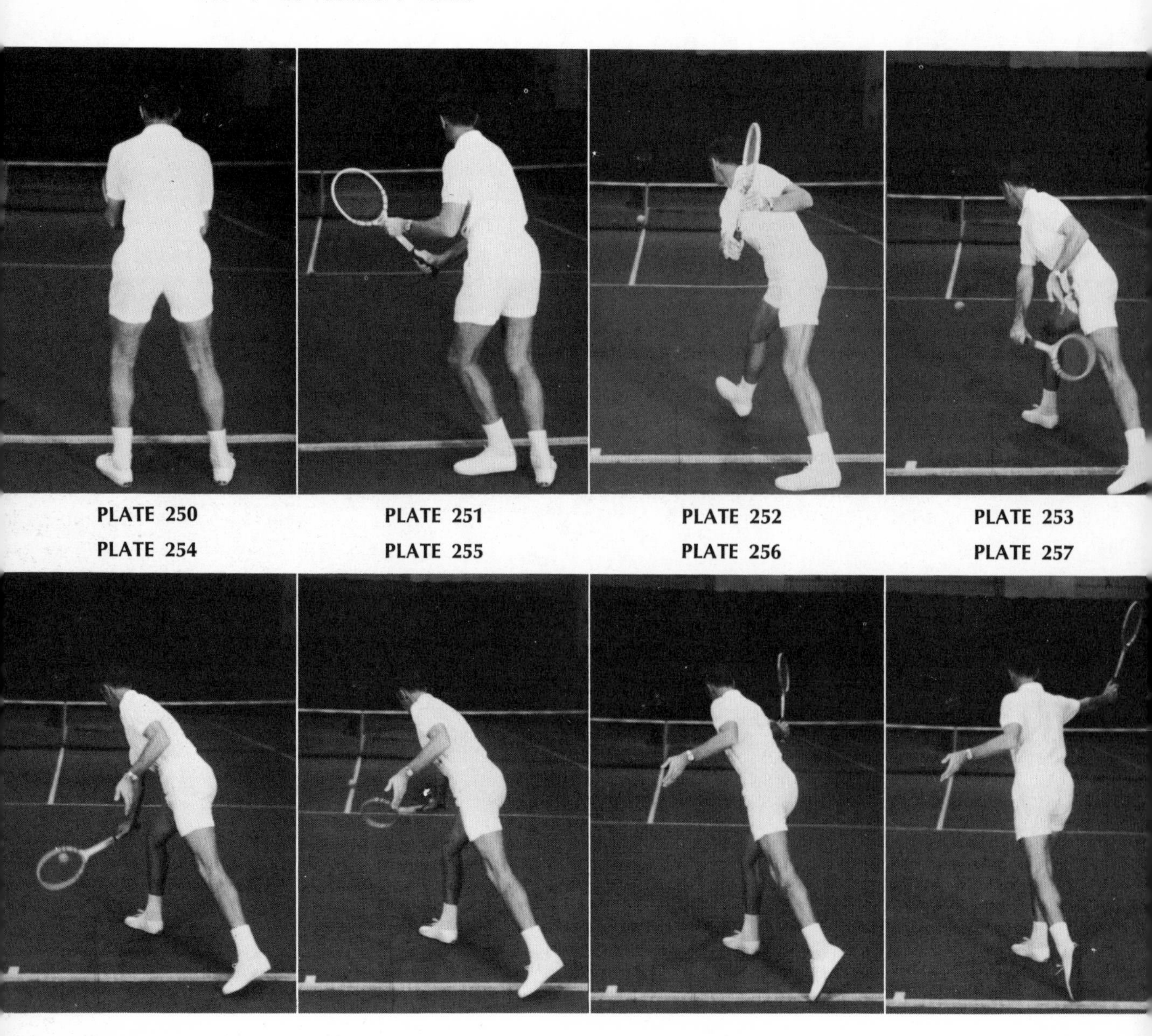

PLATE 250 PLATE 251 PLATE 252 PLATE 253

PLATE 254 PLATE 255 PLATE 256 PLATE 257

opposite your left shoulder in correct waiting position. However, instead of holding the throat of the racket with your left hand, hold a ball in it—just to the left of the throat of the racket. Extending your left arm, toss the ball up about six inches, approximately at ten o'clock on an imaginary clockface. This will make the ball land in the right spot when you pivot sideways. Now, with the ball launched, your left hand is free to take hold of the throat of the racket and bring it back as you pivot and take your step. The ball has been tossed high enough, and not underfoot, to enable you to get your racket back at the right height without bumping into the ball. Now, proceed with your backhand swing just as we described earlier.

BACKHAND SELF-TOSS *is made by tossing ball palm-up from under racket as player pivots from waiting position; immediately after toss he grasps throat of racket with left hand and makes backhand swing.*

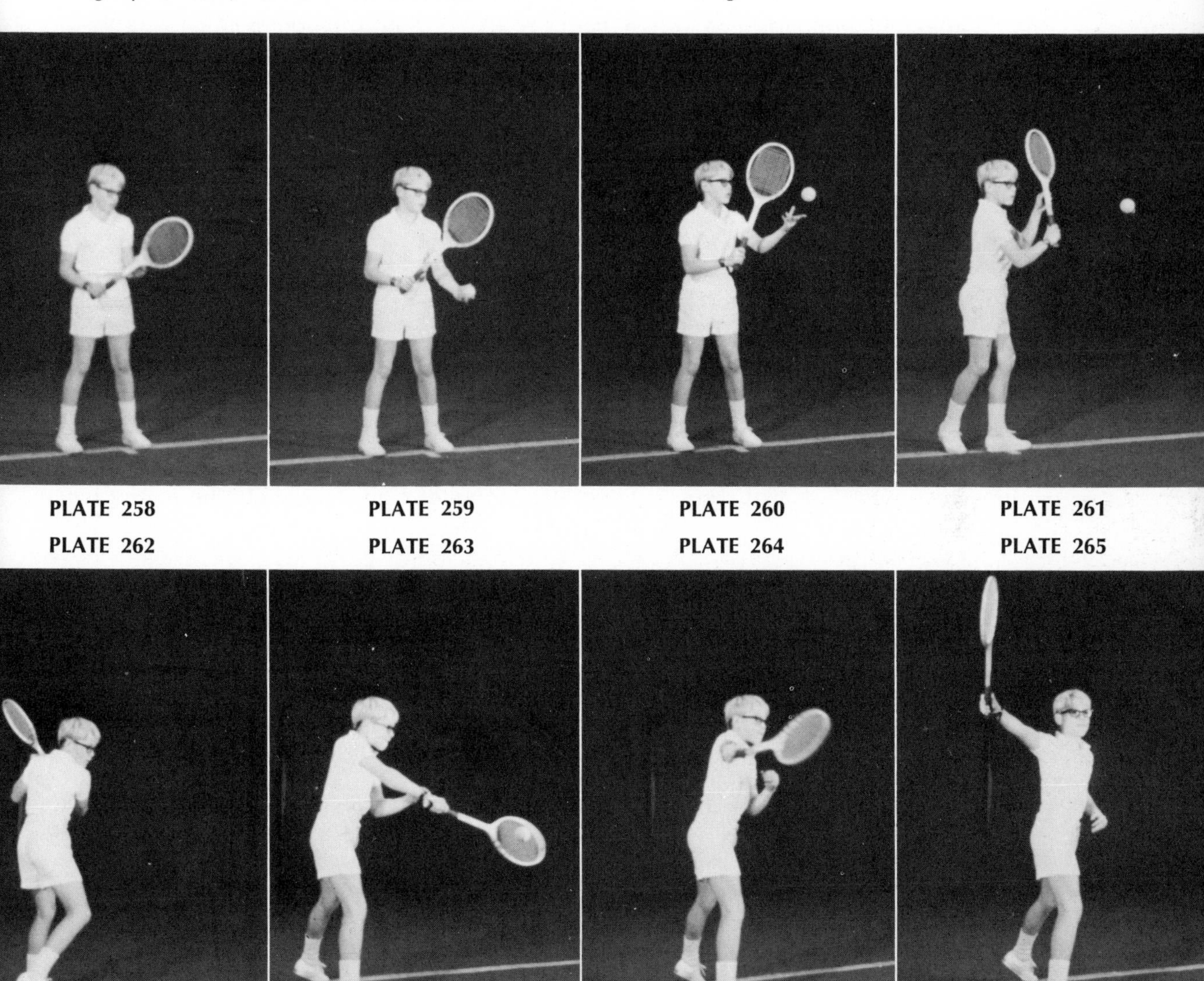

PLATE 258 **PLATE 259** **PLATE 260** **PLATE 261**

PLATE 262 **PLATE 263** **PLATE 264** **PLATE 265**

With the self-toss and swing you can now work against the board. In the meantime, your more fortunate competitor, with perhaps both a court and a friend to work with, can have balls tossed to him. He too, however, should learn the self-toss for the backhand, as it is much better to practice backhands starting from that side, even if you have better control from the forehand side. Changing grips is a little too difficult at this stage; any mistakes will only produce habits that have to be unlearned later on.

Work first on simple tosses, balls that require only one step; then try to hit them to different parts of your opponent's court. Next, hit from different parts of your own court, first easy ones requiring a right, left, right sequence of steps, then harder shots that make you move considerably. Be sure to attempt balls that come right at you and require you to get out of the way. See if you can get up to 17 out of 20 backhands on moderately difficult tries.

Teaching the Backhand

Presenting the backhand to a pupil is very little different from teaching the forehand, except that the teacher should point out the differences mentioned in the preceding section—the grip, the longer use of the left hand, and meeting the ball farther ahead—as well as the similarities. Then demonstrate the stroke, showing the pupil first the footwork, then the entire stroke. Have him try some practice swings and make obvious corrections. Again, at first toss him only balls that require one step to reach, moving up to shots that require several steps. And, of course, have him hit to specific parts of the court.

Beginner Drill 3

The Backhand

Grip

1. Place heel of hand near left-hand edge on top of handle. Put thumb diagonally across left vertical panel. Fingers should be spread at an angle to handle and index finger should be as far up as thumb.
2. Put piece of tape near left-hand edge on top as reminder where heel of hand goes.
3. Practice locating grip with eyes closed. Do ten accurate finds in a row. Check against picture on p. 103.

Waiting Position, Pivot and Swing

1. Take correct waiting position. Review, being sure racket head is opposite left shoulder, knees are bent, heels off ground. Use backhand grip.
2. Do swing and pivot. Check description on p. 104. Use mirror to check yourself or have friend check you. Do twenty swings three different times.

Practice Procedures

1. With friend holding out ball, take twenty gentle practice swings against the ball—just hard enough to feel it against your strings. Start from waiting position and take full pivot and step each time.
2. On tennis court, gym floor, or playground, have friend toss twenty balls to you underhand on one waist-high bounce to your backhand side. Try to hit ball well above net height, straight ahead, deep into opposite court. Keep track of number of good hits. Switch positions and alternate hitting and tossing until each of you have hit twenty balls three separate times.
3. Learn bounce and hit off self-toss for the backhand. See description on p. 106 and photos on p. 109.
4. On wall, mark rectangle with lower edge at net height, upper edge four feet higher, and width of about six feet. Stand thirty feet away and bounce and hit ball at target area. Do twenty shots three separate times, keeping score of hits on target.
5. Bounce and hit into target area so ball lands ten feet short of you, on your backhand. When you can do this one out of three times, try to return ball and keep it going with backhands.
6. Using backhands only, try to keep up rally. Play balls on one bounce only and try for every one. Start twenty rallies, rest, then try twenty more two separate times, noting which was the longest.

7. Do at least seven good backhands in a row against the wall and hit seventeen out of twenty into the court on easy tosses. Repeat all preceding backhand exercises two more times for good measure.
8. If you find it difficult to avoid using both hands on the backhand, use a lighter racket or try strengthening your hand or arm, but don't give in to the two-handed backhand, which limits reach and readiness to hit.

Beginner Drill 4

Switching Between Forehand and Backhand

1. With friend to toss balls for you, wait with backhand grip. Have him toss to your backhand. Make your swing, hit the ball and come back to waiting position with your backhand grip.
2. Tosser should pause long enough to allow you to get back to position and then toss to your forehand. As you start racket back, steady it with your left hand and move your right hand to the forehand grip. Continue your swing and hit the ball. Return to waiting position with the forehand grip.
3. Tosser should now alternate feeds slowly to backhand and forehand. Each time you should steady the racket with the left hand and move the right to the correct grip, returning to waiting position with that grip.
4. With tosser alternating feeds to forehand and backhand, see if you can make ten good shots (over net and into singles court) in a row. Ball must be hit on first bounce, and if you miss one, start counting again.
5. Tosser may now step up difficulty by making feeds wider, closer, deeper, shorter, and closer together.
6. Tosser may now toss to either side without warning, varying depth and width of tosses as well. With each major step-up in difficulty, try to achieve a streak of at least ten good shots in a row. If that standard proves too easy, double it.
7. A player who can hit ten or more tosses in a row alternately to forehand and backhand with little to no pause between tosses is ready to start rallying.
8. If you experience difficulty as time between tosses is reduced, slow down again, and, if necessary, reread passages explaining grip changes.

Teaching Hints 2

The Backhand

1. Show and explain the Eastern backhand grip (see p. 103). Be sure pupil understands grip by name, by sight, and ultimately by feel—with his eyes closed.
2. Review waiting position, emphasizing racket head opposite left shoulder, heels off ground, and other details (see p. 28).
3. Demonstrate the entire backhand swing without a ball. Show that the left hand guides the racket longer on the backhand backswing than on the forehand, that the ball must be met farther ahead. Next, demonstrate by bouncing and hitting a ball.
4. Go over the footwork portion of the stroke and have pupil do it correctly at least ten times.
5. Demonstrate and explain the actual stroke with the racket. Show path of racket as it goes back at shoulder height, is lowered to waist height, is swung forward into the ball, and finishes head-high with racket face kept perpendicular throughout.
6. Guide pupil through stroke.
7. Let pupil try the entire swing without the ball. Repeat five times, make corrections, do another five and correct, etc., until twenty good swings have been made.
8. Using small wheel, demonstrate how topspin is obtained by brushing up back of wheel. Also show backspin.
9. Hold ball out for pupil to swing at gently after taking proper pivot and step from waiting position. Have pupil swing twenty times.
10. Toss or hit balls to pupil till he can hit seventeen out of twenty easy ones over net and into court. Correct as you go along, but stick to major things and don't pick on every little mistake. If pupil runs into trouble, back up and review.

7
Backhand Trouble Spots

Many of the difficulties encountered on the forehand crop up on the backhand, as well. These will be pointed out briefly, while trouble spots found mainly or exclusively on the backhand will be treated at greater length.

Waiting Position

A player is more apt to lower his racket head to waist height as he starts his backswing for a backhand than he is apt to for a forehand. Even though the player waits with the racket at shoulder height, as soon as he sees the ball coming to his backhand, he drops his racket head. He may then take a straight backswing, but more likely he will bring the racket back up above ball height and slice. While a slice backhand is a useful stroke for defense, it cannot be hit hard with safety except off a high bounce. A topspin backhand, however, can be hit very hard as its spin will bring it down into the court. Just as on the forehand, if the player wants topspin, he should start his racket back at shoulder height, lower it only when it is all the way back, then brush it up the back of the ball, keeping the racket face perpendicular throughout.

If films show that the player lowers his racket head as soon as he sees a backhand coming, his entire swing should be checked. If it is otherwise correct, then he should simply start his backswing from shoulder height, for he is only doing extra work by lowering his racket after one swing and lifting it again at the beginning of the next. If, as is more likely, his whole pattern needs attention—possibly his grip as well—proceed as outlined in the following sections.

Other backhand waiting position trouble spots to look out for include the racket head opposite the midline of the body; the racket face parallel to the ground; and, the knees too stiff.

Grip

The biggest gripping problem on the backhand, as mentioned earlier, is placing the heel of the hand too far to the right on the handle. This is true of boys and girls, though girls have more difficulty getting topspin on their backhands. A player can arrive at a good forehand without any teaching—that is not uncommon. It is rare, indeed, for him to discover alone, especially if he has no good models to follow, how to stroke a good backhand.

Left to their own devices, nearly all beginners solve the problem in one of two wrong ways. If they have a Western or semi-Western grip, they cling to it, turning the racket upside down or even flipping it over in order to use the same face for both backhand and forehand. If their grip is more Eastern or Continental, they use the opposite face, yet still do not change their grip.

Even a player who has had professional instruction may have a poor backhand grip, partly because the instruction itself is at fault, partly because the player's racket may be too heavy. It appears to take a certain minimum amount of hand and wrist strength in relation to the weight of a given racket to be able to use the Eastern backhand, a point well worth detailed study. And finally, no one really likes to change his grip on the racket, particularly under the pressure of a quick return. All these obstacles must be overcome to provide your pupil with the correct grip.

The backhand grip errors we are concerned with here vary from the forehand to the Continental, including even some that pass as Eastern backhands with people who fail to note the position of the heel of the hand.

At the opposite extreme are found the people who extend their thumb straight up the back of the handle, putting the forearm at a right angle with the racket. The thumb should be diagonally across the handle.

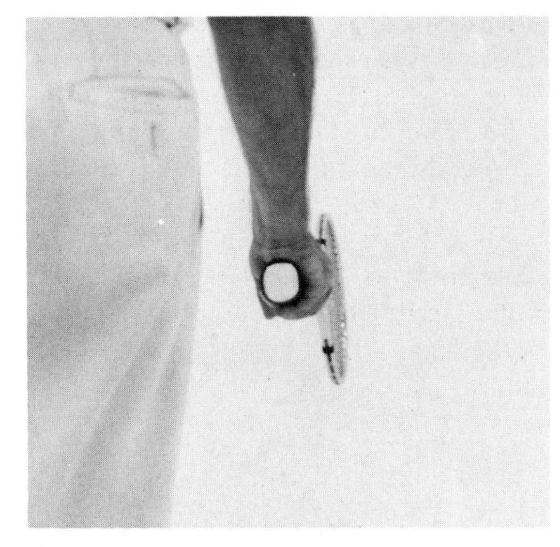

PLATE 266

HEEL TOO FAR *to right on handle opens racket face, weakens grip, forces player to slice most shots.*

PLATE 267

HEEL IN FOREHAND GRIP *position weakens grip further, causes player to curl wrist radically if he wants vertical racket face.*

PLATE 268

THUMB STRAIGHT UP *left vertical panel tilts racket face forward, puts forearm at 90° angle to racket, distorting timing and control.*

Except in the case of players using the forehand grip for their backhand, the change can be made completely and immediately. With players using this forehand grip, an intermediate change to the Continental may be necessary before going all the way to the Eastern.

The player should make sure he knows exactly which parts of the hand and the racket handle are involved (as set forth on page 26) and how they line up for the correct backhand grip (as given on page 103). By trying our trick of swinging against a doorknob, the player can get the feel of racket against ball. With imagination, he can anticipate what at first is likely to happen to his shots with the new grip—they will go down if he has been using the Continental or forehand, up if he has been using semi-Western or Western. He should start making the correction as he swings at the doorknob.

Next comes the long period of adjustment, trying the new grip on progressively harder tosses, from easy feed with the racket to easy rallies, and finally to all-out rallies and actual play.

During the course of learning the new grip, the player must watch carefully for all signs of reverting to his old one—ways that are as numerous and varied as they are ingenious. In obvious cases, the fingers will open, but often the change is not apparent during the swing. If, however, a change is suspected, check to see if the grip at the end of the swing is the same as at the beginning of the swing. In this way, the player can catch any change, regardless of how well disguised it may be. If the racket turns when he hits the ball, it is because he hit it off center, not because some gremlin turned the racket in his hand.

Any player adopting this change is likely to resist it at first. A few will get it right away and never look back. Almost any player can master it if he is willing to take the time, though it may take hundreds and even thousands of shots before it will feel normal and comfortable. If he apparently lacks the strength to do the job, he should either switch to a lighter racket or take measures to build up the strength of his hand. As we have said earlier, the best exercise for this is to swing the racket with the press on, using the proper backhand grip. Also helpful is to squeeze a tennis ball, preferably several times a day over a period of weeks.

Use of the Left Hand

Many cases of faulty backhand grip are compounded by misuse of the left hand. While the left hand plays a far greater role in assisting the backhand swing than the forehand, it can also botch up the backhand radically if not used well.

In the ideal waiting position, the left hand should be on the throat of the racket, bearing its weight. It should bring the racket back at shoulder height, set it down to waist height, and then let go at the back of the backswing. After that, its task is finished and it should stay out of the rest of the swing.

The most obvious error is not to use the left hand at all, putting a definite strain on the right hand since it must bear the weight of the racket at all times. The hand and forearm will get tired sooner and the player's hand is much more likely to perspire, causing a slippery grip in which the racket will turn even when he hits just slightly off center. In addition, this lapse usually indicates difficulty in changing grips from forehand to backhand. The player who makes no use of the left hand may simply sidestep the grip-change problem by using the Continental grip for both forehand and backhand, opening the Pandora's box of Continental grip troubles: trouble in hitting high-bouncing balls on the forehand, slicing on backhand and possibly even forehand, and rolling the racket face over on forehand when topspin is attempted. If the player does make a grip change yet fails to use the left hand to help out, he has to flip the handle from one position to another. This method is not very reliable—he may not always get the same grip and his sweaty right hand will have great difficulty keeping the racket firm.

The two most common misuses (as distinct from non-use) of the left hand are: to hold the racket at the throat but then slide the hand down during the backswing; and to start with the left hand too near the right hand. It is perfectly possible to hit a good topspin backhand with either of these errors, but the odds are against it. Such habits

UNUSED LEFT HAND *means inaccurate grip change because of flipping of racket (Plates 269 to 276); also absent are guidance of racket and rest for hand between strokes. In AFTER sequence (Plates 277 to 284) player can find backhand grip, guide backswing more accurately.*

PLATE 269 **PLATE 270** **PLATE 271** **PLATE 272**

PLATE 273 **PLATE 274** **PLATE 275** **PLATE 276**

PLATE 277 **PLATE 278** **PLATE 279** **PLATE 280**

PLATE 281 **PLATE 282** **PLATE 283** **PLATE 284**

PLATE 285 **PLATE 286** **PLATE 287** **PLATE 288**

LEFT-HAND SHOVE *(Plates 285 to 292): Player slides left hand down handle (Plate 286) and tips racket over on backswing (Plate 287). As ball approaches he swings with both hands, straightening wrists and following through below contact height, imparting backspin. In AFTER sequence (Plates 293 to 300) player adopts Eastern grip (except for extended thumb), keeps left hand at throat of racket during back-swing, then thrusts it back as he swings racket forward; swing has topspin.*

almost certainly originate because the player has either an improper backhand grip or insufficient strength in his right hand to handle the racket alone during the forward swing. He resorts to this excessive use of his left hand to cover up the weakness of his right.

In either case, the real declaration of weakness comes if the player uses his left hand to shove the racket forward. Unless the player has an authentic two-handed grip—in other words, whenever you have a player who merely shoves with the left hand—you should try to build a good one-handed backhand. If the player has a solid hold with both hands throughout the swing and has been doing it consistently for years, chances are that it would be better to try to make a good two-handed stroke of it. It is neither wise nor necessary to advise learning a two-handed stroke, since a light enough racket can always be found.

To get over the habit of having his left hand move down the handle, a player should simply concentrate on keeping it in position. It will help if there is someone

PLATE 289 **PLATE 290** **PLATE 291** **PLATE 292**

PLATE 293 **PLATE 294** **PLATE 295** **PLATE 296**

PLATE 297 **PLATE 298** **PLATE 299** **PLATE 300**

on hand to check and say "Good!" each time the player does it right, "No!" each time he does it wrong. Sometimes, if a player has been getting assistance from his left hand, it is good to go through an intermediate practice stage where he does not use his left hand at all. He should practice backhand using his right hand only—with the new, correct grip—to get the feeling of relying on his right hand to locate the ball and withstand the shock of contact. Then, once he feels at home with the right hand, he can put the left back into use. If he reverts to sliding it down the handle, almost any light, bulky material taped to the handle below the throat (a piece of plastic foam, for instance) will serve to interrupt his hand and remind him.

Another related backhand problem is the tendency of some players to reach forward with the racket before starting it on its backswing. This false motion eats up valuable time and usually leaves the player hurried or completely unprepared. In most cases, the player who does this starts from a reasonably good waiting position but works the racket free of his hand early and thrusts it forward. The way to remedy this is to have the player pull the racket back with the left hand immediately; the way to assure it is to have him check that his thumb is on the front part of the throat of the racket.

Backswing

Problems of the backswing on the backhand include most of those seen on the forehand—plus a few that are peculiar to the backhand. The objective is to have the same pattern of motion on the backhand as on the forehand: to bring the racket back at shoulder level, down to waist level, forward and up the back of the ball, obtaining topspin. Among backhand swing problems are: excessively high backswings, backswings too close to the body, straight backswings, "upside-down" backswings (racket back at knee level, forward at waist level), and too short a backswing.

Perhaps the most common of these is to start the racket back from waist level, raise it to shoulder level, and then carve down the back of the ball, imparting back-

PRELIMINARY FORWARD SWING *(Plates 301 to 308): Note forward reaching of racket in Plates 302 and 303. Backswing finally begins in Plate 304. In 305, left hand joins the action just in time to give a shove. In AFTER sequence (Plates 309 to 316), Plates 310 and 311 show backswing underway without superfluous forward motion. Left hand pulls racket back, stays on a little too long during forward swing but is nevertheless off by time of contact.*

PLATE 301
PLATE 302
PLATE 303
PLATE 304
PLATE 305
PLATE 306
PLATE 307
PLATE 308
PLATE 309
PLATE 310
PLATE 311
PLATE 312
PLATE 313
PLATE 314
PLATE 315
PLATE 316

PLATE 317 **PLATE 318** **PLATE 319** **PLATE 320**

SLICE *(Plates 317 to 324): From low waiting position, player takes racket back and opens racket face, swings into ball from slightly above and finishes below (Plate 323), arm rising long after ball is gone (324). In AFTER sequence (Plates 325 to 332), continuous pattern is evident, racket moves forward from below contact height (328), rises above to impart topspin. Change of pattern was sufficient in this case to provide topspin capability without changing thumb-around grip.*

spin. As we stated earlier, this type of swing, with its telltale spin, usually stems from a grip that is too near forehand. A player is also likely to carve in this manner when he is first learning to bring the racket back at shoulder height in an effort to get continuous motion. Apt to find himself swinging late, he has to carve in order to hit the ball at all.

With this type of backswing, it is usually wise to change the pattern of swing first, the grip later, thus setting the stage for the grip change so that it falls into place more easily. Frequently, players who have trouble with the backhand swing pattern have perfectly good swings on their forehands. Sometimes the reverse is true. In either case, a player should take advantage of this and swing on his "good" side a few times with an eye to adapting it for the other side. He should understand the similarity of the pattern of swing—with the built-in differences that on the backhand

PLATE 321 PLATE 322 PLATE 323 PLATE 324

PLATE 325 PLATE 326 PLATE 327 PLATE 328

PLATE 329 PLATE 330 PLATE 331 PLATE 332

the left hand assists the backswing longer and the ball must be met farther ahead than on the forehand.

One of the forehand backswing faults occurs even more frequently on the backhand—the shortened backswing. It is more likely to happen on the backhand because the body can interfere with the backswing, particularly if the player has not pivoted sideways. It rarely occurs all by itself and is often met with a host of other backhand maladies: grip too near the forehand, shoving with the left hand, and failure to get sideways. Often it will be cured by attending to these others, but occasionally it requires individual attention. On many shots, there is more time available for a backswing than the player realizes, particularly if he gets an early start. He should first practice the fuller swing, then try hitting a ball with it.

Racket Face Angle

The angle of the racket face during the backhand generally behaves quite differently than on the forehand. On the forehand, it is more common to close the racket face on the backswing than to have it open. On the backhand, the opposite is true. This seems natural when you consider that the arm and hand are basically in the same position whether closed on the forehand or open on the backhand.

An open racket face is not only acceptable but necessary if the player deliberately wishes to slice his backhand for tactical reasons. Many players, however, slice because they don't know how to drive the ball with topspin. Because their grip is too near forehand, the racket face is open and slides under the ball, imparting backspin—and probably some sidespin as the racket pulls around on the follow-through.

There is also found what might be called an exaggerated opening of the racket face on the backswing. Instead of angling the racket face back right away and keeping it that way throughout the swing, the player starts out with it perpendicular, brings it back to a good height, and then opens it to the heavens. It is then merely a matter of luck if he manages to straighten the racket face by the time the ball comes. Some players manage this very well—to the point where it is not worth correcting—but most have trouble with it, particularly under pressure.

To correct this type of swing, it is best for the player to work with his current grip. If it is Continental, or even farther toward the forehand, he should practice slicing with the racket face tilted back throughout. Better to have a reliable slice than no reliable backhand at all. If the grip is Eastern and the player can achieve topspin some of the time in spite of his swing, he should work on keeping the racket face perpendicu-

OPEN-FACED BACKHAND *(Plates 333 to 340): With Continental hammer grip, player brings racket back with face rotated to open position. As he swings forward, he rotates it forward to make it perpendicular at contact—a hard thing to do every time. In AFTER sequence (Plates 341 to 348 on page 128), though face is still slightly open, there is no wrist break at back of swing to be corrected during forward swing. Grip is now Eastern, contact more solid. Shoulder rotation and upflying left hand were corrected later.*

PLATE 333 PLATE 334 PLATE 335 PLATE 336

PLATE 337 PLATE 338 PLATE 339 PLATE 340

PLATE 341 PLATE 342 PLATE 343 PLATE 344

PLATE 345 PLATE 346 PLATE 347 PLATE 348

lar throughout the swing. He should take a practice swing trying to feel the racket face angle with the thumb of his racket hand. Also, the finger tips of the left hand at the throat of the racket should be able to tell him if the face is being turned.

Some players turn the racket face down on their backswing, particularly if they adopt a semi-Western or Western grip. If such a player keeps the racket face at a fairly constant downward angle and gets excess topspin, he may well have a fairly dependable stroke. The question, then, is whether to make the grip change, changing the pattern of swing, if necessary, and then the grip. As always, present effectiveness must be weighed against the time available and the ability to adjust, a decision usually best left to the teacher.

A player using a grip that is too much a forehand may close the racket face excessively on the backhand backswing if he is trying to get topspin. This sometimes is a carry-over from table tennis. (Bear in mind that a player's prior sports experience may well influence his tennis—often constructively but not always.) In such cases, the player should first improve the pattern of swing, then the angle of the racket face, and finally the grip.

The grip cannot be changed until the player has some awareness of controlling the angle of the racket face without a grip adjustment. When the player can control the ball reasonably well without the downturn on the backswing, he should then adopt the correct grip. If he finds himself hitting too low, he should reset his sights and aim higher.

Wrist Movement

People generally seem to have less serious wrist trouble on the backhand than on the forehand, perhaps because the wrist is freer to move in forehand position than in backhand. Thus, on the backhand there is less necessity to whip the racket head along to have it catch up with the arm. Even when there *is* wrist movement on the backhand, it is often converted into fairly harmless slicing action while the main part of the swing goes on—provided the player slices. But wrist habits that are relatively harmless in the slice backhand (or forehand, for that matter) are quite harmful in a topspin drive.

The first culprit is the tendency to lay the wrist back, that is, to cause the racket shaft to be at a right angle to the forearm at the back of the backswing. The best way to view this is from above (see picture); at ground level it simply looks as if the player is wrapping the racket around his body on the backswing, probably because the player has his thumb straight up the back of the handle. If the wrist angle remains in that position throughout the swing, the racket will arrive late (some beginners will hit the ball twice in rapid succession—once at the throat of the racket and once at the tip) and the only balls hit solidly will go cross court. If the wrist moves the racket head forward from this position, almost anything can happen. In either case, it is necessary to set the wrist angle properly at the beginning of the swing (45° behind the line of the racket, not 90°—see picture) and to check that it is still that way at the finish. If the thumb is at fault, set it so that thumb and forefinger extend the same distance up the handle. This will adjust the wrist angle all or most of the way.

PLATE 349

WRAPAROUND *backswing on backhand caused by thumb-straight up grip.*

PLATE 350

LOOSE WRIST *is much improved by thumb-across position and firm hold, which locks wrist.*

PLATE 351

FOREARM'S ANGLE *to racket shaft of 45° throughout swing is shown here at contact.*

PLATE 352 **PLATE 353** **PLATE 354** **PLATE 355**

PLATES 352 through 367 above and page 132

COCKED WRIST *nearly always causes backspin, results in shortened arc of swing.*

The other major wrist problem on the backhand is to lift the racket head above wrist level. Cocking the wrist is no great hindrance on the slice backhand, but it is a major nuisance on a topspin backhand since the racket head cannot drop low enough at the back of the backswing to brush up the back of the ball. The result is a mongrel swing which is neither a good drive nor a good slice. To repeat, the wrist angle must be set correctly in waiting position and stay that way. It must not be cocked but level, so that viewed from the *side* (see picture), the forearm and racket shaft are pretty much in line. To raise the racket head to shoulder height, the forearm should be raised from the elbow.

Another common quirk is for the player to push the handle back ahead of the racket head, due to the resistance from his left hand. This confuses timing since the racket head and the hand are out of phase. The tip of the racket head should lead the way back, as will happen if the player consciously pulls the racket back with his left hand.

PLATE 356 PLATE 357 PLATE 358 PLATE 359

PLATE 360 PLATE 361 PLATE 362 PLATE 363

PLATE 364 PLATE 365 PLATE 366 PLATE 367

Elbow

A major backhand difficulty found with girls, and with some boys, is the tendency to make both the backswing and forward swing from the elbow. Such a swing is usually a short, sudden poke or jab that causes the ball to fly away out of control. Such a player must be taught to get the upper part of the arm back across the body at a 45° angle at the back of the backswing. With this fuller swing, the whole arm and racket should then move forward as a unit with elbow and wrist firm. As this problem, too, stems from insufficient strength, any exercise to strengthen the arm is recommended.

PLATES 368 through 383 below and page 134

ELBOW SWING *provides chief motive power in BEFORE series (Plates 368 to 375). Note: Western grip; level, wraparound backswing; lowered racket head of forward swing, imparting sidespin. In AFTER series (Plates 376 to 383 on page 134), player has Eastern grip, continuous backswing, arm well stretched across body, meeting ball with level racket. Only quibble is slight backward leveling of racket face on finish.*

PLATE 368 **PLATE 369** **PLATE 370** **PLATE 371**

PLATE 372 **PLATE 373** **PLATE 374** **PLATE 375**

PLATE 376 **PLATE 377** **PLATE 378** **PLATE 379**

PLATE 380 **PLATE 381** **PLATE 382** **PLATE 383**

Follow-through

All of the same bugbears pester the backhand follow-through as the forehand: stopping the swing abruptly; following through below the ball, thus imparting backspin; finishing so high that contact is lost too soon; rolling the racket face over to obtain topspin; and, finishing too far around one's neck or body.

A trouble spot peculiar to the backhand is lifting the right hand so that the racket head drops on the finish, causing backspin as well as loss of power. The tip of the racket, rather than its butt or your hand, must lead the follow-through.

It is not unusual for players with excessive backhand follow-through to let their left hand fly up or out to the left. This left-hand motion is involuntary, probably the result of wrenching around too hard to the right. The left hand can and should be used not only to cure its own "flying" habit, but to aid the follow-through as well. The player should simply throw his left hand directly behind him at the same time he swings forward with his right. This backward pull will prevent him from wheeling around too far to the right, and his racket will then point, correctly, toward the opposite backstop.

PLATES 384 through 399 below and page 136

LEFT ARM FLIES UP *(Plates 384 to 391): Stroke proceeds in good form through Plate 386. In 387, left arm is out from body. As player swings racket head through low (knee bend would have helped), left arm flies out and up, shoulders rotating prematurely. In AFTER sequence (Plates 392 to 399 on page 136), arm and shoulder are under control and player concentrates on hitting into ball.*

PLATE 384 **PLATE 385** **PLATE 386** **PLATE 387**

PLATE 388 PLATE 389 PLATE 390 PLATE 391

PLATE 392 PLATE 393 PLATE 394 PLATE 395

PLATE 396 PLATE 397 PLATE 398 PLATE 399

Feet and Weight

For the most part, footwork problems on the backhand are precisely those found on the forehand—with two vital additions: Players have more trouble getting set in time for the backhand since their right arm is ahead of their body, yet getting sideways is a must (whereas, on the forehand it can be overlooked). Second, in pivoting on the backhand, too many players set their right foot down parallel to the baseline instead of pointing it toward the net post. This habit is closely associated with the use of the Continental grip, which places the arm in line with the racket shaft instead of behind it as in the Eastern grip. The result is that the player meets the ball too far behind him, and his weight does not shift into the ball as well; so setting his front foot at 45° becomes immaterial. However, once the player has made progress with his grip change and seems comfortable with it, he should turn his attention to getting that front foot at a 45° angle, bending his knee as the weight transfers onto it.

Switching Between Forehand and Backhand

We noted at the start of the section on forehand trouble spots that changing grips from forehand to backhand during play is so important the player must see himself on films if he is to have any hope of diagnosing his problems by himself. Any player, whether beginning or experienced, who is learning a new grip for either the forehand or the backhand, must incorporate the grip in his regular routine; otherwise he will only have wasted his time learning the new grips.

When rallying, a player should await the first shot with the backhand grip and, every shot after that, with the last grip he used. Thus, if the first ball turns out to be a forehand, he should await the next shot with the same grip, rather than return to the backhand grip and have to change again if the next shot turns out to be a forehand. If the next shot is a backhand, he still has time to change.

The mechanics of the change are as follows: The left hand should hold the racket steady at the throat while the right hand moves to the correct grip, the change taking place during the backswing so that there is no time lost.

In actual play, the player will start with his service grip if he is serving, immediately change to whichever side the next shot calls for, then proceed as set out above. If he is receiving, his best bet is to wait with the grip he is most likely to need, depending on which side his opponent generally serves to. However, a more important consideration might be which change the player makes more quickly and accurately—backhand to forehand or forehand to backhand. If he has a definite preference, he should by all means favor it.

GRIP CHANGE *from forehand to backhand is made by steadying racket with left hand and moving right as racket is started back and feet are moved into position. Each sequence shows finish of one swing followed by grip-change and preparation for the next.*

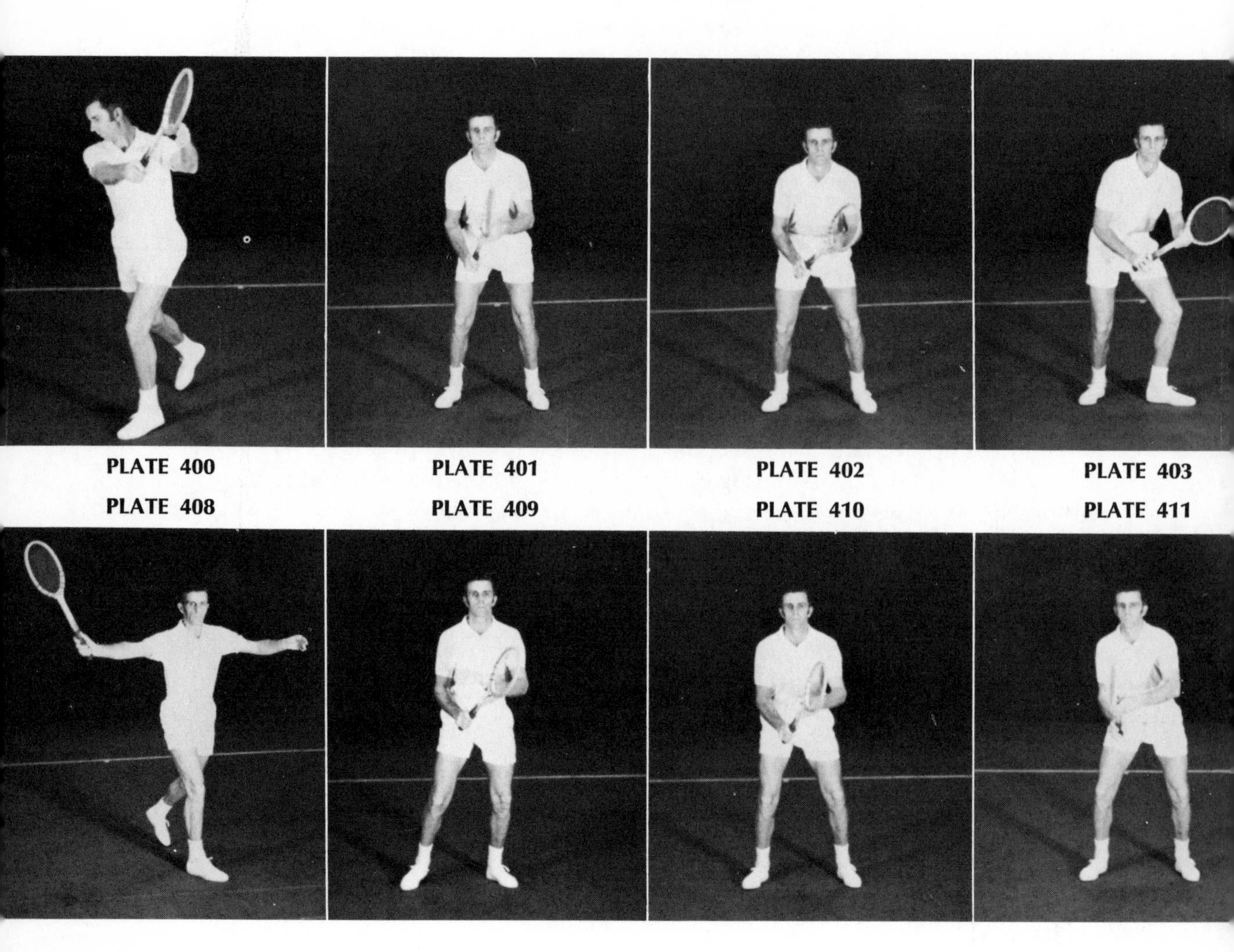

PLATE 400 **PLATE 401** **PLATE 402** **PLATE 403**

PLATE 408 **PLATE 409** **PLATE 410** **PLATE 411**

Problems in Switching

At this point, the player should examine closely the film sequence showing how he changes from forehand to backhand, looking primarily to see whether he uses the same face of the racket for both strokes. In particular, see if, at some point between swings, the racket turns completely over.

PLATE 404 PLATE 405 PLATE 406 PLATE 407

PLATE 412 PLATE 413 PLATE 414 PLATE 415

There are two ways in which a player becomes a same-sider; both stem from the use of the Western grip, the grip you would find yourself with if you picked up a racket that was lying on a table. The most obvious, if awkward, way of using the same face is to make no grip change whatever—merely turn the arm and the racket upside down while reaching for a backhand. The other trick, both more common and subtle, is just to flip the racket over, as shown on page 48.

The first step in remedying this problem is for the player to catch himself in the act. If he puts a piece of tape on the top of his racket shaft, starts each rally with the tape showing, yet doesn't see it at the end, he will know he has turned the racket over. If he sees the tape at all times, likely he has the problem under control. Nevertheless, he should keep on the lookout, for passing the test one day won't settle the matter for good.

Even with the position of the racket face solved, it may still be necessary for the player to improve his grips by reviewing the appropriate forehand and backhand sections in this book.

Backhand Trouble Spots

Problem	Why it is a problem	What teacher should do	What player should do
Waiting position 1. Lowering racket before taking it back.	Delays backswing, may cause player to slice in order to hasten swing.	Have player wait with racket head opposite left shoulder and bring it back at that height. If player always slices, see problem #4 under "Backswing," this section.	See left.
2. Racket head opposite midline of body. 3. Racket face parallel to ground. 4. Knees stiff.	See problems under forehand trouble spots, "Waiting position."		
Grip 1. Use of Eastern forehand grip for backhand.	Puts heel of hand too far to right on handle, opening racket face and weakening resistance to impact of ball. Causes slicing whether intentional or not.	Have player shift grip to Continental (not all the way to Eastern). Warn player new grip will tend to make ball go lower than usual as he no longer needs to roll racket forward to compensate for slice. Practice against a hand-held ball, then against tosses. Player may then change to Eastern once Continental has become comfortable in play.	See left.
2. Use of Continental grip.	Heel is too far right, face too open, to permit a hard, topspin drive. Biggest backhand problem there is.	Show player correct Eastern backhand grip (see p. 103) and correct pattern of motion. Warn him his shots will go down until he gives up his customary forward wrist roll to control	See left.

Problem	Why it is a problem	What teacher should do	What player should do
		height. Hold ball for him to swing against, move to easy feeds, then gradually step up difficulty.	
3. Use of Western grip (often with thumb straight up left vertical panel).	Heel too far left on (or behind) racket, tilting face forward, producing excess topspin. Because grip puts racket at 90° angle to forearm, racket head may be delayed seriously. Some players thus poke and slice.	Show player Eastern grip, particularly spreading fingers at angle to handle. Warn that first shots may go high. Hold ball to swing against, correcting pattern of motion. Feed easy tosses, gradually step up difficulty.	See left.
4. Opening fingers during swing.	Weakens grip as well as racket-face control.	Have player keep fingertips in contact with handle throughout swing. Have him adjust height by slight wrist turn rather than by grip change.	
Use of left hand			
1. No use at all.	Impedes grip change, strains playing hand, causes excess perspiration.	Show player correct use of left hand (see p. 138) in assisting grip change. Have him practice repeatedly, then hit against easy tosses, gradually stepping up difficulty.	See left.
2. Sliding left hand down the handle.	Leads to excess wrist motion. May be sign of poor grip or heavy racket since it may represent effort to help other hand swing the racket.	See problem #1—procedure is the same for sliding as for non-use. If necessary, tape cardboard collar around throat of racket to impede slide.	See left.
3. Left hand too near handle.	Usually allows too much wrist motion.	Ditto.	Ditto.
4. Using left hand to shove racket forward.	Usually bolsters weak backhand grip. Is rarely as good as either one-handed or genuine two-handed stroke.	If stroke is definitely weaker than rest of player's game and he is dissatisfied with it, change to one-handed. If player is very dependent on left hand, change to full two-handed with left hand on throughout swing. If stroke plays well, let it alone, but don't let beginners start	See left.

Problem	Why it is a problem	What teacher should do	What player should do
		that way. If changing to one-handed style, check grip and swing pattern carefully.	
5. Two-handed backhand.	Less reach, less follow-through, more trouble with control of racket-face angle since wrists tend to rotate.	Start beginners with a racket light enough to manage with one hand. With experienced players, rate the stroke against the rest of their game. If it's OK, just try to improve it; if definitely weaker, consider going one-handed.	See left.
6. Reaching forward before starting backswing.	Wastes time and effort.	Have player pull racket back with left hand as soon as he sees a backhand coming. Feel left thumb on front part of racket throat.	See left.
Backswing			
1. Excessively high backswing.			
2. Backswing too close to body.	See problems under forehand trouble spots, "Backswing."	See left.	See left.
3. Straight backswing.			
4. Upside-down backswing.			
5. Too short a backswing.	Lack of power. Many players start forward swing with arm too far out from body.	Have player bring arm back parallel to sideline before swinging forward. For this, player should start backswing early.	See left.
6. Racket back at waist height, up to shoulder height and forward (with slice pattern).	Standard slice backhand swing pattern. Good for defense but lacks power. Almost always occurs with Continental grip.	Have player change grip to Eastern and to continuous swing pattern, setting forearm down at end of backswing.	See left.

Problem	Why it is a problem	What teacher should do	What player should do
Racket-face angle			
1. Opening racket face.	Makes height and spin control uncertain.	Have player understand importance of keeping racket face perpendicular throughout swing to ensure control. Right thumb should sense this, and fingers of left hand during backswing.	See left.
2. Opening with wrist rotation on backswing.	Hard to control height and spin.	Allowing player to use current grip and swing, work to eliminate wrist rotation. If he uses slice, let him continue until wrist motion is under good control. Then teach topspin with Eastern grip and continuous motion.	See left.
3. Closing racket face on backswing.	Hard to control height and spin. May stem from Western grip.	Correct racket-face angle, then change grip if necessary.	See left.
Wrist movement			
1. Laying wrist back excessively, wrapping racket around body on backswing.	Racket shaft at 90° to forearm, forcing contact too far ahead of forward foot.	Check grip—often thumb is straight up left vertical panel. Readjust fingers and have player set wrist at proper angle in waiting position. Racket shaft should be at 45° angle to forearm.	See left.
2. Wrist cocked when attempting topspin backhand.	Does not allow racket time or room to get below ball height before contact. Result: next to no topspin. Not a serious problem on slice backhand.	Have player lower wrist in waiting position, and during backswing, deliberately lower both arms to keep racket shaft parallel to ground before it starts forward. Hit forward and follow through head-high.	See left.
3. Pushing handle back ahead of racket head.	Complicates timing.	Have player lead backswing with tip of racket.	See left.

Problem	Why it is a problem	What teacher should do	What player should do
Elbow			
1. Swinging from the elbow only—the "elbow poke."	Swing is too short and abrupt to hit ball well.	Show player full, correct backhand swing, stressing arm be parallel to sideline at end of backswing and finish with racket pointing at opposite backstop. Since new swing will take longer, start it earlier.	See left.
Follow-through			
1. Stopping swing abruptly.			
2. Following through below ball, imparting backspin.*	See problems under forehand trouble spots, "Follow-through."	See left.	See left.
3. Finishing too high, losing contact too soon.			
4. Rolling racket face over ball to obtain topspin.			
5. Finishing too far around neck or body.			
6. Lifting handle while lowering racket head.	Leads to backspin and loss of power.	Have tip of racket lead follow-through, keeping racket face perpendicular till finish.	See left.
Feet and Weight			
1. Not putting front foot at 45° angle.	Difficult to transfer weight into ball. Often accompanies Continental grip on backhand.	Change grip first, get player used to it, then change footwork.	See left.
2. For other typical problems, see forehand trouble spots, "Feet and Weight."			

*See also under backhand trouble spots, "Backswing."

8
Rallying

Learning to Rally

You have now learned how to hit the forehand and the backhand and should know the mechanics of switching from one to the other. You also know how to put a ball into play with either the forehand or backhand. Therefore, you are ready to begin rallying.

Save your rallying until the last part of your practice session, during which you should review everything basic you have learned. Go over your grip, waiting position, footwork, and swing on the forehand. Do the same on the backhand. Then practice switching from one to the other. When these are in order, practice hitting against the wall or balls tossed to you by your learning partner. Toss some for him. Then, when your eye is thoroughly on the ball, start rallying.

First, concentrate on keeping the ball in play. Hit with a full swing but at a slow to medium pace, concentrating mainly on accuracy. When you put the ball in play, make your first shot directly to your opponent. Play every ball on the first bounce and don't try to play balls that are flying out of the court. Your first aim should be steadiness, the ability to get the ball back with control. If your swing pattern is correct and not unnecessarily shortened, you will be able to add power later on.

Nothing is more crucial when you first start rallying than watching the ball during its entire flight toward you. See it when you hit it. Do not look up to see where it goes until your racket reaches its follow-through. Keep in mind that premature curiosity throws off many a shot. You can predict where the ball will go by timing your swing correctly. Almost as important is to watch the ball intently when your opponent hits it. The sooner you find out where the ball is going, the sooner you can take your grip, position, and swing.

Keep careful track of how long your rallies are. If you are practicing with your tennis-learning partner, it may be tough at first to keep the rally going for more than three or four shots. It would be very helpful if both of you, at some time, could rally with a more experienced player—preferably one who is willing to hit softly so as to give you a chance. Rally forehand against forehand at first, but when you can keep up a rally of, say, four shots each (eight in all), mix in some backhands. When you can do a fourteen- or fifteen-shot rally, then try hitting backhand against backhand.

After about fifteen minutes of rallying (by no means any more than that in your early stages), try several rallies to see who can win the point. Start by hitting a shot directly to your opponent but well back in his court, then play the point as if it were an actual game. Do this for five minutes, take a breather, and see if you can get in another similar practice session later in the day.

By this time, too, you can play a scaled-down version of an actual tennis game, amending the rules if it will improve the quality of your practice. One way is to use half the width of the court, starting the point with a self-toss-and-hit forehand into the service box directly across the net. All subsequent shots must be in that half of the court. This keeps the ball within running range but at the same time gives you a chance to attempt shots your opponent cannot return. Another way is to use the full court, but alternating service boxes each time, just as in a real game. Still another version would be to use either full or half court, but starting the point by hitting into the opposite backcourt instead of the forecourt. This will increase the challenge should the receiver be consistently putting the serve away.

All of this mock play is the means of getting much of the enjoyment of tennis before actually knowing how to serve.

Teaching Rallying

In this last section we outlined a number of drills for players who are teaching themselves and each other. These same exercises can be used by you, the teacher, whether you are working with individuals or groups. In rallying with pupils yourself, always proceed gradually from the simple to the difficult. Constantly remind your pupil to resume waiting position between strokes and get back to the middle of the court. Have him be on his toes, ready to start his swing and his run for the ball as soon as it crosses the net—even earlier, as he improves. Be sure he hits all balls on the first bounce or on the fly. See if he can acquire a feel for his court so that he won't play balls which are certain to go out. Finally, set him a good example by practicing what you teach!

9
The Serve

From a tactical standpoint, the most important stroke in the game is the serve—at least until a player can serve really well; then his most important stroke becomes the return of serve. Very often, one of the first two strokes of a rally establishes a player's dominance for that rally.

A really top-notch server combines a high percentage of first serves in with a low incidence of double faults. To this, he adds good placement, variety in spin, and—a big factor only if the others are present—power. Here, our emphasis at first will be on a serve that is reliable. This at the same time lays the groundwork for placement, spin, and power.

Learning the Serve

The serve, quite obviously, is a more involved stroke than either the backhand or forehand, since both hands must be coordinated and the right arm and body have more difficult tasks to perform. On the other hand, *you* completely control the serve; moreover, you can practice it all by yourself.

BASEBALL THROW *should be understood before serve is learned. Arm is fully extended on takeback, then bent when upper arm is parallel to ground. While stride is desirable for throw, pupil should understand it is not used on serve.*

The motion of the right arm in the serve is almost exactly like an overhand baseball throw. The footwork is different and the left hand has a vital job to do, but the right arm motion is the same. It is therefore a good idea at this point to give yourself a throwing lesson, preferably in front of a full-length mrror. The best ball would be a lightweight, perforated plastic one that you can throw without damaging the furniture. Do so, paying no particular attention to your aim, but watching your throwing motion carefully in the mirror. Did you bring your hand back past your thigh with your arm at full extension, or did you bring it past your right ear? Did you bend your elbow when your arm was in back of you, or did you keep it straight the whole time? If you brought your arm back past your thigh and bent the elbow when your arm was behind you, you were in general doing the right thing. Try throwing with the full windup, that is, bringing the arm back past your thigh. Then, when you get your arm out parallel to the ground behind you, bend your elbow and then reach up and throw. Be sure to follow through and time your release of the ball so that it will go where you want it to.

If you have any trouble letting go of the ball cleanly as you throw, you may have a faulty throwing grip. You should be gripping the ball like a baseball player, that is, between the thumb and the first two fingers with the other two curled against your palm.

Ball-throwing is something to practice long after you grasp the general idea and its relationship to the tennis serve. Set up a target for yourself—one good way is to draw a picture of the baseball strike zone on a wall—and throw against it. Do it for fairly short periods, but regularly; you'll soon acquire a smooth motion and a stronger arm, as well as better control for your serve.

With the motion in mind, you are now ready to apply it to the service swing, without a ball at first. Draw a straight line on the floor to simulate the baseline of the court. (Remember, you are still standing in front of that mirror.) Take hold of your racket with the forehand grip, or the Continental, if you feel confident you can do it.

The service position calls for placing the left foot just behind the baseline at a 45° angle to it, the right foot a comfortable distance behind the left and parallel to the baseline. A line drawn from the toe of your front foot to the toe of your back foot

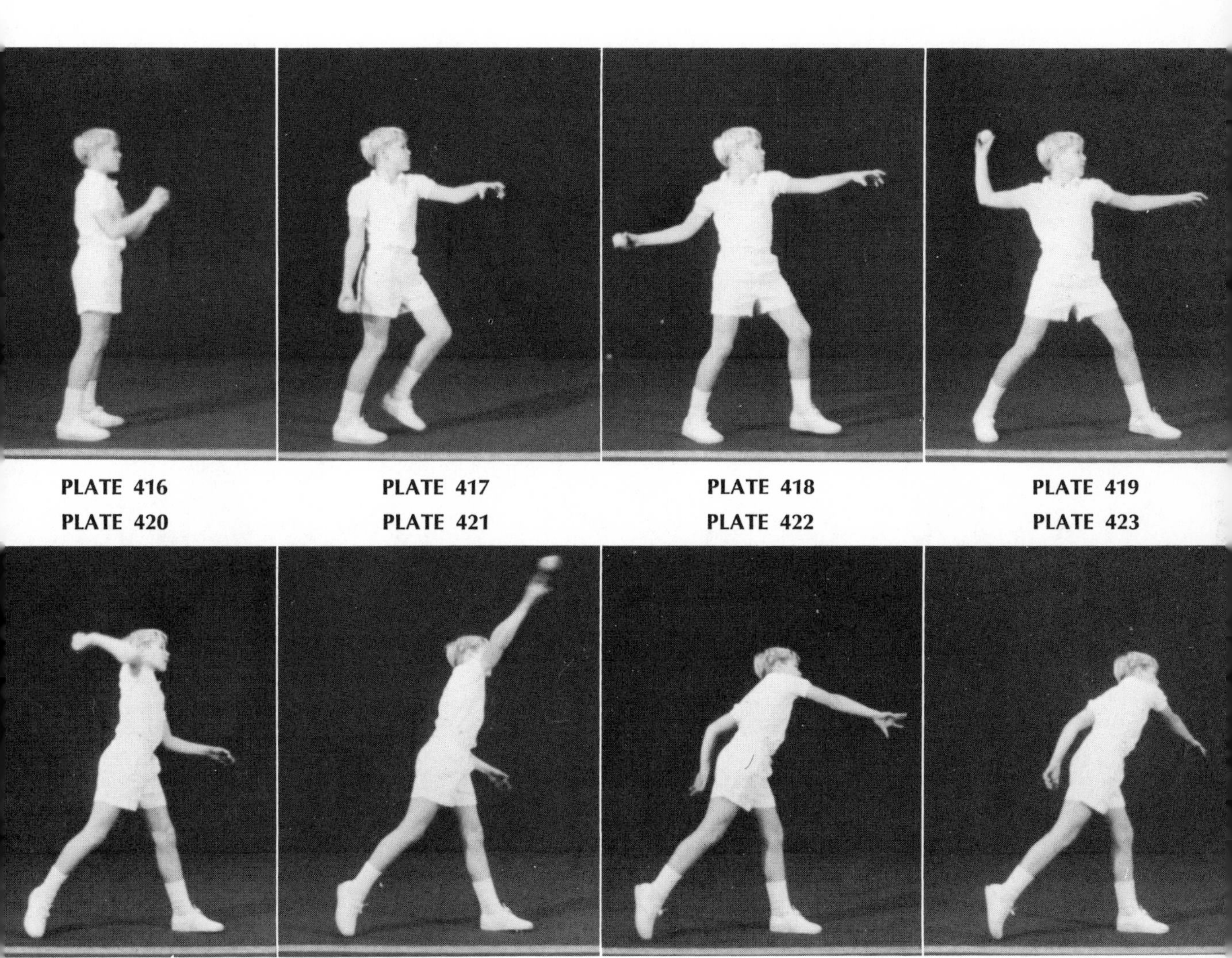

PLATE 416 **PLATE 417** **PLATE 418** **PLATE 419**

PLATE 420 **PLATE 421** **PLATE 422** **PLATE 423**

PLATE 424

SERVICE FOOT POSITION: *Left foot at 45° to baseline, right foot parallel to baseline; line from shoe-tips, when extended, should pass through middle of service box being served to.*

should point to the middle of the service box diagonally opposite. (You will have to wait till you get on the court to work this out exactly; for the time being, just estimate.)

Next, hook the middle finger of your left hand around the shaft of the racket about halfway between the handle and the throat. It will join the index finger under the ball you are going to toss up, once it lets go of the racket throat. Your arms should be moderately extended in front of you.

PLATE 425

SERVE *begins with racket in Continental grip where possible, Eastern forehand otherwise; left hand holds balls, middle finger hooking shaft of racket.*

Now you can guide yourself through the swing. Start your hands down together. When they arrive at waist level, they should part, your left hand pausing a moment while your right continues until it is as far from the body as the left. Now raise both arms. Your left goes up for the toss while your right goes on back in the throwing motion till arm and racket shaft are out parallel to the ground in back of you. Then, bend your elbow and drop the racket head behind your back. At this point, your left arm will be at the top of the toss. Now, swing forward and hit an imaginary ball, following through with your racket face down by your left shin.

Try it again, checking yourself in the mirror and comparing your performance with that in the pictures on page 58 which show the seven critical stages: the starting stance, the parting of the hands, arms moving out from the body equidistant, the racket out parallel to the ground, the elbow bent with the toss at its full height, the moment of contact, and the follow-through.

Do a number of practice swings in front of the mirror before heading out to the court. When you feel ready to graduate to the court, take a couple of balls in your left hand and take your stance at the baseline center mark. The first thing to work on is your toss. Start your motion, hands down, up and toss, but do not swing your racket forward. Instead, stop and catch your toss—if you can, that is. Try it again, concentrating on tossing the ball straight up so that you can catch it without significantly moving your left hand (see picture). Imagine that you are trying to toss it up a six-inch diameter pipe without hitting the sides.

PLATE 426

CORRECT TOSS HEIGHT *can be gauged by holding racket in contact position and tossing ball six inches to a foot above the tip of the racket.*

To determine how high you should toss the ball, reach up over your head with your racket. The toss should be at least as high as the tip of your extended racket, perhaps a few inches higher, but nothing beyond that. Toss the ball slightly to the right of your head if you are using the forehand grip, just about on a line with your head and the service court if you are using the Continental grip.

Practice your toss this way a number of times, making sure you coordinate it with your right arm. Not to coordinate the motion of one arm in the serve with the other cancels the whole purpose of your practice.

It is now time to stand up to the baseline, arrange your feet correctly, and

TOSS TEST *consists of starting serve motion with both arms, tossing the ball and holding left hand still to see if ball will return to it. Inaccuracies are readily apparent.*

PLATE 427 **PLATE 428** **PLATE 429** **PLATE 430**

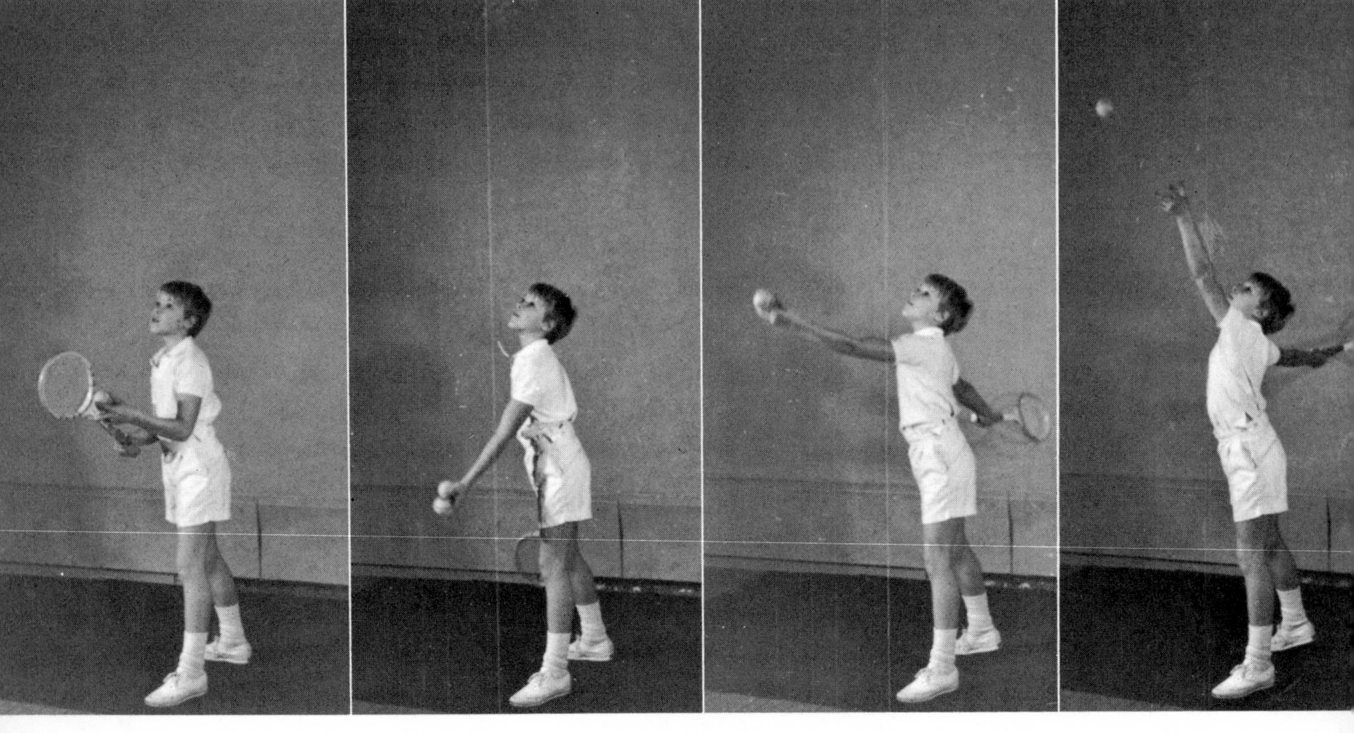

serve. Be sure you have a good supply of balls on hand so as not to disturb your concentration. Take plenty of time between serves and think through the steps before you try each serve. If it doesn't go well the first couple of times, go back to practice swings and tosses. Then try again. Continue practicing for about fifteen minutes, then switch over to your ground strokes. Later, before you call it a day, try another five minutes of serving.

As soon as you are making fairly regular contact with the ball and clearing the net, you should start to work on controlling your serve so that it will go into the appropriate service box and, ultimately, to a specific spot in the service box. To do this, you must learn how to control height, direction, and length.

PLATE 431 **PLATE 432** **PLATE 433** **PLATE 434**

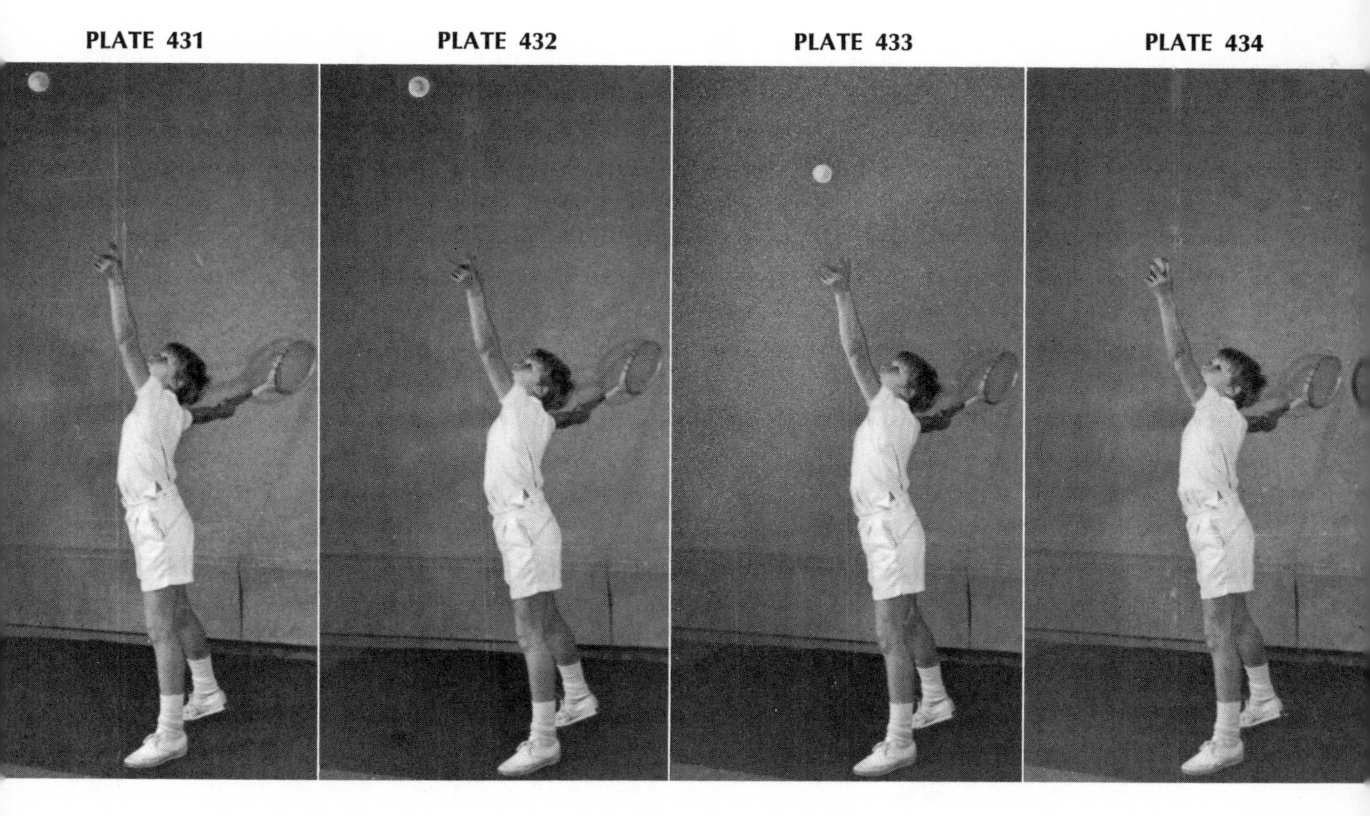

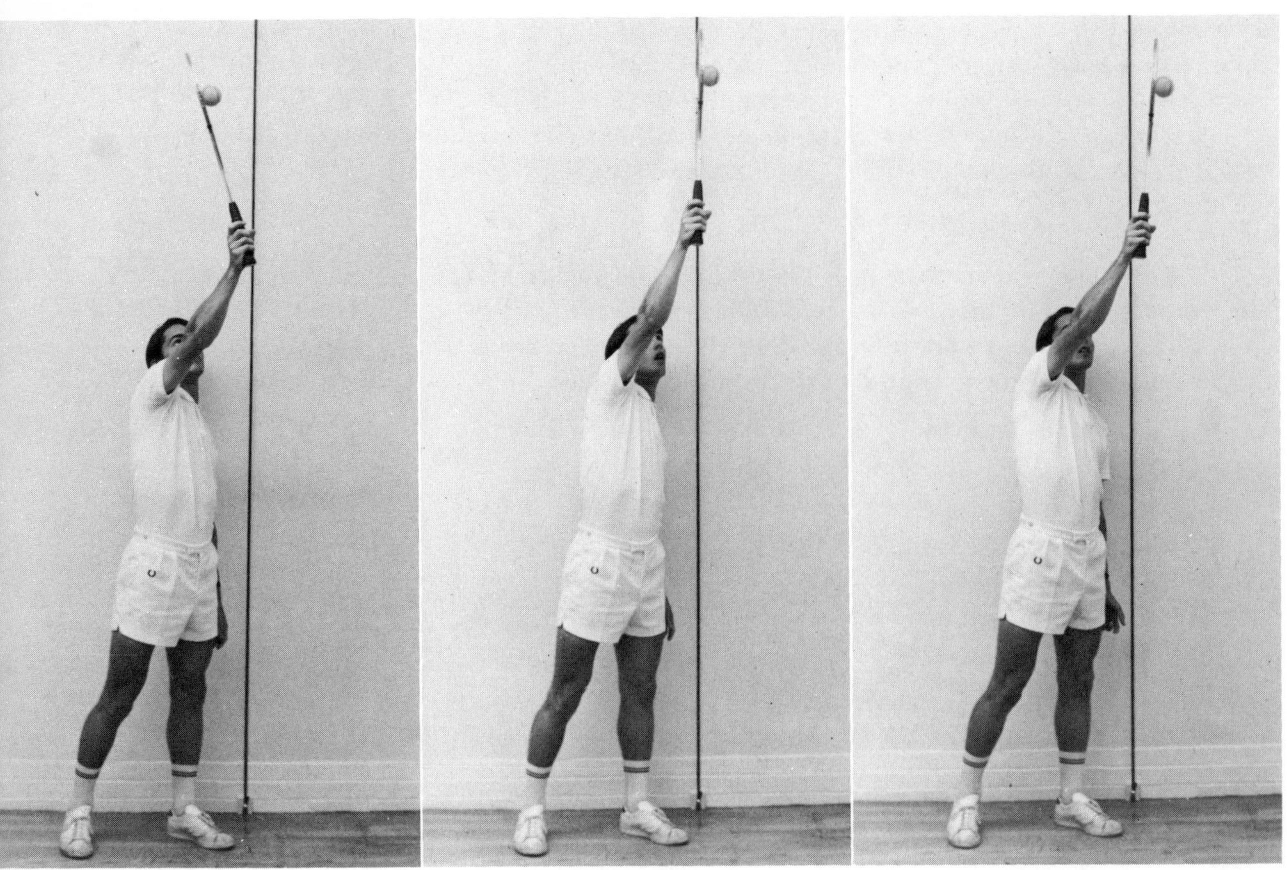

PLATE 435 **PLATE 436** **PLATE 437**

CONTROL OF HEIGHT *in* **flat** *serve is determined by how far back (Plate 435) or forward (Plate 437) racket is tilted.*

If you are using the forehand grip, you can control the height of your serve as it heads for the opposite court just by varying your wrist angle slightly. If you tilt it back as you meet the ball, the ball will fly higher; if you tilt it forward, the ball will fly lower. Side-to-side control (direction, that is) comes from rotating your wrist to either the right or left. Control of depth is a combination of how hard you hit the ball with how you tilt your racket—forward or back.

With the forehand grip, which causes a flat impact of racket on ball, the harder you hit, the less control you have. When the ball is hit flat at considerable

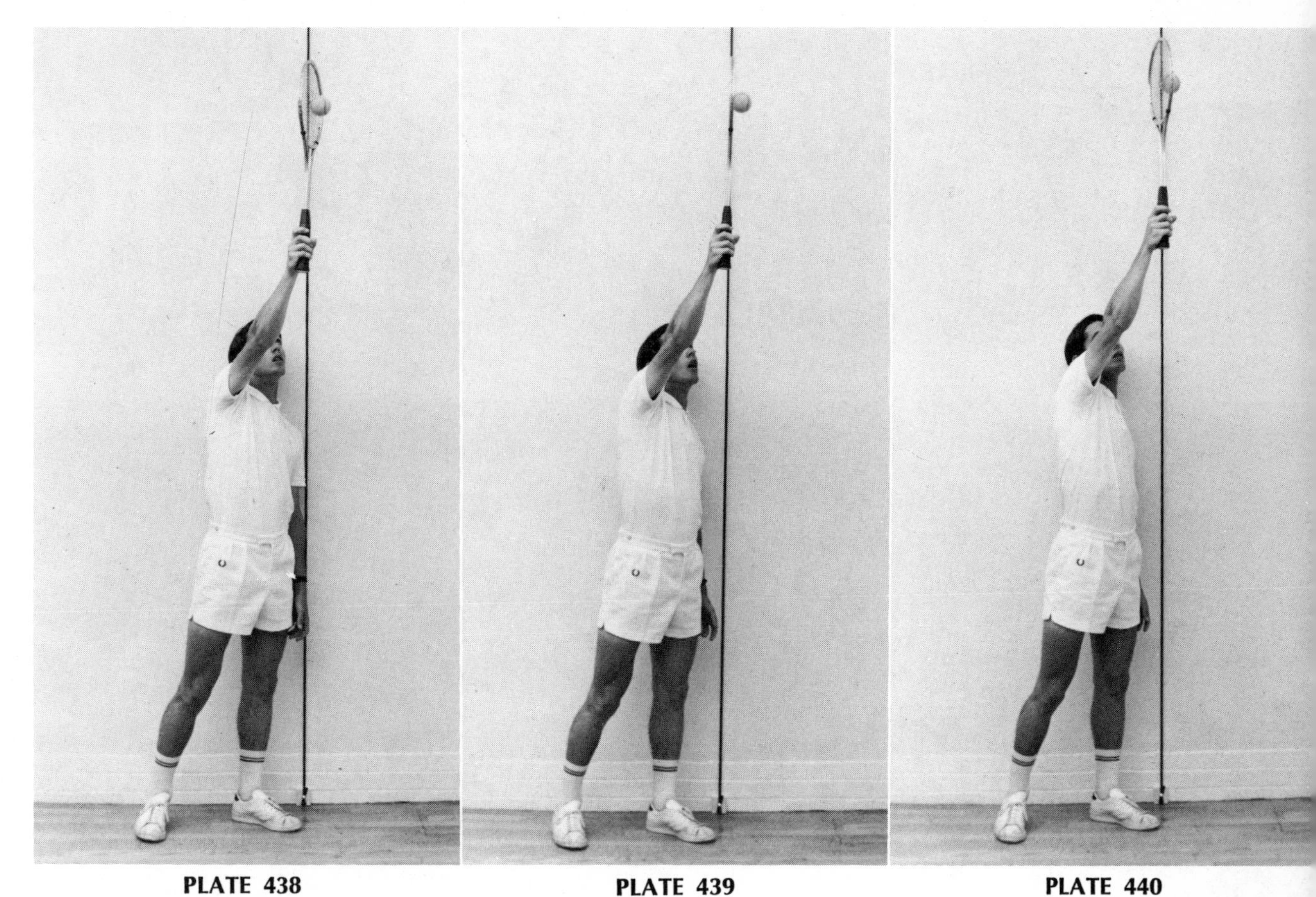

PLATE 438 **PLATE 439** **PLATE 440**

CONTROL OF DIRECTION *in* **flat** *serve is determined by extent to which racket is turned to right (Plate 438) or left (Plate 440).*

speed, it travels in such a straight line (trajectory) that, hit too high, it will go out, while hit too low, it will be stopped by the net. That is why people with only flat serves have good days and bad days—mostly bad.

PLATES 441 through 464 on pages 158 and 159

FLAT SERVE *requires toss further to right of head, racket coming through with shaft straight up and down. All other features are identical with spin serve (pages 160–162)—and should be, so that intent is not telegraphed.*

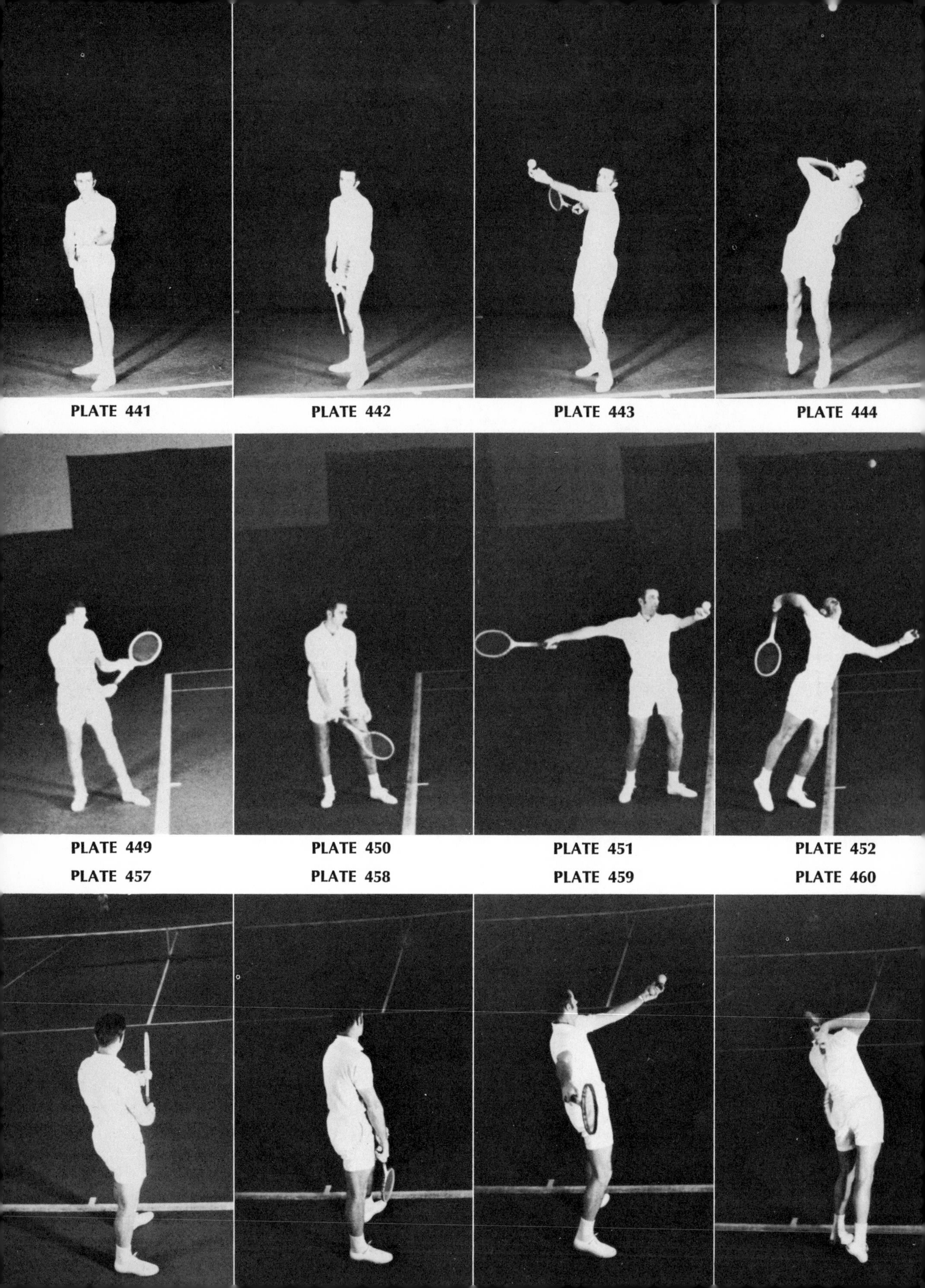
PLATE 441
PLATE 442
PLATE 443
PLATE 444
PLATE 449
PLATE 450
PLATE 451
PLATE 452
PLATE 457
PLATE 458
PLATE 459
PLATE 460

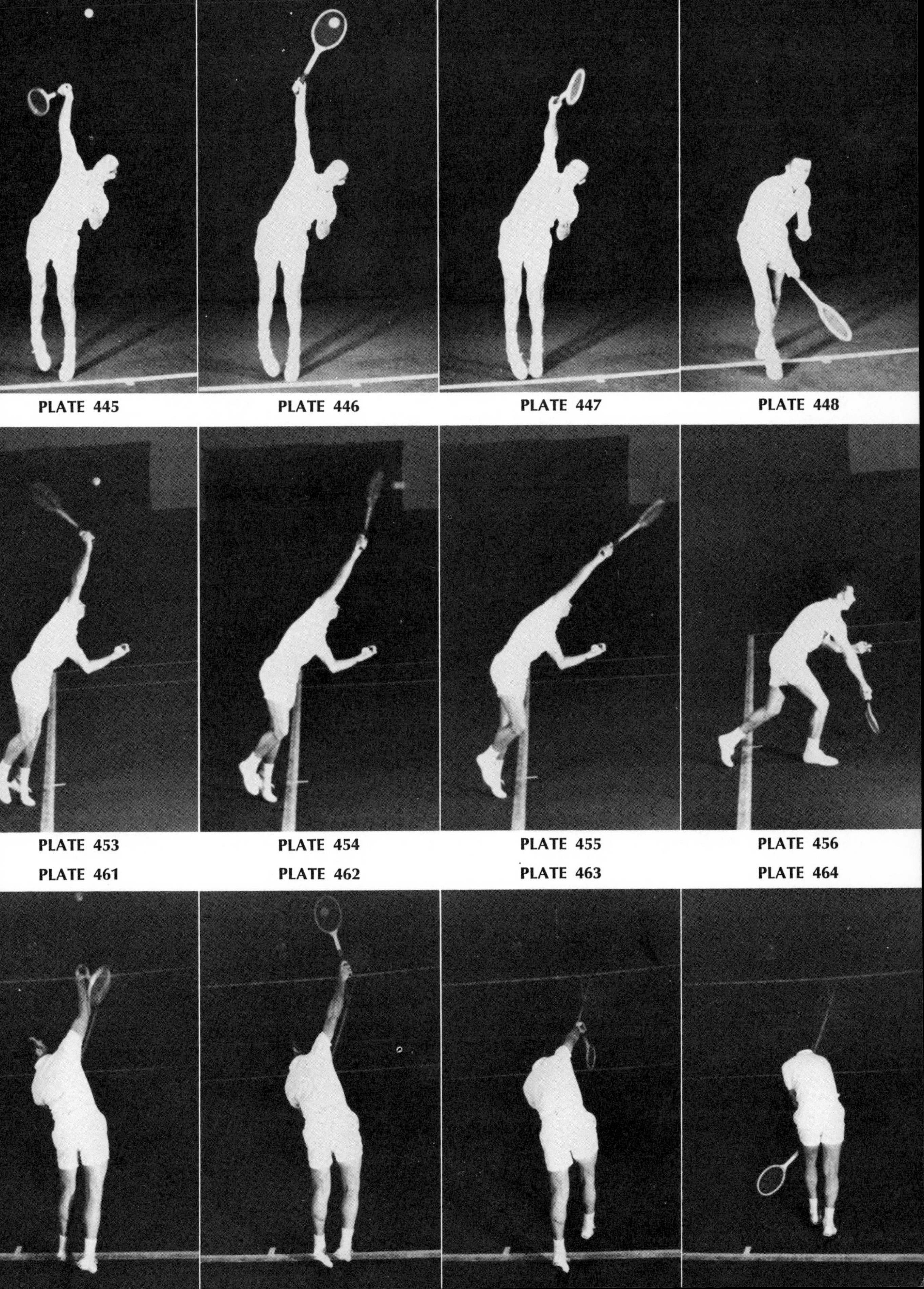

PLATE 445 PLATE 446 PLATE 447 PLATE 448

PLATE 453 PLATE 454 PLATE 455 PLATE 456

PLATE 461 PLATE 462 PLATE 463 PLATE 464

With the Continental grip, control with power is made possible by using spin. To get a spin serve with Continental grip, the ball must be tossed in line with your head and the service court. When the racket head makes contact with the ball, the shaft of the racket is about 45° off the vertical (see picture), even though the arm is fully straightened. The racket imparts forward spin to the ball by moving upward and from left to right, bringing the ball down sooner than would a flat serve hit on the same trajectory. Thus the ball can safely be aimed higher, since it will clear the net more dependably yet land in front of the service line. Furthermore, as it is possible to

PLATE 465 **PLATE 466** **PLATE 467** **PLATE 468**

PLATE 473 **PLATE 474** **PLATE 475** **PLATE 476**

PLATES 465 through 488 below and page 162

SPIN SERVE *features racket moving upward so as to impart top- and sidespin to the ball. See this in Plates 468, 469 and 470. More general features to note are stance, arm position, completeness of arm bend, angle of racket face as spin is applied, follow-through opposite left shin. Player leans forward at start, brings weight back, arches body forward, leans into ball, catches self with right foot.*

PLATE 469 **PLATE 470** **PLATE 471** **PLATE 472**

PLATE 477 **PLATE 478** **PLATE 479** **PLATE 480**

PLATE 481 PLATE 482 PLATE 483 PLATE 484

PLATE 485 PLATE 486 PLATE 487 PLATE 488

take a full-strength swing with this spin serve, once you master the technique, it won't be necessary to let up radically on your second serve. Far too many players resort to a softer, safer second serve if they fault with their first. In doing so, they sacrifice the advantage the server holds; more important, as pat-ball serves are apt to be put away, they sacrifice the point as well.

Control of height with the Continental grip is obtained by tilting the racket face up or down at the moment of impact with a slight bending of the wrist, forward or back. Side-to-side control is obtained by rotating your forearm so that the racket faces either to the right or to the left at the moment of impact. You can visualize this by holding your racket over your head at the point where you would meet the ball and assuming these positions.

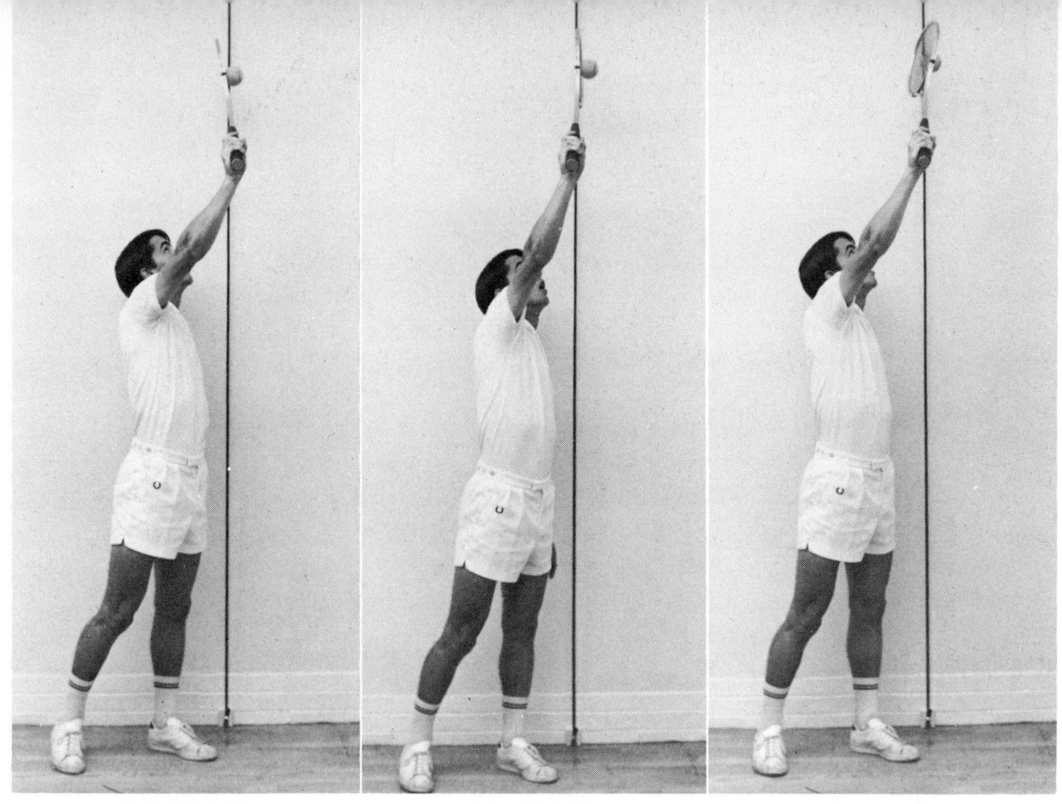

PLATE 489 **PLATE 490** **PLATE 491**

CONTROL OF HEIGHT *in* **spin serve** *is determined by rotation of racket face up (Plate 489), perpendicular (490) or down (491).*

CONTROL OF DIRECTION *in* **spin serve** *is determined by rotation of forearm to the right (Plate 494) or to the left (Plate 492).*

PLATE 492 **PLATE 493** **PLATE 494**

With the Continental grip, depth control is achieved through spin. This spin is applied by swinging upward and forward simultaneously. The upward effort results in spin, the forward effort in power. Thus ideal depth control combines spin with forward motion or power.

Do not attempt serving with the Continental grip until you have developed some consistency at moderate speeds using the forehand grip. Then, experiment with your serve by moving your toss slightly to the left and hitting up the back of the ball so as to impart both topspin and sidespin. The better you are able to coordinate this type of swing, the easier it will be to adopt the Continental grip. Don't, however, be in a great hurry to use it (it has become something of a status symbol among servers, and deservedly so) for while it works for the good server it often discourages the novice.

Teaching the Serve

With a beginner, the teacher should of course begin with the basic fundamentals of the serve. With a pupil who has played some, the teacher should first see how he serves, since anything he does correctly can be put to good use.

From the teacher's point of view, the serve is the toughest and most challenging—therefore, the most interesting—part of tennis instruction. It has more moving parts, in more directions and capable of stranger detours, than any other stroke. The teacher must be able not only to explain the serve to a beginner, but also to map out a constructive plan of change for an experienced player with a minimum of dislocation to the player.

First of all, the teacher should read over the previous section on the basics of the serve and how the self-taught player can learn them. There the teacher will learn the serve action we recommend—or more properly, describe, since most players follow this action instinctively. There, too, he will find a learning process which he can direct.

It makes use of two visual aids, the mirror and photographs, and calls for the pupil to compare his performance as seen in the one with that shown in the other. (Picture series on pages 165 and 166 gives greater detail.) The teacher can use these or any other aids he may be lucky enough to have access to (i.e., movies, a videotape or disk recorder).

If the teacher will now skip to the next chapter, he will doubtless recognize many of the trouble spots discussed; hopefully, he will find a basis for attacking them

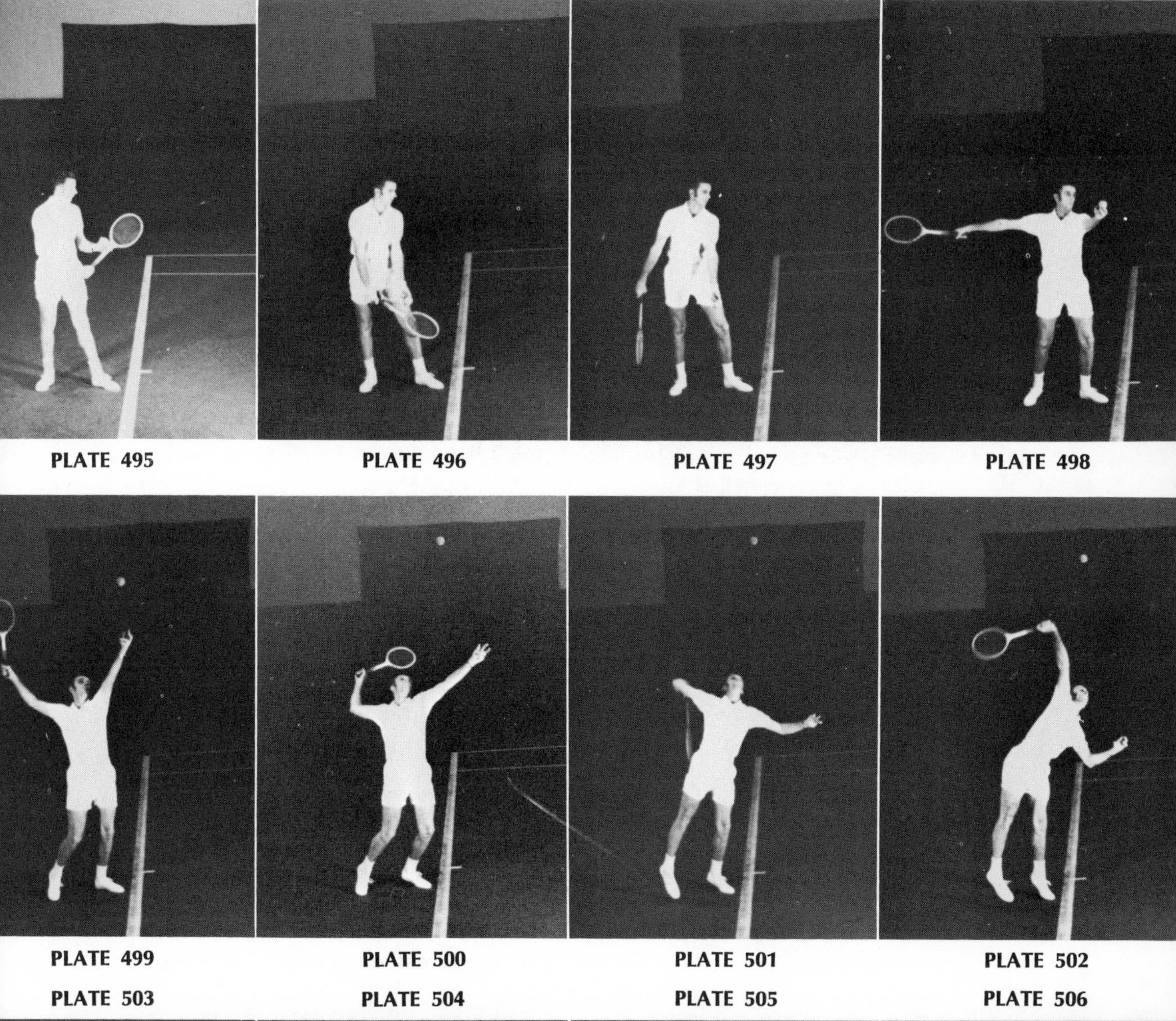

PLATE 495 **PLATE 496** **PLATE 497** **PLATE 498**

PLATE 499 **PLATE 500** **PLATE 501** **PLATE 502**

PLATE 503 **PLATE 504** **PLATE 505** **PLATE 506**

PLATE 507 PLATE 508 PLATE 509 PLATE 510

that makes sense and is orderly. Furthermore, if he has a thorough knowledge of these problems, his beginners may avoid them altogether.

With or without visual aids, the teacher's presentation of the serve should emphasize the similarity between swinging the right arm and throwing a ball. Then, if there is a major error in the player's throwing motion, he can correct it. Once the player shows some improvement, the teacher should demonstrate the serve very slowly and explain it in detail: grip, stance, position of hands, downward motion, upward motion, impact, and follow-through. Then, he should guide the player through the serve, let him try some practice swings, and finally, some actual serves. After that, the teacher will very possibly want the pupil to work on his toss, drilling the player on starting the serve motion with both hands, tossing the ball "up the pipe," and trying to catch it without moving his left hand significantly.

Serve Practice

The serve should be practiced regularly for short periods throughout the entire year—whether the player has access to all-weather courts or not. Serving can be practiced on a gymnasium floor, or against a wall, on a snow-covered hard court—or even without a ball. A player's shoulder should always be kept in good physical condition for serving and a few practice swings daily, even through the dead of winter, will help keep the arm in shape. Under no circumstances should a player try serving until he has warmed up, slowly and carefully, on ground strokes.

Checking his toss periodically, the player should practice a number of serves by himself, aiming toward targets on the court. These can include towels, hula hoops, chalk or tape marks, or whatever else can be made to work on the surface the player picks. The target area should be large at first, then increasingly small, always with the emphasis on control—height, direction, and depth. A running record should be kept of the number of successes vs. the number of attempts.

Most important, the player should practice his own particular weak points, checking up on them periodically with a teacher or with films.

Beginner Drill 5

The Serve

1. Stand before full-length mirror, throw lightweight or plastic ball using overhand baseball motion; note how your throwing motion compares with that illustrated on p. 151.
2. If you haven't already, adopt the three-finger baseball throwing grip.
3. If your throwing motion seems noticeably different from that recommended, practice throwing against a wall using the prescribed motion. Do twenty or thirty throws (more if your arm will take it) each time you go out to practice your serve.
4. Take recommended service stance (see pp. 158–160) and do twenty practice swings without balls.
5. Moving to baseline of court, take stance and reach racket up over your head to measure approximate height required for toss, namely six inches to a foot above tip of outstretched racket.
6. Having established height, practice coordinating toss and racket-arm motion, as follows: start both arms down together and up together, toss ball, then hold left hand still. See if ball will return to stationary left hand. If so, toss is excellent.
7. Do twenty tosses and catches in this manner, moving left hand as little as possible to catch ball. Be sure both arms start together and right stays in motion as long as left, or else drill is valueless.
8. Go through entire serve motion, tossing ball and hitting it. Take plenty of time for each serve, watching ball carefully, particularly when you hit it. Aim high enough over net to send ball deep into correct service box. Hit easily and try for control.
9. Do twenty serves in a row, taking plenty of time. If results come quickly, do another twenty keeping track of how many go in. If you are having difficulties, do not be discouraged: recheck the directions, rest awhile, and try another twenty.
10. When you can get ten out of twenty serves over net and into or near proper service box, study (p. 156) methods of getting more exact control in serving. Using these methods, do five serves each, aiming high, low, to right, to left, long, and short.
11. Serve twenty balls from right court and twenty from left, recording the number you get in.
12. Serving from the right, aim ten serves to right-hand corner of service box (near center service line). Aim ten to left-hand corner.

13. Repeat, serving from left court.
14. Repeat following exercises regularly each time you practice service: throw ball against target with right hand; practice swings without ball; practice tosses coordinated with racket backswing (catching ball without moving left hand if possible); twenty serves from right court, twenty from left.
15. Having completed preliminary study of forehand, backhand, and serve, you would be wise now to have films taken of each stroke and to compare with "Trouble Spots" section for each stroke.
16. When a level of fifteen out of twenty serves in court at good speed can be maintained in play, you are ready to try change to Continental grip on serve. This calls for heel on top, large knuckle on right bevel.

Teaching Hints 3

The Serve

1. If pupil has ever served before, observe serve carefully, step by step; then make recommendations in accordance with those in "Service Trouble Spots" section.
2. If pupil is beginner, start by checking throwing form, that is, see how well he can throw a ball with his racket hand. If his form needs improvement, demonstrate, then have a catch with him. Have him practice throwing briefly each day he practices serve.
3. Demonstrate serve from beginning to end, explaining stance, motion, where ball must go, etc.
4. Explain rules for serving, its importance in tennis tactics, then demonstrate. Explain exactly what you did while serving. Show how hands start together, right follows motion of baseball throw, left simply goes down and up for toss. Show how and why feet are positioned at beginning of serve and end. Full explanation starts on p. 149.
5. Have player take correct stance, forehand grip on racket, left hand hooking racket throat, two balls in left hand, then guide him slowly through motion. Omit only actual release of ball in toss. (Tossing arm should go down and up in unison with right arm motion.)

6. Show player exactly how high and where toss should go; have him practice toss by starting motion, tossing, and seeing if he can catch ball without significantly moving left hand. Repeat ten times or until you are satisfied he has a 50-50 chance or better of being able to hit ball.
7. Pupil should now try serve. Correct serious misunderstandings or faults but let minor errors wait till player begins to get feeling of hitting ball.
8. Have pupil practice serve frequently before next lesson, striving to get ten out of twenty serves in court.
9. Explain and demonstrate methods of controlling serve. Have pupil continue to accumulate serving experience, keeping score on number of serves in.
10. When pupil can manage fifteen out of twenty serves in court at good speed and has some control over ball, teach Continental grip and show pupil how to put spin on ball. See p. 169, #16 for explanation.

10

Service Trouble Spots

Like any other stroke, a serve should be judged first by the results it gets. If the player gets a high percentage of first balls in, rarely double faults, gets consistent depth, power, spin, and variety of placement, the instructor is in no position to quarrel with his form. There is, however, a high correlation between good form and the good results described in the last chapter.

A teacher who seeks to analyze a player's serve should thoroughly examine both its effectiveness and its form before drawing any conclusions or making any changes. This applies to all players except complete beginners, though many of the problems cited later on will occur, at least temporarily, with beginners. If possible, the teacher should see his pupil serve under the pressure of actual play and make at least a mental count of how many first serves he gets in, how often he double faults, how deep the serves are, etc. Asking the player to articulate his serving troubles may reveal some problem the teacher might otherwise miss. In turn, the teacher should do his best to memorize the pupil's motion in detail, trying to describe it in words from beginning to end. The teacher should improve his powers of observation by seeing how few serves of his pupil he can watch and still get all the essentials.

Our self-teaching player is obviously going to have a more difficult time evaluating his own serve. He can have a friend watch him play to count the number of first serves in and double faults out of total serves and to keep track of the depth and placement of the serves. And, most helpful of all, he can compare films of his service with those shown here.

Both teacher and pupil should examine the serve in the following order: the placement of the feet, the handling of the body weight, the tossing arm and its coordination with the serving arm, and, finally, the grip and the swing.

There is a special reason for analyzing the serve observations in this fashion, for though it is completely contrary to what happens in actual play, it is the best order in which to introduce improvements. First, get your feet under control. Next, direct your attention to the toss and its coordination with your racket arm, then to your racket arm itself, and, finally, to your grip. If all the other elements are in reasonable shape, you may proceed directly to working on your grip, but it is generally better to leave that till the end.

Eliminating excess foot movement gives the player a new awareness of his two arms. Once he stops moving around, he can concentrate on making his toss more accurate and will soon be serving better no matter what type of grip or swing he uses. With these distractions eliminated, the real problems of coordinating the arms and making a good swing will show up much more clearly. And, finally, if the player has a grip problem, it can now be tackled without upsetting everything else.

In your mental snapshot of the correct ready position, you should note the position of your hands, your grip on the racket, and the position of your feet. File the first two for future reference.

Feet

To repeat, the proper way to line up is with your left foot at a 45° angle to the baseline and your right foot parallel to the baseline, so that a line from shoetip to shoetip would point to the middle of the court being served into. Your left foot should not move at all except for a lifting of the heel well off the ground at the moment of impact.

The most common mistake made at the outset is for the player to have his front foot parallel to the baseline. This prevents him from transferring his weight forward, since, if he did, he would only fall over sideways. Thus, he is apt to resort to any one of several bad expedients. First, and very common, is to take a forward step with the left foot, correcting its angle. Second is for the player to leave his foot parallel, but then jump and turn it as his racket comes through and hits the ball. Both of these gyrations seem a rather heavy price to pay for not putting the foot at a 45° angle in the first place.

PLATES 511 through 566 below and page 174

LONG STEP AND JUMP *complicate serve control—even if player, unlike this one (Plates 511 to 518), starts way behind line to avoid foot-faulting. In AFTER sequence (Plates 519 to 526 on page 174) player has kept left foot in place, controlled toss and weight and thus obtained better control of serve.*

PLATE 511 **PLATE 512** **PLATE 513** **PLATE 514**

PLATE 515 **PLATE 516** **PLATE 517** **PLATE 518**

PLATE 519 PLATE 520 PLATE 521 PLATE 522

PLATE 523 PLATE 524 PLATE 525 PLATE 526

In addition to stepping with the left, many players bring their right foot through too soon. This moves their right shoulder up under the ball—perhaps even past it—making it necessary to reach back to hit it. The serve thus has nothing on it.

Another more complicated foot pattern is to bring the right foot up alongside the left with the knee bent outward in an awkward position, then pushing off with the right foot so as to jump forward while hitting. This maneuver was not legal until the foot fault rules were liberalized in 1959 to allow jumping. Even when used by a top player it adds next to nothing to the serve, except the illusion that he is putting something more into it. With less gifted players—most of whom have picked it up by imitation rather than through their own invention—it is a costly affectation, since it varies too much from serve to serve. Suffice it to say that, among the biggest bombers, neither Gonzales nor Budge nor Vines required it, and neither did Riggs who was a great server in spite of his size. Conversely, Hoad did use it—indeed, he was probably the first—and it didn't make him a better server than Gonzales, though he was close enough to Gonzales so that a real breakthrough in service technique might have made the difference.

In all cases of foot-wandering, a two-stage remedy is called for. First, the player should line up properly, and then, keeping both his feet still, serve without any weight transfer at all. If he presses his left foot against the ground, he can feel that it is staying in position. He will have to toss the ball a little closer to himself so he can reach it easily without being tempted to step. While he may find this procedure handicapping at first, his teacher can help by demonstrating just how hard a ball can be served without transferring any weight at all. (If the teacher has never tried this himself, he will be quite pleasantly surprised!) The player should practice serving this way until he gets used to not moving his feet. He may then resume his normal toss and weight transfer. Most players soon find they have a better sense of where the ball is and where their racket is when they keep their feet relatively still.

There are a couple of other errors of stance which can be corrected right away by a player, though he may need frequent reminders. One is either to face the court too much (open stance) or to face away from it too much (closed stance); the other is to have the feet either too far apart or too close together.

With too open a stance, the player gets almost the same result as if he stepped too soon and too far with his right foot, or tossed too far back over his head. He has to reach behind himself to hit the ball and his serve will be higher and weaker. With too closed a stance, the player is off-balance. He is likely to work out some complicated way to get his weight into the ball, such as taking a big step to his right, or crossing his right foot over his left on the follow-through.

With his feet too close together, the player is apt to take a step with his left in order to restore his balance, and may well footfault as a result. If his feet are too far apart, he is likely to bring up his rear foot, perhaps pushing off from it and throwing off his timing.

Weight

Body weight in the serve follows a somewhat more complex sequence than on the ground strokes, where there is a simple transference from back to front foot. In the serve, the player can either start with his weight forward and rock back on his backswing and toss, or he can start with his weight back. In either case, because his back is arched, a part of his weight is sent forward before all the rest follows. The player's left foot actually bears most of his weight at this point; but once his racket arm comes forward, so does his weight, and the only thing resisting his momentum now is the impact of racket on ball. Finally, he reaches forward with his right foot on the follow-through to stop himself, literally, from falling. If his knee is properly bent as his foot comes down, he can spring either forward toward the net or back behind the baseline as his opponent's return demands.

There are many ways to mishandle weight transference in the serve, most of them stemming from misplacement of the feet or peculiarities in the toss. Moreover, most of them involve getting one's weight in too soon and, often, too violently.

In general, many of these problems work themselves out by concentrating first on the feet and then on the toss. Unless bad weight use is really the only thing wrong with a player's serve, it is a serious mistake to focus any attention on it. If a teacher talks weight to a server with a bad toss and wandering feet, it is only likely to add to his difficulties. The same can be said for trying to get a player to arch his back, a movement that should come naturally because the rest of the motion is sound or else be skipped altogether. Anyone who has difficulty arching his back is a fair bet to get a backache as his reward. Both authors can attest that back trouble is bad trouble.

Toss and Coordination of the Arms

To review, we recommended that in ready position for the serve, the player should have the middle finger of his tossing hand hooked around the throat of the racket, which should be pointed toward the court being served into. This places the hands at the same height and assures that they part company simultaneously and are therefore able to keep in time with each other throughout the delivery. It is one of nature's symmetries that if the hands start together in this fashion, the ball will arrive at the top of its toss at the precise moment the racket is ready to smack it.

There are several variations from this starting position—some of relatively minor consequence, some a good deal more serious. The most minor is for a player to have his hands at the same height but without linking his middle finger to the shaft of the racket, hence possibly having no contact at all between his left hand and the racket. Another method is to rest the shaft of the racket on the wrist of the left hand, which, like the middle-finger hook, makes for a clean parting of the ways. A less effective type of linkage is to hook onto the racket with the left thumb so that the racket rests between the thumb and the ball. Unfortunately, the player's racket may well jar the ball loose as it breaks away, creating an uncertainty that affects the rest of his serve.

PLATE 527

NO LINK: *Hands start at same height but are not linked in any way—acceptable if they work together.*

PLATE 528

WRIST REST: *Racket shaft rests on left wrist. Acceptable if disengagement is clean.*

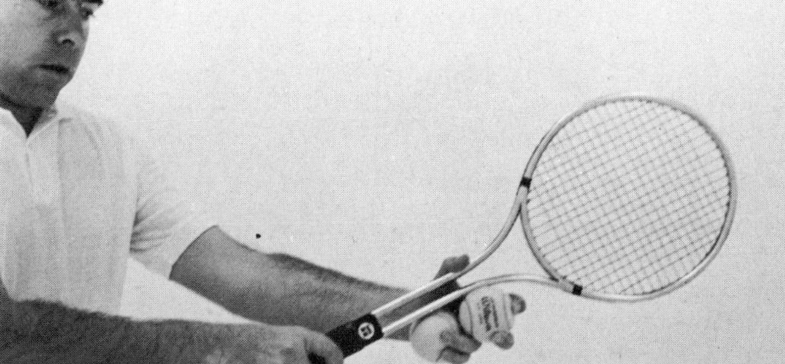

PLATE 529

THUMB HOOK: *Racket shaft is between thumb and balls at start; player must pull racket to right to disengage. Not recommended.*

One of the most commonly taught starts is to hold the balls against the strings of the racket. While this method permits a coordinated start and a convenient perch for the balls, it has complications that don't occur if the hands are somewhat closer together. Frequently, players starting this way lead their backswing with their elbow, turning the hitting face of the racket backward, so that they have trouble untangling themselves as the serve progresses (more of this later under "Racket Arm").

PLATE 530

BALLS AGAINST RACKET: *This start can lead to snag in which racket head's progress is arrested and it never catches up with player's hand.*

Occasionally, a player may start with his hands at the same height and with a sound linkage but will start the toss first. To remedy this mistiming, the player should start with his hands high enough that they can descend together. The left hand should drop a little below waist height before it starts up again for the toss, though, actually, both arms can start up once they are out a bit and equidistant from the body.

No problem should occur with the player who starts with his hands apart but at the same basic height (say, waist level), and lifts them in unison. It is quite rare to discover such a player, however. Trouble comes when the racket starts high and the tossing hand low. The two arms pass each other heading in opposite directions; the toss gets there first, and the racket arm—whipping around vainly trying to catch up—often leaves out such essential parts of the swing as the elbow bend. Sometimes, a serve of this sort is prefaced by several other twitches and twirls before arriving with the racket up and the tossing hand down. There is no end to man's creativity with service oddities.

PLATES 531 through 546 below and page 180

HIGH-LOW START (Plates 531 to 538): *With racket head high and tossing hand low, player tosses long before swing is ready. He tosses extra high to use up time, causing wild toss which makes him step with left foot and jump. In AFTER sequence (Plates 539 to 546 on page 180) arms go down together and up together. Toss need not be so high, is more accurate and left foot can remain in place.*

PLATE 531 PLATE 532 PLATE 533 PLATE 534

PLATE 535 PLATE 536 PLATE 537 PLATE 538

PLATE 539 **PLATE 540** **PLATE 541** **PLATE 542**

PLATE 543 **PLATE 544** **PLATE 545** **PLATE 546**

To deal with this problem, the player should realize that the serve works more easily if the hands start together at the same height. Look at the pictures above which show how the hands descend and rise together, allowing the player to get his toss in the right spot at just the time he wants to hit it. The player should then try it, making sure his hands travel down together.

Even with that basic coordination problem resolved, there is much that can go wrong with the toss. First, the player should have a clear idea of exactly where he is trying to toss the ball—how far to the right or left, how far forward or back, and how high. The answer will depend on what type of serve he is attempting. If he is hitting a comparatively flat ball with a forehand grip, as will be the case with many beginning or inexperienced players, he should toss slightly to the right of his head, about a foot into the court, and about as high as he can reach with the racket. If he is using a spin serve, he should toss more in line with his head and the opposite court (in other words, about six inches farther to the left) the same distance ahead or perhaps a little closer, and just a shade less high.

It is absolutely vital to have a completely dependable toss. Many ways have been devised to learn it, and one of the best is detailed on page 153. To start with, note the path the left arm should travel on its way down and up. When the left arm and the racket are in their starting position for the serve, they should both be pointing at the middle of the appropriate service box. The left arm should continue to point in this direction throughout its *entire* motion; any deviation is likely to cause a bad toss. We stress this highly because one of the most common tossing errors is to lower the left arm pointed correctly, but then to bring it up parallel to the baseline. This results in a "rainbow" toss, where the ball moves in a lofty arc from right to left and the server's racket has to chase the course of the ball. A racket has so much momentum that it generally ends up wrapped around the outside of the ball.

Less frequently, the left arm comes back quite a ways with the racket and then tosses the ball up and forward. Such a toss is generally made backhanded, that is, with hand knuckles up instead of the palm. As this type of toss has the virtue of being more in line with the path of the racket, it is not surprising that there have been some successful practitioners of it, such as Jack Kramer and the late Rafael Osuna. For the rare player who can do it, well and fine, there is no point in changing; for the young player with a tendency in this direction, it is best to discourage it.

For all these tosses, the player should lower and raise his left arm along the same vertical line and practice it for awhile (try it in front of the net post, for instance). The muscles of his left shoulder must move the whole arm, with little or no bending the elbow, and as this is a fairly delicate job to assign to such large muscles, it takes a little conditioning. Then the player should practice the toss in coordination with his serving arm, seeing how little he has to move his left hand to catch his own toss. A good exercise is to toss twenty times in this fashion and then serve ten balls; repeat the exercise several times. If the player has any difficulty catching the ball in his left hand when he already holds one, have him do this drill with one ball only. (This method is valuable for any player whose toss is giving him trouble.)

There are several other major errors that the tossing arm can commit on its downward motion. One, often seen with beginners whose coordination is faulty, is to swing the arm way to the left, almost to the hip. This eats up so much time that the racket has to wait for the ball and loses its momentum. The opposite of this mistake is to abbreviate the downward motion of the left arm and get the toss up too early. In both cases, the player should be sure that his left arm gets down to waist height, but no farther.

On its upward course, there are two frequent misadventures for the left arm. The more common is that it stops so abruptly that control is lost, whereupon the ball usually goes too high and to the side. To cure this, the player should move his arm up smoothly and not release the ball until it is above his head.

The other error in tossing the ball is to bend the forearm, which only causes the ball to go back over the player's head. The left arm must move up as a unit, just as in golf a certain stiffness is necessary in putting.

The player should note how to hold the balls in his left hand. The best way is to use the same basic grip that a baseball player uses, that is, with the thumb and first two fingers, the other two fingers curled behind the ball unless they are holding a second one.

The ball should never be rolled off the extreme tips of the fingers, nor should it be tossed from the palm of the hand as often happens with players who find themselves unable to hold more than one ball at once. The latter should make certain they hold that one ball correctly. The fingers should grip the ball lightly and open up as it is launched, definitely not in a squirting fashion. The player should then make sure he moves the second ball in place if his first serve is a fault.

In general, beginners and all other players using the forehand grip will toss too far to the right. Most girls will also toss too low, so as to avoid extending their serving arm. Stress a higher toss, not too far to the right, as the best groundwork possible for a proper swing.

The Racket Arm

In reviewing the basic motion of the serving arm, remember that it starts out in front of the body with the racket pointing toward the correct service box. The face of the racket is perpendicular to the ground while the player's forearm is parallel. At the beginning of the swing, both arms may simply fall with the right arm extending back as it passes by the player's right leg. When both arms are equidistant from the body during their downward fall (about ten inches away from and as high as the pants pockets, as seen on page 158) they move up until the right arm is parallel to the ground and pointing directly behind the player. During this 180° arc, the racket and arm have behaved exactly like a pendulum—a freely moving object anchored at one end. The plane the arm swings through should be that which passes by the shoetips to the opposite service box. At the beginning of the swing, the hitting face of the racket faces to the player's left; when it is extended behind him, it faces to the right.

At this point, the player should cock his elbow, leaving his upper arm parallel but relaxing his wrist so that the racket head drops down behind his back. Now, the racket starts up again and forward, the arm extending throughout the swing until the follow-through carries the racket face down opposite the left shin. The arc of the arm in its forward motion should be much the same as that described in the backswing.

In observing a serve either filmed or live, the player or teacher should note what the right arm does at each of four stages: the backswing, the elbow bend—or lack of one, the moment of impact, and the follow-through. Watch the entire motion from beginning to end, then concentrate on each successive stage. Then watch it all over again until it is imprinted in your mind.

The Backswing

Length of backswing is the first thing to look for. Basically, the fuller the backswing, the greater the power potential. While it is true that most of a serve's power generates after the elbow is bent, that power depends to a great extent on how much momentum is built up during the backswing. The shorter and higher the backswing, the less momentum. The longer the backswing, the greater the momentum. On the other hand, many people feel a short backswing is more reliable and controlled, and so it is, unless the full backswing truly behaves like a pendulum—in which case its path is predetermined and it is no more out of control than a railroad train or a trolley.

The next things to look for are errors of the elbow or wrist. The elbow should not lead the backswing unless the player works out an efficient way to lift the racket over his head and position it correctly for the forward swing. Nor should the wrist be allowed to droop during the backswing; it should be relaxed but not limp. If it is too limp, the racket head will be so far behind the swing of the arm that even a strong forward snap will not speed the racket head through on time. If the wrist is comfortably relaxed while the elbow is cocked, it can snap forward just before impact for added power. Happily, most people who take quickly to the proper serve motion are able to use their wrist naturally in the serve without special attention.

Other backswing errors on the serve stem from swinging off the main line that points to the service court. The worst of these is to pull the racket arm back past the right hip almost parallel to the baseline, and the left-arm toss tracing the same course on its side. This results in the player's energy going entirely to waste. As he wraps his racket around the ball, the serve will go wild, without even topspin to bring it down into court.

The most subtle of all backswing quirks is the mismanagement of the racket face. It should be examned closely during the backswing to make certain that it opens 180°—no more and no less. At the start, the racket should be perpendicular, and its hitting side facing the player's left. When the arm is parallel to the ground during the backswing, the racket face should be facing to the right. Too many players delay the opening of the racket face so that it stays closed all the way up to the top of the backswing. Our term for this is the "snag." With some beginners, this may become so serious they are unable to get a serve over the net, and a timely explanation may result in dramatic improvement.

The player can also open the racket face too far and too soon on the backswing, though this is rare.

All these backswing problems can be dealt with directly, whether the self-taught player recognizes them on film or has them pointed out by his teacher. In the case where the player errs by veering off the backward-forward arc, he will almost certainly have to correct his toss as well. With the snag, the correct path of the racket should be explained and the player should be encouraged to rotate the wrist outward as the racket goes back.

The Elbow Bend

Starting the forward motion of the serve from the bent-elbow position is only now coming to be understood. Although its use became widespread after World War II, it was more the result of imitation than comprehension. Perhaps the main reason for America's domination of world tennis just after the war was its big servers—Kramer, Schroeder, and Gonzales. Once the Australians, led by Sedgman and McGregor, spread these methods to all their players, the balance of power went the other way. The rest of the world soon followed and the elbow bend has been present since in nearly all big serves.

The significance of the elbow bend is simply that the muscles that straighten the arm at the elbow can generate an awesome power. Leaving them out of the swing reduces the power potential greatly.

Serve motions without any elbow bend at all are fairly rare, but those without enough are quite common. In either case, a throwing lesson is indicated, and if the player has a hard time putting the idea to use in his serve, the throwing practice should

PLATES 547 through 562 below and page 186

INCOMPLETE BEND *and round-arm swing are coupled with curved-arm, "rainbow" toss (Plates 547 to 554). In AFTER sequence (Plates 555 to 562 on page 186), player gets almost complete elbow bend plus truer toss.*

PLATE 547 **PLATE 548** **PLATE 549** **PLATE 550**

PLATE 551 **PLATE 552** **PLATE 553** **PLATE 554**

PLATE 555 PLATE 556 PLATE 557 PLATE 558

PLATE 559 PLATE 560 PLATE 561 PLATE 562

be continued. Explain carefully the path the arm should follow, how the mere act of straightening the arm generates power even when the upper arm and shoulder are held stationary.

From time to time, you will come across players who bend their elbow properly, but are unable to straighten it sufficiently so that their serves are cramped. Often, the fault lies in the toss—it is too low—rather than the swing. Stress the importance of tossing high enough to allow the racket arm to straighten.

Two of the most difficult elbow problems, which often go hand in hand, are the premature bend and the tuck. The tuck usually accompanies the premature bend but it also crops up by itself. In the premature bend, the player starts bending his elbow almost immediately after the racket has passed his right leg. Often, he keeps his upper arm pressed against his body, and if he continues to keep it pressed against the body until the end of his backswing, his affliction becomes the tuck.

The tuck can also occur with a backswing that starts out normally. The player may even get his whole arm out parallel to the ground in back; then, just at the moment he bends his elbow, his upper arm collapses against his body and the swing becomes impotent. With the upper arm tucked against his body, the player cannot drop the racket head down behind his back; consequently, his upward thrust doesn't travel far enough to generate either good spin or real power.

The remedy here is to have the player delay his elbow bend until his arm is out parallel to the ground. Then, when he makes his bend, have his elbow continue to point directly behind him until he starts to swing forward. While these are difficult problems and require much hard work, films will help the player greatly.

Girls tend to bend their elbow but leave their upper arm parallel to the baseline, instead of pointing it behind them. This results in a restricted swing that derives all its strength from the straightening of the arm and none from the forward thrust of the upper arm. Perhaps partly because their shoulder socket is constructed somewhat differently, girls are even more prone than boys to the upper-arm tuck.

One of the most bizarre trouble spots in the serve backswing, and one that is well beyond the present capabilities of most experienced tennis teachers to correct, is the player who hits himself in the middle of the back with his racket. It is extraordinary to see a person of presumably sound mind and no known masochistic tendencies repeatedly punish himself in this manner—yet it occurs. Until more is known about this idiosyncrasy, the best prescription is to get everything else about the serve into working order—the footwork, the toss, the timing, and the grip—and pay as little attention to the back-pounding as possible. Meanwhile, it is up to us tennis teachers to bring this and other coordination eccentricities to the attention of scientifically trained people to look for fundamental causes and remedies. Experts in kinesiology (the study of the movement of the muscles), whether they are physical education professors, physiotherapists, neurologists, physiologists, or what have you, are the people who should be consulted.

Moment of Impact

Certain problems show up clearly at the moment of impact just by observing the behavior of the ball. It is quite obvious when the ball has been met too low and the player has not given himself room to straighten his arm, since the ball will fly up and, probably, out. The kind and amount of spin applied can be seen from the type of impact made. Does the player get good topspin or are all his serves flat, with excessive sidespin or even reversed spin? Any exaggerated lay-back of the wrist will also show up, generally in the form of backspin.

The moment of impact is too brief for a player to try to adjust his action at that point. If correction is in order, it must be made well ahead of the "moment of truth," so to speak, to have any effect.

The Follow-through

The follow-through should end up on the left side of the body with the hitting face of the racket opposite the player's left shin. The most common variations are to finish on the right, or with the forearm only while the upper arm stops. Another is to finish with the frame of the racket face edge first. If the right edge of the frame leads the way, the serve probably has excess sidespin; if the left, the serve probably has a reverse spin.

In the case of the abbreviated follow-through finishing to the right, a straightforward explanation, with possibly a review of ball-throwing, is usually enough. With the racket frame finishing edge first, however, a more fundamental approach to the problem of spin is necessary. As it may well involve grip, too, these issues will be discussed two sections below.

Timing of the Swing

When the teacher or the player has analyzed the various parts of the right-arm motion, he should review the entire motion, studying its timing especially. Many players start their backswing with a tremendous rush, but then slow down as the swing goes on. It is far better to build up momentum gradually, expending greatest effort just as the arm starts out of the bent-elbow position. The racket should build to its climax, not dissipate it before the moment of impact. Attention to this timing factor is the best way for a young player with sound serve mechanics to get power, but keep in mind that those mechanics must come first. Until he begins to acquire the necessary muscle to do the job, a young player should forget about power and concentrate on a smooth, gradually accelerating swing.

Grip and Spin

We come now to two of the most tricky teaching problems on the serve; how to hold the racket correctly and how to apply spin. The two are treated together here because they are inseparable in actual play. Without the correct grip, it is difficult to get spin; without spin, a serve with any speed on it tends to be unreliable. Unfortunately, it is as hard to get used to the correct grip as it is to achieve proper spin; nevertheless, it is very much worth doing.

Servers use every grip ranging from the extreme Western forehand to the Eastern backhand. Furthermore, many players even start their serve with one grip and change it once, or even twice, during the swing. The teacher should examine this process very closely. First, ask the player what grip he *believes* he uses. Then, catch hold of the player's racket hand at the end of his follow-through to see if he still has that same grip. The teacher may have to move quickly, since some alert pupils can actually get back to their original grip by the time they recover their balance.

While we said earlier that grip should generally be tackled last among serve problems, there is one exception. If a player uses the Western or semi-Western grip, it should be moved over one notch .(from Western to semi-Western or from semi-Western to Eastern) right away. The reasoning is this: With the Western or semi-Western, the racket face at hitting position faces to the right. With the Eastern forehand, it faces straight ahead and therefore provides the best chance for a hard, flat hit. With the racket in Continental forehand or Eastern backhand position, it faces to the left, so that the player may feel he is going to hit the ball with the front edge of his racket frame, or only brush it weakly with the strings.

Moving the grip from Western toward Eastern is thus likely to feel somewhat better to the player, while from Eastern forehand toward Continental, or beyond, is likely to feel awful. The player should not attempt to move from one extreme on the grip scale to the other, all at once, for he will just be frustrated and lose valuable time.

In changing from Western to semi-Western, or semi-Western to Eastern forehand, the player should be warned that his early attempts with the new grip will probably make him serve farther to the left than he does ordinarily. The reason is, that to control his serve with his former grip, he had to curl his wrist forward; that

SEMI-WESTERN GRIP, *long step with left foot, and jump are features of this commonly seen serve pattern. While step and jump are sometimes seen with top servers, semi-Western serve grip never is, since it won't permit adequate spin control. In AFTER sequence, player controls grip, step, and jump, and produces much tidier swing.*

PLATE 563 PLATE 564 PLATE 565 PLATE 566

PLATE 571 PLATE 572 PLATE 573 PLATE 574

same wrist curl will now turn his racket face too far, and he must aim well to the right to compensate.

It may be necessary to wait quite some time before moving on to the Continental—which, incidentally, is an extreme enough grip for most people. The full backhand grip is too tough for all but the most coordinated women and top-notch men players. There is no need for the player to be in a big hurry to get over the

PLATE 567 PLATE 568  PLATE 569  PLATE 570

PLATE 575  PLATE 576  PLATE 577  PLATE 578

hump to the Continental. For a player taking weekly lessons, it might take anywhere from six weeks to a year to make the full change. It is more important that he build solidly for the long run, practicing his serve regularly and trying to use what he has been taught in play.

Changing the grips during the serve nearly always occurs because the player has been taught a new grip yet cannot help reverting to his old one. What he must do is keep his fingers glued to the racket throughout the swing, gripping as firmly as possible. If he can acquire an open mind about what happens to the ball under these circumstances (almost certainly it will go too far to the left), he can then adjust his wrist angle to send the ball on its proper path.

PLATE 579 PLATE 580

PLATE 581 PLATE 582 PLATE 583

PLATE 584 PLATE 585 PLATE 586

FINGERS OPEN *during backswing of this serve (Plates 579 to 586), causing player to lose control of racket face. Change occurs as player tries to return to semi-Western grip from Continental. He was told to keep fingertips in contact with handle and to adjust racket face by wrist angle instead of grip change. In AFTER sequence (Plates 587 to 594) he controls fingers as he should.*

PLATE 587

PLATE 588

PLATE 589

PLATE 590

PLATE 591

PLATE 592

PLATE 593

PLATE 594

A trouble spot for many beginners using the forehand grip is to lay the wrist back so much that the racket face is open to the sky, much like a waiter's tray. One good remedy is for the player to stand up about ten feet from the net and try to serve over it into the opposite service box. Even an experienced player will have trouble at first getting his racket head through. Eventually, however, the player will work out the wrist adjustment necessary to get the ball down into the court, at least when serving from the baseline.

Once the forehand grip is firmly established, the player may work on applying spin with it. Though it won't be easy, spin is possible, and the effort required will help edge the player toward understanding the wisdom of acquiring the Continental grip.

To repeat, the player should be sure that his elbow bends enough to allow the racket head to drop behind his back, but that his upper arm stays parallel to the ground when his elbow is bent. He can then experiment to see how the upward motion of his racket imparts spin to the ball. He should toss the ball farther to the left (in line with his head and the court he is serving into) than he has been, keeping the racket shaft at a 45° angle to the arm when it meets the ball. (See picture on page 160.)

The teacher can demonstrate how spin is applied to the ball by using a small wheel and axle. By brushing his hand up the back of the wheel he can show topspin; and by tilting the wheel's axle about 45° to the right, he can show that the ideal spin to strive for is a combination of topspin and sidespin, not pure topspin.

As the player tries it out, he should be sure to aim well over the net so that he actually sees how the spin brings the ball down into the court. At first, he may be able to see it more clearly if he stands near the opposite service line while his teacher serves a few times. Often, the most difficult part for able young players is to get them to trust their new spin serve in actual play. If they serve a good spinning ball on their first serve which just misses the court, instead of trusting themselves to make the correction on their second serve, they hit a flat pat-ball. They should realize that the way to get the ball in is to accentuate the spin—by increased upward motion of the racket. By sacrificing a little power on the second serve, and replacing it with greater spin, the player thereby controls depth.

Many servers get plenty of spin but not the right kind. The least useful, because it is the least dependable, is reverse twist. This twist serve generally stems from use of the Western grip; it is far less common than it used to be, because today there are far fewer Western grippers.

In the reverse twist, the racket passes from right to left on the ball, causing it to spin to the receiver's right, bouncing away from his backhand (or in, on top of his forehand). Unfortunately, as the arm must turn in an awkward way, it is hard to execute a proper follow-through. Furthermore, the racket face tends to be tilted back so much on the reverse twist serve that the ball frequently goes long. With all its drawbacks, when this serve is controlled, it can be very deceptive and confusing, particularly to those who do not play against it often. The odds against its successful use are quite high, however.

PLATES 595 through 610 below and page 196

REVERSE TWIST *(Plates 595 to 602) can occur inadvertently if player's grip is near semi-Western or Western and he tosses too far to his right. Racket finishes on left side of ball instead of on right. In AFTER sequence (Plates 603 to 610 on page 196) he tosses farther to his left and makes racket finish on right side of ball so that ball spins correctly.*

PLATE 595 **PLATE 596** **PLATE 597** **PLATE 598**

PLATE 599 **PLATE 600** **PLATE 601** **PLATE 602**

PLATE 603 PLATE 604 PLATE 605 PLATE 606

PLATE 607 PLATE 608 PLATE 609 PLATE 610

Usually, the problem in the reverse twist is that the player's toss may be even more at fault than his grip. When the toss is made too far to the right, the player has a hard time getting his racket around the right side of the ball. If he moves it over to the left, he will begin to get the correct motion. If he moves his grip East at least one notch, he will begin to feel the spin. Examine the pictures of the player above and note the position of his toss in the before-after sequences. It was necessary to change his grip only slightly. It had been just a little West of Eastern forehand and was moved to Continental with a minimum of dislocation.

Excess sidespin on a slice serve is not so much a problem of technique as a matter of its priority in the player's repertoire. It should be neither his principal serve nor his principal second serve, but no well-equipped player should be without it. He should use it for variety, as an element of surprise, against opponents for whom it will cause the most trouble, or on smooth court surfaces where it will be the most effective.

First, the player must learn a serve that is predominantly topspin and totally reliable: the serve we have discussed here at length. Then he must learn to disguise his slice service delivery so it looks as much as possible like his topspin delivery. For the slice, the ball is thrown farther to the right and the racket comes severely around the right side of the ball. For the topspin serve, the toss must be moved to the left with the upward motion of the racket emphasized.

Service Trouble Spots

NOTE: Before working on specific aspects of a serve, observe it very carefully from several vantage points: on the baseline just to player's right; directly behind him, looking in direction he is serving; finally, from receiver's position on other side of net. If player is experienced, play as many points as are necessary against him to give you feeling of how effective serve is in actual play. Weigh its effectiveness and reliability against difficulty of any contemplated changes. Make observations in this order: 1) feet and body weight; 2) toss and coordination with racket arm; 3) racket arm itself; and 4) grip. (This is generally the best order for introducing changes, as well.)

Problem	Why it is a problem	What teacher should do	What player should do
Feet and body weight			
1. Front foot parallel to baseline.	Prevents player from sending weight out onto toe of that foot, causes him to step with left foot, jump, or spin in place on it.	Have player put foot at 45° angle, keeping it there by maintaining pressure on front of foot throughout swing.	See left.
2. Stepping through with right foot.	Moves right shoulder up under or even past ball, so server must reach back to hit, losing power.	Have player leave right foot back until ball is hit. If necessary, have player keep right foot in place throughout serve.	See left.
3. Right foot brought up alongside left, jump launched from right foot while hitting.	Adds almost nothing in power but complicates control since player is moving around while swinging.	Have player keep right foot back, both feet on ground until he becomes accustomed to not jumping. He may then lean forward while hitting, but keep right foot back till contact has been made.	See left.
4. Stance too open or closed; feet too far apart or close together.	Each complicates control and fluent movement of racket and body.	Show player correct stance and have him get accustomed to it. Simple concentration may be reinforced with regular reminders.	See left.

Problem	Why it is a problem	What teacher should do	What player should do
5. Weight misuse.	Interferes with serve control, often robs serve of its swing.	Usually solved by correcting footwork, often aided by eliminating weight transfer so player can see how little his major gyrations contribute.	See left.
Toss and coordination of arms			
1. Hands start at same height but no link of left hand to racket.	Relatively minor as long as hands work together.		
2. Racket shaft rests on left wrist.	Ditto, though this may encourage "rainbow toss," which see.	In all four cases see if player can adapt quickly to hooking middle finger on racket shaft. For those who can't, be sure arms are lined up correctly and working in unison.	See left.
3. Hooking racket shaft with left thumb.	Ditto, but may create uncertainty because racket shaft could dislodge balls.		
4. Balls held against strings of racket.	May cause elbow to lead racket backswing, racket head may "snag" (see under "racket arm") and lead to rainbow toss.		
5. Racket held high, tossing hand low. (Note: player may start correctly, then go into this position; others have preliminary gestures, often quite ornate, before going to this position.)	Tossing arm gets up before racket is ready to hit ball, so player tosses too high; the higher the toss, the harder to control. Body action usually awkward, also.	Start hands together, hooking middle finger on racket shaft. Maintain contact with that finger as hands go down, part below waist height, and go up together. Toss will be lower since serving arm will be ready sooner.	See left.

Problem	Why it is a problem	What teacher should do	What player should do
6. Ignorance of where toss should go.	Makes both toss and serve inconsistent. For flat serve with forehand grip, toss is slightly to right of head; for spin serve, directly in line with head and court being served to.	Inform player and have him drill using toss and catch method (see p. 154).	See left.
7. "Rainbow toss" (i.e., lowering left hand perpendicular to baseline and lifting it parallel, so ball arcs across player's front).	Player wraps his racket around the ball instead of hitting straight into it; requires radical change of racket path if toss is not perfect.	Explain problem to player and show him how to move left arm in the same channel. Have him drill repeatedly, using toss and catch method, p. 154.	See left.
8. Tossing arm comes back too far with the racket arm; sometimes produces backhand toss.	Player has difficulty controlling toss; therefore loses accuracy.	Ditto. Show player exactly where left arm should stop on downswing and its route on upswing.	See left.
9. Left arm lowered too far.	Wastes time; racket is ready before toss.	Have player stop left hand just below waist level and start it up as racket is lifted.	See left.
10. Left arm not lowered far enough, halted abruptly.	Ball up too soon, toss is extra high to use up time while racket gets ready.	Ditto.	See left.
11. Stopping left arm abruptly on way up.	Control is lost.	Have player hold on to ball until near top of toss, then lift arm up smoothly.	See left.
12. Bending forearm upward.	Toss arcs back over head.	Have player keep arm fully extended on way up.	See left.
13. Incorrect ball hold.	Poor finger control causes erratic tosses.	Have player hold ball with index and middle fingers underneath and thumb on top. If other ball is in hand, other two fingers hold it. If first ball is a fault, second should be moved up and gripped like the first, with baseball throwing grip.	See left.

Problem	Why it is a problem	What teacher should do	What player should do
14. Tossing too low.	Restricts arc of swing. Many girls do this through lack of strength, real or imagined.	Have player toss higher, attempt fuller swing. If really taxing, have player try to strengthen arm and loosen shoulder.	See left.
15. Tossing too far to right and low.	Many men using forehand or semi-Western grip do this, lose downward thrust into court.	Have player move toss a little to left and higher, allowing fuller swing, more downward hit.	See left.
Racket Arm Backswing 1. Extending the racket arm less than at full length, or otherwise shortening the backswing.	Loss of momentum and freedom of motion, hence loss of power.	Have player let arm swing down and back like a pendulum (see pp. 158-160).	See left.
2. Elbow leads backswing.	At very least, arc of swing is shortened; also racket may become snagged. Racket head is late arriving at ball, has hard time controlling it.	Ditto.	See left.
3. Wrist droops.	Racket head lags behind arm, may not catch up. Control erratic.	Have player firm up grip slightly and keep racket head in time with arm.	See left.
4. Swinging back almost parallel to the baseline. Usually goes with rainbow toss.	Player wraps racket around ball, gets excess sidespin, no topspin, often hits wild to the left.	Have player line arms up towards court being served into and move arms in that plane.	See left.
5. Racket face stays closed too long during backswing so that it snags.	Player gets racket tangled as he tries to lift it and loses control of racket head.	Racket face should make gradual 180° turn. Hitting surface should face to player's left at start, to his right when racket arm is parallel to ground during backswing.	See left.

Problem	Why it is a problem	What teacher should do	What player should do
Elbow Bend 1. No bend at all. 2. Not enough bend.	Leverage and power are lost since muscles that straighten arm are not used.	Have player practice throwing overhand using correct bend; have him take practice swings with racket; then have him try new motion while swinging at ball. Pay careful attention to timing of toss since player requires more time to get full motion.	See left.
3. Failure to straighten elbow.	Likely to be result of too low a toss.	Explain problem, have player toss higher and try to straighten arm.	See left.
4. Premature bend (i.e., bending elbow as arm passes body on backswing).	Player usually straightens arm too soon, thereby putting full dependence on shoulder muscles to move racket. Besides losing power, player has difficulty getting spin.	Show player correct motion, have him practice throwing, then have him practice swing with racket and finally have him serve with ball. Take plenty of time with each step.	See left.
5. Tucking elbow in against body just before swinging forward.	Restricts arc of swing; more important, prevents racket head from getting down behind player's back in backswing so he can swing up and get topspin.	Ditto.	See left.
6. Elbow bent but upper arm parallel to baseline or even pointing towards net.	Common problem with girls. Restricts swing, reduces power.	Show full arm swing, have player practice throwing to develop shoulder muscle strength sufficiently to allow him (or her) to point elbow straight back just before swinging forward.	See left.
7. Back-pounding.	Usually racket face is too open and player cannot straighten it out soon enough to control ball.	Try to get all other parts of serve in order: footwork, toss, timing, grip; pay as little attention as possible to back-pounding.	See left.

Problem	Why it is a problem	What teacher should do	What player should do
Moment of Impact			

NOTE: the moment of impact provides opportunity to observe if ball is being met too low, what type of spin, if any, player is using, whether there is any excessive layback of wrist. Moment is too fleeting, however, for player to try last-minute adjustments—he must plan ahead.

Problem	Why it is a problem	What teacher should do	What player should do
Follow-through 1. Finishing on the right.	Not appropriate for flat or spin serve. Power is lost since effort is not in direction player is serving.	Have player try to finish with hitting face of racket opposite left shin on follow-through.	See left.
2. Finishing with forearm only.	Abbreviated forward motion of upper arm limits power of swing and player's control of motion.	Have player get used to idea of following through without inhibition. Practicing overhand throw with full follow-through will help.	See left.
3. Finishing with right-hand edge of racket face leading way.	Indicates player has gotten excess slice, not enough power for his effort.	See under problem #8 in "Grip and spin" section following.	See left.
4. Finishing with left-hand edge of racket face leading way.	Indicates player has gotten reverse spin, which is hard to control.	See under problem #7 in "Grip and spin" section following.	See left.
Timing of swing 1. Excessively fast backswing.	The faster and more frantic the backswing, often the more feeble the forward swing.	Have player take racket back fairly slowly till elbow is bent, then swing forward with full power.	See left.
Grip and spin 1. Changing grip during swing. Often occurs with those learning new grip.	Causes uncertainty in racket-face control.	Observe closely how and when player makes change. Explain better control results when grip is unchanged throughout swing. Have him keep fingertips in contact throughout and control racket face by wrist adjustment instead.	See left.

Problem	Why it is a problem	What teacher should do	What player should do
2. Use of Western grip.	Turns racket face too much to right, making topspin nearly impossible. Often causes reverse spin.	Have player switch to semi-Western, and when comfortable, to forehand. Warn player he will hit too far to left unless he compensates by adjusting wrist angle.	See left.
3. Use of semi-Western grip.	Turns racket face too much to right; topspin difficult, reverse spin likely.	Have player switch to forehand grip. Warn player he will hit too far to left unless he compensates by adjusting wrist angle.	See left.
4. Use of Eastern forehand grip.	A virtue in beginner, becomes detriment to experienced player, since it prevents adequate topspin.	Have player switch to Continental grip. Warn him he will hit too far to left unless he compensates by adjusting wrist angle. Emphasizing upward motion while swinging forward will obtain topspin.	See left.
5. Excessive wrist layback.	Racket face laid back when arm reaches zenith of forward swing. Player meets ball too low, has no spin but much trouble controlling length and height.	Have player move up inside own service line and attempt serving. Will force him to speed racket head through so it is at its peak when arm is.	See left.
6. Hitting patball second serve.	Likely to be clobbered by opponent and not as reliable as good spin serve. Often a problem with player who knows, but is afraid to trust, spin serve.	Teach spin serve if player's grip and swing will permit. If player already knows technique, help him over fear of using it.	See left.
7. Reverse twist.	Hard to control; player usually hits long whenever he tries for extra power. Also, works contrary to natural arm bend.	Grip is usually semi-Western or Western, toss too far to right, so path of racket is from right to left. Follow-through has left edge of racket leading. First correct toss, have player hit more directly into the ball. Then ease grip over towards forehand, eventually, Continental.	See left.

Problem	Why it is a problem	What teacher should do	What player should do
8. Excess sidespin.	Harder to get power than with topspin serve. A good change-of-pace serve, however, and useful on certain court surfaces.	Explain change-of-pace value of this serve but its inadequacy as spin serve. Show player how to make racket move up back of ball, imparting combined top- and sidespin instead of wholly sidespin.	See left.

11
The Volley

By now, you have laid the foundation for your ground strokes and your serve and can carry on a match. You should be able to have some good long rallies, get plenty of exercise, and perhaps have a few victories to your credit. But there is no denying that there is something of major importance missing from your game. Perhaps you have already discovered what it is.

It is quite likely you have had to move up to the forecourt to get to a short shot hit by your opponent and then wondered whether you should retreat to the baseline or advance to the net. If the latter, and your opponent's shot was too hot to handle, you found out one basic thing about the net—it's a risky place to be. If you had the good fortune to get a fairly slow, high return that you could close in on and kill, you found out something much more important about the net—it can also be a very rewarding place. If you stop and think why, it makes good sense. The farther forward in the court you are, the easier it is for you to hit a wide-angled shot out of your opponent's reach; similarly, the higher and more floating the shot, the easier it is to hit it down into the court.

The reason the net is a risky position is that the ball comes at you much faster than when you play it near the baseline on a bounce. If you expect to play at the net, you must develop the right reactions and then practice so they are available at split-second notice. If your reactions are fast but incorrect, you must improve your style. If they are slow but correct, you must work to develop your eye to its theoretical limit and to improve your physical condition so that your court coverage increases.

The stroke usually used at the net is called the volley. A volley is any shot hit on the fly. Naturally, some shots played by a person at, or approaching, the net fall so short they are played on the bounce. There are forehand volleys, backhand volleys, and overhead volleys—simply called "overheads."

The word "volley" should not be used to mean an exchange of shots. The word that tennis players use and understand for that is "rally." Furthermore, there is no such thing as volleying (or even rallying) for serve, for the choice of serve is determined by spinning the racket. Saying "volley" when he means "rally" has been a way of telling the tennis greenhorn from the aficionado almost since the game began.

The volley, as you will have discovered if you've tried it, doesn't leave you much time to swing. Furthermore, it should be clear that you don't need a very big swing anyway. The ball has so much momentum of its own that you need only hold on to your racket firmly and move it forward just a little bit to return it.

If you were to stand about ten feet from the net, midway between the sidelines, and attempt to volley (without prior instruction), you would soon find that your ground-stroke swing is no help in playing low balls, since most will go into the net and the rest will fly out of the court. In fact, it may not work very well on higher balls either, since a ground-stroke swing takes up too much time.

It should now be clear that the swing for a volley must be short and must provide you with a way of getting low balls up over the net while at the same time giving you strength on medium-high and high volleys.

The Volleying Grips

For the forehand, the grip is the Continental, with the heel barely on top of the racket handle, the base knuckle of the index finger on the right bevel, and the thumb around the racket handle. For the backhand volley, the heel of the hand can be shifted just a bit to the left if time permits, though not as far as for a backhand ground stroke. The distance the hand moves between forehand and backhand volley

PLATE 611

FOREHAND VOLLEY GRIP: *Heel barely on top, toward right-hand edge, base knuckle of index finger on right bevel, thumb around.*

should be kept minimal—just enough to provide strength on both swings. As you can see, these grips tend to open the face of the racket somewhat, a valuable asset in handling low balls.

The Volley Swing

For the forehand volley swing, stand about halfway between the net and the service line, midway between the sidelines. Be sure you have the correct volley grip, the heel barely on top of the handle and the base knuckle of your index finger on the right bevel between the top and the side. If your waiting position is correct, the head of your racket will be opposite your left shoulder and your left hand will be on the throat of the racket. As the ball comes, turn your shoulders to the right so that they face the sideline. When the racket head is almost opposite your right shoulder, let go of the racket throat with your left hand and bring the racket back, at most, a few inches to the right of your right shoulder. You need no more backswing than this. Now, take a step toward the net with your left foot, being sure to put it down at a 45° angle, and swing your racket forward and down. Meet the ball a little ahead of the left side of your body. This is farther ahead than on a forehand ground stroke, but it must not be so far ahead of you that you've used up your swing by the time you meet the ball. As you hit the ball, transfer your weight into it and follow through with your racket pointing at the

FOREHAND VOLLEY *starts from usual waiting position, player turns shoulders to right and puts racket head back opposite right shoulder. He then steps with left foot and moves racket forward and down in brief stroke, finishing with racket pointing toward net. Wrist is cocked and laid back throughout swing. Racket face is slightly opened to help impart spin, more opened on lower balls.*

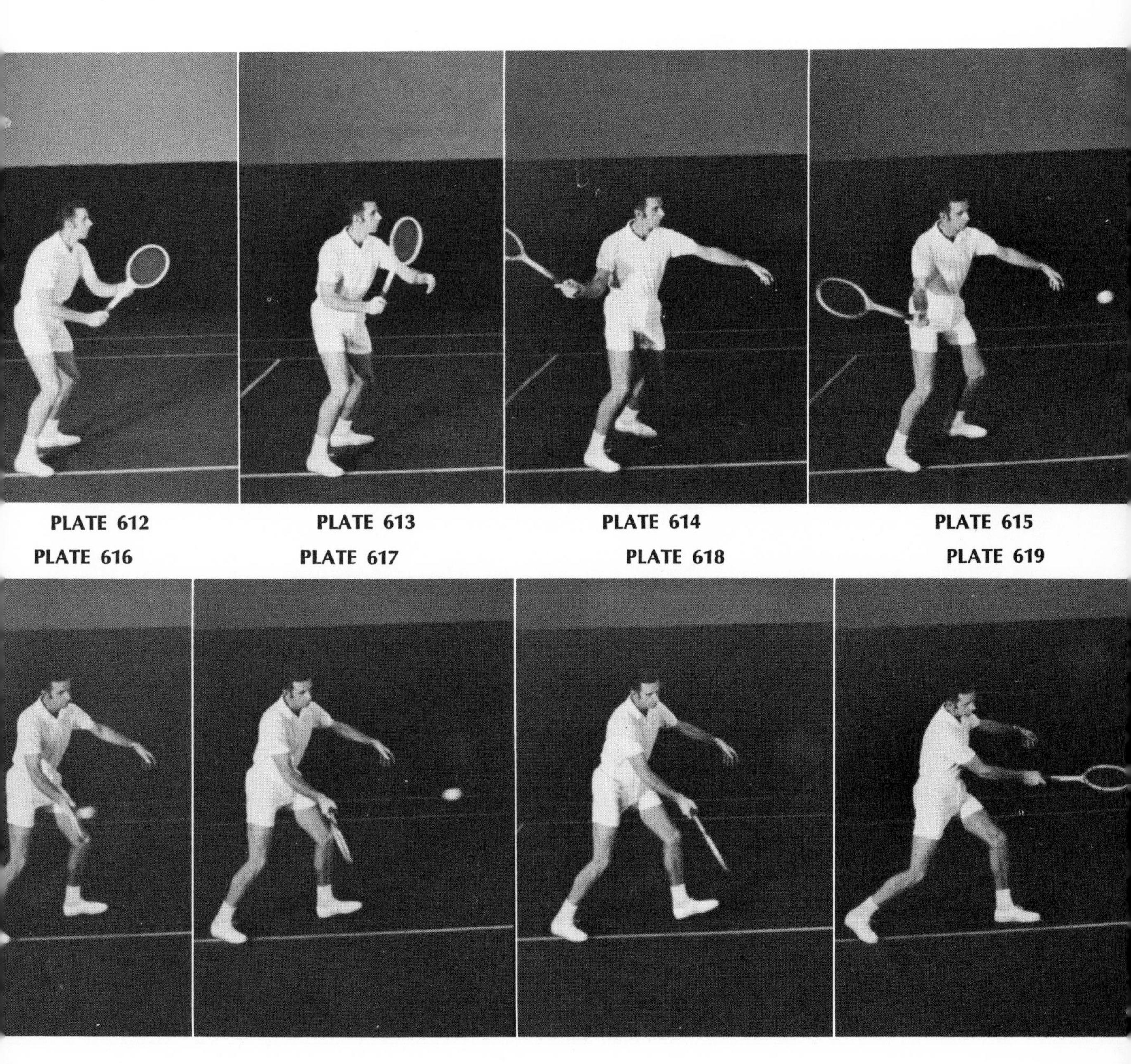

PLATE 612 **PLATE 613** **PLATE 614** **PLATE 615**

PLATE 616 **PLATE 617** **PLATE 618** **PLATE 619**

net. While swinging, you should keep the racket head above hand height and lay your wrist back somewhat. The racket face should be just about perpendicular to the ground when you meet a shoulder-high ball, more open on lower balls in order to help them clear the net.

The Backhand Volley Swing

For the backhand volley, rotate the heel of your hand slightly to the left, start at waiting position, then simply apply the same principles as on the forehand. Turn your shoulders to the left, bring the racket back no farther than your left shoulder, let go with the left hand, take your step forward with the right foot, swing forward into the ball and down somewhat, meeting the ball well ahead of you and finishing with the racket tip pointing at the net.

Learning the Volley Swings

Practice the swings in a mirror and compare your performance with the pictures on pages 209 and 211. It is very important that you feel the difference between the volley swing and the ground stroke. In the former, the racket must move downward

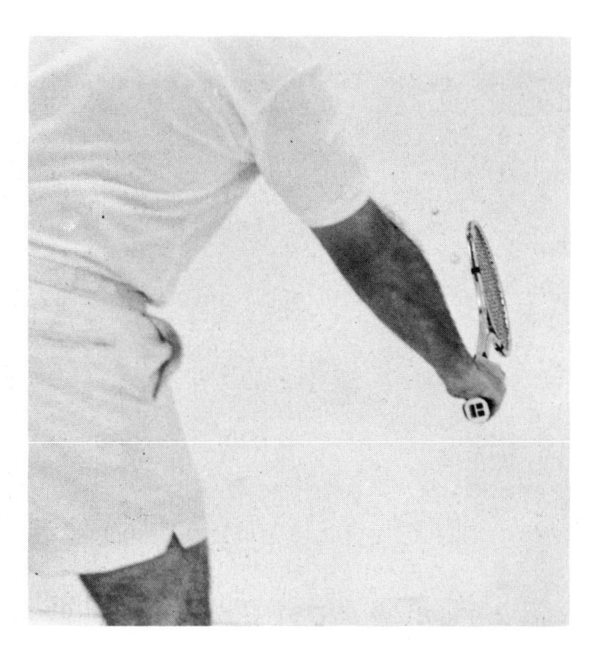

PLATE 620

BACKHAND VOLLEY GRIP: *Heel moves slightly to left and thumb is extended onto left vertical panel if time permits. If not, player should hold forehand volley grip.*

BACKHAND VOLLEY *swing starts as player turns shoulders, pulls racket back with left hand so that racket head is opposite left shoulder. Player then swings racket forward and down while taking step toward net with right foot. Racket head is cocked and face is slightly opened.*

PLATE 621 **PLATE 622** **PLATE 623** **PLATE 624**

PLATE 625 **PLATE 626** **PLATE 627** **PLATE 628**

as well as forward so as to put backspin on the ball. In the latter, the racket should move upward as well as forward so as to put topspin on the ball.

Your next step is to take a number of balls out to a practice wall and station yourself about fifteen feet from it. Check your volleying grip, face the wall in waiting position, turn your shoulders, toss a ball up with your left hand, to your right and about three feet in front of you, step with your left foot and punch your racket forward, down, and into the ball. Do this over and over until you begin to get the hang of it. Then, take your backhand volley grip and try the same thing. Remember, your self-toss must be made from above the racket and high enough so that you can free your left hand in time to have it help out in getting your racket back.

If you can return any of these shots, it will be indeed remarkable; really, it is better not to waste time trying. You now need your friend to toss balls to you on the court, preferably with plenty of balls on hand. Take your correct position at the net, with your friend standing on the opposite side but out of the line of fire so that you have room to hit straight ahead without endangering him. Your friend should start by tossing you simple, shoulder-high forehands. Be sure you start correctly, bringing your racket back above the ball, getting your shoulders sideways, and stepping forward to meet the ball out ahead of you.

Next, your friend should give you some high backhands. Hit into them in the same manner. When you can hit ten in a row of each (not counting any really bad tosses), start in on low forehands. For these, you must bend your knees, keeping your racket head up and its face open, and watching the ball with extreme care. With a low volley, the object is to hit into it as solidly as possible and to get as much depth as conditions will allow. The low volley is one of the hardest shots in the game, almost impossible to achieve with both depth and pace, one that requires the keenest concentration, and one that is often popped up—even by the best players. Perhaps the most difficult, yet most effective, low volley is that which clears the net at minimum height and at maximum angle, hit preferably in the opposite direction from where your opponent is heading.

Now proceed to work on tosses to the low backhand volley. When you can do ten in a row fairly effectively, you are ready to try out the volley with someone hitting balls to you. At this point, help from an experienced player who can hit balls to you with good control would be invaluable. However, if that is not feasible, get help from your tennis-learning partner and provide the same for him. With you at the net, he should stand just behind the service line so he will be able to get better accuracy. He should hit the ball gently at first and keep it where it is easiest for you to hit—about a racket's length from your body.

PLATE 629

FOR LOW VOLLEY *player should stand sideways, bend knees, cock racket, lay it back and open racket face, moving racket forward or even upward to get ball over net. Positions are similar for forehand (Plate 629) and backhand (Plate 630).*

PLATE 630

Go through the same routine as with the toss. First do shoulder-high forehands, then shoulder-high backhands; next, low forehands and then low backhands.

So far, we have suggested neither rallying nor even alternating feeds to forehand and backhand. Not until you can do ten in a row of each (and don't be discouraged if this takes quite awhile) are you ready to try alternating. At first, your feeder should allow plenty of time between shots so you can change grips correctly. There should be no real problem if you have been using the correct grip for the forehand, since it is only a matter of moving the heel of the hand slightly to the left and going ahead with the backhand swing. To prepare for a forehand, simply rotate the heel back to the right at the same time you start your backswing. Remember that your left hand steadies the racket while your right hand starts to bring it back. Problems you may encounter in grip-changing are discussed later on.

Gradually, your friend should cut down the time between feeds so you are forced to speed up your preparation. All of this time you should be trying to volley firmly to the baseline, straight ahead of you. If your friend's feeds are improving in accuracy, he should now move back to the baseline and begin rallying, that is, he should now try to return your shots. Spend only about five minutes on this at first, then switch back to separate feeds. Now, however, your friend should step them up in pace, hitting them farther away from you, right at you, and switching them from forehand to backhand without warning.

When a ball comes right at you, slide to your right or left (it is usually easier to play such a ball on your backhand) and try to step forward and get your weight into the ball if time permits.

Once again, when volleying, you must remember to keep your weight on the balls of your feet and your heels off the ground. There is not much point in even going to the net unless you are prepared to be as agile and active there as possible. It's a wide net and you have to move quickly to cover it.

Now you should be ready to start incorporating the volley into your pattern of play. Go at it gradually. First, stand on the service line. As your friend hits the ball, move in as far as you can get and volley the ball straight ahead and deep. He should try to return your shot, and if he does, move in as close as you can and try to angle your next volley. One of the keys to successful volleying is to keep moving to the net if at all possible. A player should never consider a specific spot at the net as "the" right position: It is strictly a way station and he should be ready either to charge the front line or evacuate it, instantly.

After trying this sort of rally, move back, say, midway between the baseline and the service line, and move in again as your friend hits the ball. Keep working your way in. Score one point for every rally he wins, three for each you win with a put-away volley. See who can get to twenty or so, first.

Next, have your friend start a rally with each of you in his respective backcourt. He should hit a somewhat short shot to you, at moderate speed. Make your approach shot straight ahead and then head for the net. Pause just as he returns your approach shot, then volley it deep and straight ahead and move farther in. If his next return permits, angle it off for a winner. Practice this general formula, adding your own variations, making sure you attempt volleys on both your backhand and forehand.

Teaching the Volley

By reading over the previous section carefully, you will find the forehand and backhand volleys as they should be taught to your pupil. There, too, appears the proper approach: working from grip and practice swing to tossed balls, to racket-hit balls, and finally, to rallies. In particular, the teacher should make certain his pupil grasps the idea of the correct volley swing.

One of the biggest problems will be to get a player accustomed to the forehand volley grip. Some hands adapt to this instantly, while others find it quite difficult. If properly taught, beginners catch on sooner or later, provided the teacher shows just the right amount of persistence. As with many things that are hard at first, or even hard for weeks, months, and years, a reminder later on at a key moment may find the player much more able to respond. This is particularly true of younger players, who may be stumped by a task one year, only to find it simple the next.

The forehand volley grip requires the wrist to be turned at a fairly uncomfortable angle, at least until the player realizes that it feels right when he hits the ball. Many players have so much difficulty hitting the ball in the center of the racket with that grip that they cannot justify its use, and, quite rightly, dislike it. To get the player used to positioning his arm and racket correctly in the backswing, the teacher can stand behind him and slightly to his right, and superimpose his own hand over the player's racket hand. Then, as the ball is tossed by another person or a ball machine, he can help the player hit the ball. Any means the teacher can devise which allows a pupil to hit a stationary ball with the right kind of swing will also help him greatly in grasping the basic idea.

The forehand volleying grip is a soundly conceived one, particularly for medium-high and low balls. One of the main jobs in volleying is to resist the impact of a fast-moving ball. This is why the wrist is laid back, since it puts the bones of the forearm more directly in back of the racket. Because the wrist is laid back, the ball must be met farther in front of the player. The racket head is kept above wrist level so that when it is knocked back by the impact of the ball (just try holding your left hand in back of your racket head as it meets a backhand volley if you want to find out), it recoils in such a way as to help lift the ball up over the net. If the racket head is at wrist level or below at the moment of impact, the racket drops away and the ball skittles off. Another virtue of the Continental forehand grip is that it opens the racket face. This helps on low volleys in getting the ball up over the net, and accentuates backspin on higher volleys. Finally, because the Continental forehand and backhand grips are one and the same, it can be used without changing at all.

With the backhand grip, it is much the same story. If the proper wrist adjustments are made, the grip is sound and will hold up in most circumstances. Moreover, most people find the backhand grip more comfortable for volleying.

The most complicated trouble spot in the forehand grip is same-siding the racket for forehand and backhand and usually stems from a Western or semi-Western forehand grip. In this case, the player either uses the same grip and turns his racket upside down to play the backhand, or else flips his racket halfway around to something approaching an Eastern backhand. Either way is awkward and time-consuming. The teacher must get the player to change correctly, by gradually revising his forehand grip.

At first, feed your pupil only forehand volleys. You can drill him on other aspects of the game, but keep all volley work confined to the forehand. Start him with the Eastern forehand, and when that goes well, move up to the Continental. Then drill him on making the change correctly, first without the ball, then with it. Go very slowly and carefully, making sure your pupil is correctly prepared each time.

In today's rapid-fire game, particularly in doubles, no player can afford the time-consuming handicap of being a same-sider. Preventing or curing this problem will be a real service on the part of the teacher.

Volley Practice

No serious player can do without volley practice for long. Peak sharpness of eye and reflex can ebb away from anyone in a matter of a few days. The eye requires constant exercise to be at its best and volleying challenges the eye to its limit—and beyond.

In practicing, a beginner or a player who is making extensive changes in his volley technique should be allowed plenty of time for preparation between shots. As his technique improves, the time should be cut down and the variety and speed of the shots increased.

Volley rallies with each player at the net (similar to baseball's pepper game) are an excellent warm-up for players at a high level of play. Moreover, they are surprisingly valuable between a pupil and his teacher if the former can grasp the general idea and the latter can keep his volleys soft enough to give his pupil ample time. The pupil should use proper form and try to keep the ball in play as long as he can. The continuity he gains will improve his volley under progressively more difficult conditions. It will also help develop his eye and reflexes for all shots.

Another most valuable drill is the one Roy Emerson wrote of in the October, 1966, issue of *World Tennis*. Two players use half the width but the full length of a tennis court, including the doubles alley. One is at the net and the other in the backcourt. With about two dozen balls available, one is put into play by either man and they then play it as if it were a serious point in a match. The net man tries to volley the ball away and the backcourt man tries to pass him or lob over him. Score can be kept or not, as the players choose. A game of 21 makes a good unit. As soon as one ball goes out, another is put into play without pause, so that both players are kept constantly on the run. This drill provides tremendous eye and reflex training, as well as physical conditioning. And once again, this exercise can be surprisingly effective between an inexperienced player and a teacher who can control the ball.

Perhaps the most challenging volley drill, again using half the width of the court, is for both players to start in the backcourt and try to force their way into the net against each other, playing ground strokes on the rise and volleying hard.

Beginner Drill 6

The Volley

Grip and Waiting Position

1. The volleying grip for forehand has heel barely on top, base knuckle of index finger on right bevel, thumb around handle.
2. For backhand grip, move heel of hand slightly to left (about to edge between left bevel and top of handle).
3. Try forehand volley grip with eyes closed, ten times.
4. Try backhand volley grip with eyes closed, ten times.

Volley Swing and Self-Toss

1. Take waiting position with forehand volley grip and practice forehand volley swing (p. 208), if possible, in front of mirror, checking swing against pictures on p. 209.
2. If forced to work alone, go to practice wall or tennis court with good supply of balls; toss and hit with forehand volley stroke for ten or fifteen minutes steadily, repeatedly checking grip, wrist angle, elbow position, and other key points in swing.
3. Follow same procedure on backhand, tossing ball by reaching forward *under* your racket with left hand.

Practice on Court

1. With friend, take positions on opposite sides of net, you in correct volleying position (on center service line, midway between net and service line) and friend same distance but slightly off the line of a straight-ahead shot by you. He should then toss balls shoulder high to your forehand until you can hit ten in a row.
2. Try high backhands.
3. Low forehands.
4. Low backhands.
5. Have friend hit shots to you from just behind service line. He should then gradually move farther back, hit slightly higher and lower, hit somewhat harder, cut down the time between feeds. Work on shots to forehand only, then to backhand.
6. Have friend alternate feeds to forehand and backhand, at first allowing plenty of time between feeds, then shortening the interval, using different ball for each feed. Player should make all volleys straight ahead and deep.
7. If net man is now able to control most shots, feeder may try to return ball to keep up rally. Backcourt man should do his best to get all shots on first bounce.
8. Net man should slide to right or left for balls right at him (whichever gives him a better chance to handle

the ball) and step forward as he hits. Keep heels off ground while ball is in play.

Intermediate Practice

1. Have would-be volleyer start on service line; as feeder hits ball (aimed for shoulder-high forehand), volleyer moves forward, volleys deep; feeder tries to return ball so volleyer has chance to put it away. Repeat this routine regularly while learning volley.
2. Have volleyer start midway between service line and baseline; follow routine in step 1.
3. Have volleyer start from baseline, play ball on one bounce, make a forcing shot, and move in to volleying position.
4. Using this routine, have feeder gradually vary shots and step up their difficulty. Proceed slowly and if performance goes off, step down difficulty to level where performance is adequate.
5. Have each player practice volleying at net. Stand a yard or two deeper than normal, so rallies will be longer and players will get more practice on low volleys. Hit easily and right to opponent at first, then gradually speed up shots and make them tougher.

Advanced Practice

1. Proceed as above, but with players standing in doubles alley, trying to pass or lob over opponent into doubles alley.
2. Do Emerson drill (see p. 217).
3. Using half the width of the court, have both players rally and try to move up to net.

Teaching Hints 4
The Volley

1. Follow practice routines outlined in beginner drill section for players just learning to volley.
2. For pupils experienced in volleying but having mechanical problems, play enough points to determine nature of problem; then rally, letting pupil take volleying position, in order to confirm diagnosis.
3. Explain problem to pupil, suggest remedy, then rally, making sure shots are easy enough and well enough spaced out to encourage pupil.
4. Gradually step up the difficulty of your feeds until the pupil has more success with new method than old one.

12

Volley Trouble Spots

In the volley, many of the troublesome aspects of the forehand and backhand ground strokes show up, some of them in much exaggerated form. There are also errors peculiar to the volley. In general, most good players have comparatively fewer problems with their volleying mechanics than with those of serve or ground strokes. Their net troubles usually stem from lack of aggressiveness, insufficient drill to be really sharp, lack of imagination, lack of depth, or the like. Less advanced players tend to have more serious mechanical problems, stemming largely from a complete misconception of how the volley should be hit.

Waiting Position

If waiting position is important for ground strokes—and it is—it is just about twice as important for volleys, since the player has only half the time in which to decide what he is going to do with the ball. Alertness is the first essential. But equally vital is keeping the racket head opposite the left shoulder between strokes. Why? Because the backswing is apt to have to be shoulder-high on most volleys, even on the low ones when the shoulder goes down along with the rest of the body as the player bends his knees. It is vital that the racket be brought back at least a little above ball height, even if the volley is made off the shoetops. Think again of a free-spinning wheel: If you were to brush your hand down its back, you would impart backspin to the wheel. Similarly, when your racket imparts backspin to a ball it aids control, keeping the ball so low that your opponent will hit it up higher than he means to. It is much easier to put the racket above ball height at the back of the backswing if it is already at that height in waiting position.

One of the most difficult things for a player to determine is whether he uses the same face of the racket on both forehand and backhand when he is at the net. The beginning player who applies the volleying methods of this book (or whose teacher more or less uses our approach) should not have much trouble if he has followed instructions closely. But before the experienced player tackles any other aspect

USE OF SAME FACE *of racket for forehand and backhand volley can be seen in this sequence (note circle). Player uses semi-Western forehand grip though with essentially correct swing. After hitting ball he flips racket over, losing valuable time and racket control while preparing for backhand.*

PLATE 631

PLATE 632

PLATE 633

PLATE 634

of volleying, he must first find out if he is a same-sider, and if so, whether he thinks it worth changing.

To find out, put a piece of tape on the top of your racket handle. Stand at the net and have someone hit balls alternately to your forehand and backhand. After every few strokes, check to see if your tape is still up where you can see it. Better yet, show the pictures on page 221 to your friend (or a knowledgeable tennis person) and ask him how your performance compares. Once again, this is a situation where a tennis teacher is best qualified to help you.

Just as with ground-stroke grip troubles, the diagnosis and cure are one and the same. If that tape is not upright at all times, you are at fault; if a minute adjustment in grip by a minimal movement of the heel of the hand will keep the tape upright, you are cured.

Grips

There is no doubt that gripping is a distinct problem in volleying. Players who have had some instruction tend to volley using an Eastern forehand, and just a slight variation of it for their backhand. They have a fairly good pattern of swing, yet on the forehand they have considerable difficulty with low balls, and on the backhand they have trouble getting any real punch. It is not uncommon to see such players trying to make backhand volleys with an out-and-out forehand grip. A serious weakness like this is easy to detect in a match and a player should train himself to look for such mechanical weaknesses in his opponents and exploit them.

If the player's swing pattern is adequate, he should change his volley grip to Continental for the forehand. For the backhand, he should move the heel of his hand just slightly left. He should drill with these grips extensively, until they feel comfortable and he can make the change under all but the most pressing conditions.

Use of the Left Hand

The left hand is essential in positioning the racket for the first volley in any given rally and for any subsequent volleys where time permits. In rapid-fire exchanges at the net, the left hand is likely to go unused, but players who get into such exchanges and survive them usually have a strong enough racket hand that they can pass up the assistance of the other hand.

The player should be sure he makes use of his left hand between strokes to rest his racket, to relax his racket hand, and to facilitate any grip changing.

Pattern of Swing

The most important and major error in volleying is to use a ground-stroke-like swing. Such a swing completely ignores both the court's geometry and the time factor, thus making volleying an even more chancy business than it already is. By using top-spin, a player risks netting the ball. By using too long a backswing—the other major characteristic of a ground-stroke swing—the player eats up too much time.

Changing to a proper volley swing is as essential for experienced players as for beginners. While it is not easy, a volley made with the proper swing pattern can be executed even with the Western grip. A player contemplating a grip change should go by stages—Western to semi-Western to Eastern to Continental—preferably under a teacher's supervision. Once each grip change has been absorbed, the player should move on another notch until, finally, he is comfortable with the Continental. He should expect that his new grip will at first make him volley up more than he means to, because up to this point he has been using his wrist instead of the correct grip to open the racket face.

Certain errors in swing pattern are committed by players who otherwise have the right idea and are achieving backspin. One is to overemphasize backspin by carving down too much and not punching forward enough. Another is to have too long a backswing; sometimes, in the process, the racket head hangs down from the wrist, somewhat in the manner of a serve backswing, so that it has to be thrown forward at the ball, with wildness the inevitable result.

Racket Face Angle

Assuming the player's grip has now been corrected, he may still have trouble regulating the racket-face angle. He must get the feeling of how much angle is required at various heights and test it out till he has command of it under stress. Most players will tend to open the face a little too much, getting more backspin and/or upward flight than they need or want. If the player tends to the opposite—to close the racket face, or worse, to roll it forward—woe be unto him. He must be made to understand that this destroys his control of height, that he must try to keep the face angled back more.

Wrist

Quite a common problem on the volley is the misuse of the wrist. Many a top-flight volleyer is said to have "touch," to have a "facile wrist," or to display "delicate wristwork"—and so he does. Most of this wristwork consists of setting the angle of the wrist correctly at the beginning of the stroke and keeping it there, or letting the wrist give somewhat at the moment of impact so as to absorb much of the force of the shot and send it back softly. This is so-called touch. Many a player, however, gets the misimpression that the volley is therefore a wristy stroke. He sticks his arm out rigidly and then waggles his wrist as the ball comes, only to find that the ball falls right off the racket. This may cause him to question the quality of his wristwork, but not to question the mechanics of its use. The joints which do the moving in the volley, as in the ground strokes, are the shoulder and the elbow. The wrist has special duties in the volley—to set the correct angle for each shot—but its ultimate duty is to hold still.

Elbow

A player does not need as much swinging room for a volley as for a ground stroke. In fact, it is better to be somewhat closer to the ball, by keeping the elbow a little closer to the body at the start of the volley. The arm extends fully as the ball is met; the so-called punch in a volley is simply this straightening of the arm. A teacher should be sure, therefore, that his pupil does not roll his racket face over by straightening his arm prematurely and trying to hit the volley with a roundhouse motion. The farther he is from the ball, the more likely the player is to hit it with a straight arm; and the straighter his arm, the more likely his shoulder muscles are to roll his arm—and thus his racket face—forward.

Follow-through

A volley is a fairly abrupt stroke but it should not lack follow-through. The volleyer should make a definite impact on the ball, not merely let the ball bounce off his racket. On the finish, the racket head should be pointing to the net. It should move a couple of feet past the point of impact for a hard, point-ending volley or a deep, forcing volley. With an angled or stop volley, of course, the finish is much shorter and, as stated earlier, the wrist gives slightly so that the racket head falls back somewhat at the moment of impact. Occasionally, a player makes all his volleys this way and thus lacks firmness of impact. If he emphasizes his finish, he will add a great deal more punch to his volleys and be a much more effective volleyer (see picture on page 225).

PLATES 635 through 650 below and page 226

LACK OF FOLLOW-THROUGH *(Plates 635 to 642): Backswing starts well with racket head cocked, laid back and opened, but racket hardly moves after meeting ball (Plates 640, 641, 642). Impact is limp. Player was told to accent finish and follow through pointing to net. In AFTER sequence (Plates 643 to 650) racket travels into ball and impact is much firmer.*

PLATE 635 **PLATE 636** **PLATE 637** **PLATE 638**

PLATE 639 **PLATE 640** **PLATE 641** **PLATE 642**

PLATE 643 **PLATE 644** **PLATE 645** **PLATE 646**

PLATE 647 PLATE 648 PLATE 649 PLATE 650

Feet and Body Weight

Far too many volleyers face straight ahead or take their step with the foot nearest the ball. It is essential on all volleys to get the shoulders sideways, and if possible, the feet, too. The weight should be directed forward into the stroke in any event, and the step must be taken with the foot *farthest* away from the ball. This allows for better weight transference and much greater range in reaching a ball that is well wide of the volleyer. Of course, if the ball comes right at the player, he may want to pull his near foot back so as to get himself sideways.

Volley Trouble Spots

Problem	Why it is a problem	What teacher should do	What player should do
Waiting position 1. Racket head too low.	Leaves player unprepared or poorly prepared.	Rally with player at net, reminding him, with each shot, to get racket up.	Rally with friend, taking care to be ready on each shot.
Grips 1. Use of same face for forehand and backhand.	Consumes time when player can least afford it; also puts racket face at awkward angle.	Move player gradually from Western or semi-Western towards Continental on forehand; show correct change.	Diagnose problem by checking to see if distinctive marking on top of handle remains there or is turned over as you switch. Review correct grip-change (p. 221), then gradually shift forehand grip towards Continental.
2. Use of forehand grip on backhand.	Weak grip, incapable of resisting impact of ball.	Have player shift grip as far towards correct backhand as possible, feeding him backhands till he gets used to it.	Check grip against pictured grip, correct it, then try your luck against easy tosses, easy feeds and, finally, hard shots.
Use of left hand 1. Failure to use it.	Puts strain on right hand, causing poor grip-change. Particularly important between approach shot and first volley.	Have player alternate forehand and backhand practice swings correctly, slowly at first, then faster. Have him try correct method on slow-paced feeds and, finally, at full speed.	See left, and have friend feed shots.
2. Use of left hand on backhand during forward swing.	Sign of weak grip with right hand, restricts reach.	Show player correct grip on backhand and let him get used to it, so he will realize left hand only hampers good backhand volley.	Check backhand grip of right hand. Correct it, and practice with it at slow speed, gradually taking on tougher shots.

Problem	Why it is a problem	What teacher should do	What player should do
Racket-face angle 1. Open too much.	Player either pops ball up or imparts too much backspin.	Show player how this hinders control and power. Explain only slight backward tilt of racket face is needed, and that the higher the ball, the less is needed.	Volleys will pop up or have excess backspin. Films will confirm player is opening racket face too much. Experiment with tilt of racket face until solid impact results regularly on the volley.
2. Rolling forward.	Player nets volleys frequently.	Continuously changing racket-face angle during swing all but destroys control. Player must keep forearm from rotating forward.	See left.
Wrist 1. Moves during swing.	Makes control too difficult.	Tell player to set wrist at proper angle and keep it firm during swing, principally by gripping tightly.	See left.
Elbow 1. Too stiff.	Leaves out a main source of power, often accompanied by rotation of forearm, throwing off player's control.	Have player pull elbow in closer to body while preparing swing, extend it only as he hits.	See left.
Pattern of swing 1. Ground-stroke type swing.	Excessive backswing uses up too much time, topspin risks netting ball.	Show player correct swing pattern, stress brief backswing and downward path of forward swing for imparting backspin.	Observe films of yourself volleying and compare swing pattern with pictures on pp. 209 and 211. If backswing is excessive, shorten it. If topspin results, try to chop ball slightly. Work from very easy tosses to hard shots.
2. Excess chopping (overemphasis on downward path of forward swing).	Detracts from speed of shot, often giving opponent time to get to ball.	Show player how to hit into ball giving greater emphasis to *forward* aspect of swing.	If severe backspin results on all volleys, you are chopping too much (films will confirm your observation). Check path of swing and compare with pictures on pp. 209 and 211. Hit forward into ball, not down so much.

Problem	Why it is a problem	What teacher should do	What player should do
3. Excess backswing.	Even if player's swing pattern is correct, excess backswing eats up time, may force racket off main line of swing.	Show player how this swing eats up time, may derail his swing. Have him put racket head opposite rear shoulder, wait for ball, and punch it at impact.	On court you will feel hurried and, may flub easy volleys. Films will show big windup, possibly with extra bend in backswing. See picture, pp. 209 and 211; limit backswing to same extent as model's, i.e., opposite rear shoulder.
Follow-through			
1. Lack of finish.	Weak shots result, which opponent can get to.	Have player follow through farther, so racket tip points at net on finish.	See left.
2. Elevated finish.	Leads to topspin, detracts from control.	See problem #1 under **Pattern of Swing.**	See left.
Feet and body weight			
1. Stepping with foot nearest ball.	Minor problem on forehand, **if** shoulders are turned (though it detracts from power). Major problem on backhand since it impedes backswing.	Have player arrange feet as does model in pictures on pp. 209 and 211.	See left.
2. Failure to turn shoulders.	When shoulders are not turned sideways (and it is not always possible to turn them in time), swing will lack power.	Have player at least turn shoulders, and set correctly whenever possible, so as to get maximum power potential from swing.	See left.

13
Supplementary Strokes

Armed as you are with a forehand, backhand, serve, and volley, you still lack some of the strokes you need to become a tennis competitor. These are the lob, drop shot, overhead, and half volley. With your present knowledge and some ingenuity, you could teach yourself all these strokes without reading further. If you were to jump right into competition without them, you would have to learn them somehow, by trial and error. It is better to add them to your repertoire right now, especially since the job is not that difficult.

The Lob

The easiest of these strokes to learn is the lob, though it's probably as hard as any of the others to do well. The lob, which we touched on briefly before, is that high, lofting shot a player uses when forced badly out of position. Though generally thought of as a defensive weapon, the lob, at its best, can be used for repeated point-winners, or to turn the tide in favor of a player under heavy siege by a net rusher. Used at the appropriate time and in the appropriate way, it can be the straw that will break the back of the strongest sort of game. This applies to singles as well as doubles, for in a fast game, where taking the net is the objective of all good players, the lob is the best way to drive an opponent back.

There are two main types of lob: the backspin and the topspin. By far the easier and safer of these is the backspin lob. It is the one you should learn first and the one you should use the majority of the time. The topspin lob requires more timing and touch, but today's young players are learning it earlier and using it as an outright point-winner.

Lobbing Grips

The grips for lobbing are the same as for volleying. For the forehand, the heel is barely on top of the handle, the thumb around the front of the handle, and the base knuckle of the index finger is on the right bevel. For the backhand, the heel of the hand rotates slightly to the left. The reason for using these grips is that they open the face of the racket and allow the player to hit the ball up and apply backspin.

The pattern of motion for the lob is almost identical with that of the forehand or backhand drive, except that the racket face must be tilted well back to loft the ball, and the backswing is often much shorter. The head of the racket should be above the height of the hand throughout the stroke. At impact, the racket face must pass under the ball so as to give it backspin; at the end of the swing, the face should be open even more—to accentuate the backspin. See Plates 651-666 on pages 232-233.

To repeat, the primary purpose of backspin is to give control of depth, so that you can swing fairly hard and still keep the ball in court.

To learn the lob, you must first be convinced of its usefulness—and that you are not in the least fainthearted or weak if you use it. Young sluggers scorn the lob as a sissy stroke, particularly if they are beaten by "pushers." But the lob is a vital part of the game, and a player must know not only how to play against it, but how to use it effectively himself. If you can lob well and at the right time, your opponents will gripe but you will win.

There are two principal times to use the lob: when you are out of position and when your opponent is rushing the net.

To perfect the lob, you can either do the preliminary work by yourself or have your friend toss to you. Bring along plenty of balls and go out to a court. The lob is one stroke which is fairly difficult to practice except on a court, since only there can you tell whether you are hitting high enough and far enough. Stand behind the base-line and take your Continental forehand grip. Using the self-toss, take a brief backswing

LOB SWINGS *call for Continental grip and backward tilt of racket face. Follow-through should be high and racket face is opened even more as swing progresses.*

PLATE 651 PLATE 652 PLATE 653 PLATE 654

PLATE 659 PLATE 660 PLATE 661 PLATE 662

PLATE 655 PLATE 656 PLATE 657 PLATE 658

PLATE 663 PLATE 664 PLATE 665 PLATE 666

and lift the ball up high over the net and way back to the baseline of the opposite court, tilting the racket head back as you follow through.

Try for a height of fifteen or twenty feet over the net and for as much depth as possible. You should strive for real accuracy under relaxed conditions so that you will be able to lob under progressively more difficult—and typical playing—conditions. The only way to get to this point is to lob a couple of hundred balls in a row, alternating courts every two dozen balls or so. It shouldn't take you more than fifteen or twenty minutes, after which you should go on to something else. Then, come back to lobbing practice again, for only by countless repetition will you be able to develop the sense of touch that tells you just how much force is needed to get that ball over your opponent and back to his baseline.

The rest of your course you can almost outline for yourself. First, try backhand lobs in the same way, from the self-toss. Next, have your friend toss to your forehand and backhand, then have him hit from across the net to your forehand and backhand. Finally, try the lob out during rallies. Hit him a short shot to force him to the net, then lob over him. Repeat this sequence over and over with progressively tougher shots. Later, once you have both learned to hit an overhead, one of you will be able to work on that while the other practices lobbing. The Emerson drill described on page 217 is ideal for lob practice under heavy pressure.

The Topspin Lob

There are two effective ways a lob can be used; offensively and defensively. Offensively, it can be used either to win a point outright or elicit an error. In the first instance, the ideal lob is of minimum height (but, still over the head of one's opponent), combined with maximum depth, so that the net man can neither reach it nor overtake it in time. The second, more modest, offensive lob simply dislodges the net man from his advantageous position. Here, depth is the most important thing, and for safety's sake the lob can afford to be a little higher. Defensively, the lob can be used to gain time, so that when a player has been forced badly out of position he can scramble back. Here, height is more important, since it consumes time and offers the best chance for recovery.

The topspin lob is used only offensively, either to win the point outright or to put such pressure on one's opponent that he will hit a setup one or two shots later. Topspin, of course, is forward spin. When the topspin lob clears the outstretched racket of the opponent, the ball drops quickly and then takes a fast, high bounce that is almost impossible to overtake.

This is primarily a forehand stroke and not an easy one to make; only the very best players can use it with any hope of success on their backhand. Generally, when a player lobs, he is forced to play the ball on the rise; consequently, the ball quite naturally tends to have backspin on it as it leaves the lobber's racket. But to lob with topspin, it is necesary to counteract this force by reversing the natural spin of the ball. This requires very good hand-to-eye coordination.

The topspin lob stroke is much like an ordinary ground stroke except that the swing starts from below the level at which the ball will be hit, the racket face is slightly closed, and the racket is given an exaggerated upward motion to apply excess topspin. The Eastern forehand grip or even the Semi-Western is good for the topspin lob.

TOPSPIN LOB *is made by lifting racket abruptly as it comes forward and making ball seem to stick to racket momentarily before releasing it with exaggerated topspin. Face of racket must be closed slightly. Great care is needed to direct effort into production of spin rather than power, or open racket face will send the ball far out.*

PLATE 667 **PLATE 668** **PLATE 669** **PLATE 670**

PLATE 671 **PLATE 672** **PLATE 673** **PLATE 674**

The backswing is identical to that of a ground stroke and the more it looks like it, the more deceptive the shot will be. The follow-through, however, must be much higher than that of a ground stroke. The racket face should make a glancing upward impact. If the player hits through the ball and thus too squarely, he is likely to get too much depth.

Teaching the Lob

By following the pattern outlined in the previous section, the teacher can cover the backspin lob quite adequately. His main job is to prevent the errors detailed below from being committed.

Trouble Spots on the Lob

Any stroking error that upsets the ordinary forehand or backhand ground stroke can upset a lob as well, but there are certain ones that occur primarily in the lob.

1. *Grip.* The player may have difficulty getting his grip set in time. The tougher the opponent's shot, the more need for a lob, and the less time available for grip changes. Most lobs are hit from the backcourt where ground-stroke grips are used. The important thing is that the player gets in the habit of returning his left hand to the throat of the racket immediately after every shot, so that it is there and ready to help on the grip change. The player should also practice grip changes without a ball, trying them at increasingly rapid speeds while preserving accuracy.
2. *Swing.* In the backspin lob, the player may jab stiffly at the ball with the result that he cannot control its flight. He should slow his motion down and be sure he follows through, bearing in mind that he must keep his racket on the ball as long as possible in order to control it. Many players stop their swing because they do not want the ball to go too far—instead, that is precisely what happens.
3. *Follow-though.* Instead of following through with an upward motion, the player may follow through with his racket finishing below the point of contact. Again, if he hits with any power, the ball is likely to fly too far. He should follow through with the racket head finishing well up, but it should pass under the ball to impart backspin.
4. *Racket Face.* The player may roll his racket face forward during the course of the swing. For self-diagnosis on this point, a player can suspect some such thing if he is having all kinds of trouble controlling height on

simple lobs. He will not know it for sure, however, unless he sees films of himself lobbing. The player who is being carefully taught by a teacher should have this problem pointed out to him early. The remedy is simply to resolve to keep the racket face open and to open it still further on the follow-through.

5. *Backswing.* The player may try to take too big a backswing, especially when retrieving a hard-hit ball. The harder the ball, the less backswing he'll need. His main effort has to be directed at getting the center of the racket face into the path of the ball; otherwise, a hard-hit ball will merely twist the racket in his hand and the ball will go wild. The rule, then, is that on a hard-hit ball the player should use a short backswing, concentrate on getting the center of his racket into the path of the ball, and be sure to follow through properly.

6. *Body Movement.* The player may find his weight is moving back instead of forward while he hits the ball. This is much more likely to happen on a hard-hit, sharply angled, or deep shot than under less pressing circumstances. Quickness and anticipation will help a great deal to eliminate this difficulty. But if a player is moving as fast as he can, yet is simply too sorely pressed, he can compensate for the backward motion of his body by pushing the racket through a little bit farther than he ordinarily would. This sort of expedient helps a player make the most out of a bad position.

The Drop Shot

This is a delicately-hit shot that lands just over the net. If perfectly executed, it takes its second bounce before the opponent can get to it. It is a stroke that every great player has used—even those who rely mostly on power. It can be used to win points outright, to tire an opponent, to force him to make weak returns, to break up his rhythm and concentration, and even to irritate him. Like the lob, it can turn the tide of a match that might otherwise be lost.

Unfortunately, today's emphasis on power tennis has caused the drop shot to be neglected. A player intent on hitting every ball hard—especially an inexperienced player—has great difficulty in slowing down his swing while still retaining control. When he tries a drop shot, he nearly always hits it too hard and it turns into a setup his opponent can get to easily and put away. Then the power hitter grumbles, "There, you see, it just isn't my kind of stroke."

A by-product of today's power game is the headlong rush for the net, and net-rushing is another reason why the drop shot is less frequently used these days. If both players are moving in to the net, the odds are against either of them being able to use the drop shot. Often, though, only one player is coming to net and he can try a drop shot either on his way in or when he arrives. If the former, he hits the ball on the fly. This is a drop volley, a somewhat more demanding shot, but made similarly.

Because the drop shot has fallen out of fashion among many top flight players, it is not taught as frequently as it should be. As a result, many otherwise well-schooled players have an unorthodox and thus erratic drop shot. If a player cannot rely on a given shot and has difficulty making it cleanly, chances are he will avoid using it. In the case of the drop shot, knowing how to make it is vital; knowing when to use it is everything.

A drop shot should be made from the attacking position. Let us suppose that a player has forced his opponent back behind the baseline with a strong, deep drive. The opponent replies with a fairly short ball but stays rooted to the baseline. The player can then hit either another drive or a drop shot. As long as the danger exists that he may do either, his opponent will be in doubt as to whether he should stay where he is or move in and either shot will be that much more effective.

If you are a teacher trying to convince your pupil of the value of the drop shot, one sure method is to make him the victim of it. Tell the player, in an innocent way, that you would like to rally with him to see how his ground strokes are progressing. Be sure he understands that he is expected to get to every ball on the first bounce or the volley. Then, during the rally, maneuver him out of position and win the point by means of a drop shot. Repeat this several times and see if it arouses any curiosity in your pupil. Ask him if he noticed what kind of shot you used to win those points and explain to him why it worked so well.

The drop shot is made almost exactly like a backspin lob. The grip and swing are the same, except that the latter is less severe. And needless to say, as the ball is not aimed as high, the racket face need not be tilted so far back.

To review, the grips are the same as those for the forehand and backhand volleys, that is, about halfway between those for the forehand and backhand ground strokes. To execute the swing, the player turns sideways as he moves the racket back,

DROP-SHOT SWING *is miniature version of that used for lob. Grip is Continental, racket face open, cocked, and turned under slightly during swing. Follow-through is slightly elevated. Player must be sure to follow through gently, not merely stop the swing.*

PLATE 675 PLATE 676 PLATE 677 PLATE 678

PLATE 679 PLATE 680 PLATE 681 PLATE 682

PLATE 683 PLATE 684 PLATE 685 PLATE 686

PLATE 687 PLATE 688 PLATE 689 PLATE 690

his right hand with the correct grip on the handle, his left hand on the throat guiding it back. The racket head goes back past his shoulder and then moves forward into the ball. On a waist-high ball, the racket is tilted back slightly at impact so as to open more on the finish. The racket head must slide under the ball and impart backspin, then follow through well past the point of impact. On a shoulder-high ball, there is more downward motion. On a knee-high ball, the racket moves forward and up.

If a player wants to teach himself the drop shot, it is best to follow the procedure he used to work on the lob. However, instead of standing near the baseline, he should start at about the service line. Using the form just described, he should try a drop shot off the self-toss, not gripping too firmly, and keeping the shot as soft and short as possible.

The player should do this over and over, then try it on both his forehand and backhand, first with balls tossed to him by his friend, then with balls hit to him. Once the player feels he has the basic technique and is getting the feel of the stroke, he should move to the backcourt position and try this simple drill: Your opponent hits you a fairly deep ball; return a shot that he can handle; he then hits a short ball, and on this one you can try your drop shot. Keep this routine going as long as possible, gradually increasing the difficulty of the chances as and when they come within the limits of what you can do.

The object of this extensive practice, of course, is to perfect your drop shot so that you no longer have to concentrate on how to make it but can begin to learn when to use it.

The most important element in a successful drop shot is surprise. The key to surprise is disguise. The backswing for the drop shot should look no different from that of a lob or a ground stroke. The realization that a drop shot is being made should not dawn on your opponent until the last possible split second. At that instant, your racket head tilts back slightly and slides under the ball.

To improve the disguise, practice the same drill as before, only this time alternate between hitting a hard ground stroke and a drop shot, using a motion as nearly alike as possible for both. Here, your friend's ability to detect what you are up to is very important. He should study your moves and criticize anything you do to tip off your intention. No matter how good an actor you are, you cannot tell whether your act is working unless your "opponent" is fooled by your actions—or is not, and tells you so.

As a player starts to use his drop shot in actual play, he may fall into several errors. The most common *technical* error is to chop down into the ball too hard, overdoing the spin and hitting too far. The most common *tactical* error is to attempt a drop shot from too deep a position. Assume that the player has driven his opponent well behind the baseline; his opponent replies with a high-bouncing, deep return and the player then attempts a drop shot. Chances for its success are very slim. However well-made and disguised, the shot has to travel so far just to clear the net that his opponent will have time to get to it. Or, suppose his opponent moves in to the net behind a shorter approach shot than he intended. It is obviously not the time for the player to try a drop shot—unless he sees his opponent retreating to his baseline. Similarly, a drop shot is often a player's best reply to a drop shot if his opponent has tried one while moving up to net on an angle. Then the player can catch his opponent off balance and out of position with a drop shot to the opposite side of the court.

The Overhead

We have just described the two supplementary strokes that are the greatest help in breaking up a power game—the lob and the drop shot. Now we move on to the stroke that is most essential to a player's own successful power game—the overhead. An overhead shot (or smash, as it is sometimes called) takes place, of course, when a lobbed ball is still at a point over the player's head. It is an opportunity for both sensational putaways and spectacular fluffs. A good, decisive overhead, which puts away all but the very best lobs, makes the net player all but impregnable. A poor overhead, no matter how well the net player prepares his approach and volleys low-flying balls, is a fatal chink in his armor.

Most players don't realize that merely knowing how to make the overhead is not enough. The average player shies away from practicing overheads 1) because they are difficult and 2) because it is boring for him or his opponent to push up lobs to be smashed. But regular practice is more necessary on the overhead than on other strokes because its timing is the most difficult. As the lobbed ball descends at right angles to the path of the stroke, there is only a fleeting instant when the time is right to hit the ball. Once this instant passes, the ball is difficult—even impossible—to play, and the advantage gained (being able to smash the ball down into the opponent's court) is lost. The difficulty of such timing is so great that even first-rate players must practice their overhead incessantly.

This timing factor is not the only problem in the overhead. Like the serve, it requires a long and rather intricate swing. More important, an overhead requires more difficult footwork than any other stroke: The player must turn and run back while simultaneously keeping his eye on the ball and his body sideways enough to be able to make his stroke at the right moment.

Though the overhead is obviously no cinch, it need not be too hard to learn. In the first place, knowing the proper motion for the serve already reduces a good portion of the difficulty. Secondly, if you start by having balls tossed or hit right to you, your footwork problems will be kept to a minimum for the time being. Then, if the practice tosses or shots are high enough, you will have time to complete your backswing and won't have to resort to a clumsy partial swing.

The overhead swing is exactly like the service swing except for its backswing. Whereas in the serve backswing the racket head passes the player's leg on the way back, on the overhead it passes back about waist height.

The most important elements in the overhead are concentration on the ball and correct positioning under it. Before you try your first overhead, make up your mind you are going to watch the ball better than ever before and get into position promptly and accurately. You will need to, because while the ball takes a long time to reach you, you must keep your eye on it and get set for that brief moment when it is right to hit it.

Start off by taking up volleying position on the court (halfway between net and service line and midway between the sidelines), but without your racket. A friend should stand on the opposite baseline with a couple of dozen balls and either hit or throw good high lobs to you. Your job is to move under them and catch them. His shots should be fairly shallow and aimed near you at first, then they should gradually get a little tougher. From this exercise you will get an idea of how much you have to move and how long you have to wait for a ball to get down to you. For the next half-dozen practice periods work on your overhead in this way for at least ten or fifteen minutes before you actually start hitting balls.

When you are ready to start hitting overheads, await them with your forehand volleying grip. When the ball approaches, start turning sideways while you bring the racket back past your waist to the bent-elbow position. From this point on, the swing is exactly like that of a flat serve. The racket should travel forward and into the ball, with your arm fully extended at the moment of impact. You must get behind the ball so as to meet it well out ahead of you and slightly to the right of your head. The follow-through should end up with the racket's hitting face just about opposite your left shin and your weight forward on your left leg.

Strive to hit your overheads deep and straight ahead, since a deep overhead, even if it goes right at your opponent, is hard to return and much more sure of landing in the court. Furthermore, this type of overhead ensures your getting a good piece of the ball each time. Short, angled overheads should not be tried until the simple, straightforward version is under good control.

OVERHEAD *requires accurate judgment of ball's flight so that ball will be just to right of head and high enough to allow full racket extension. Turning feet in direction of runback is helpful. Right knee must absorb momentum of the runback and recoil player back toward the net as he swings. Swing is identical to flat serve swing except for abbreviated takeback.*

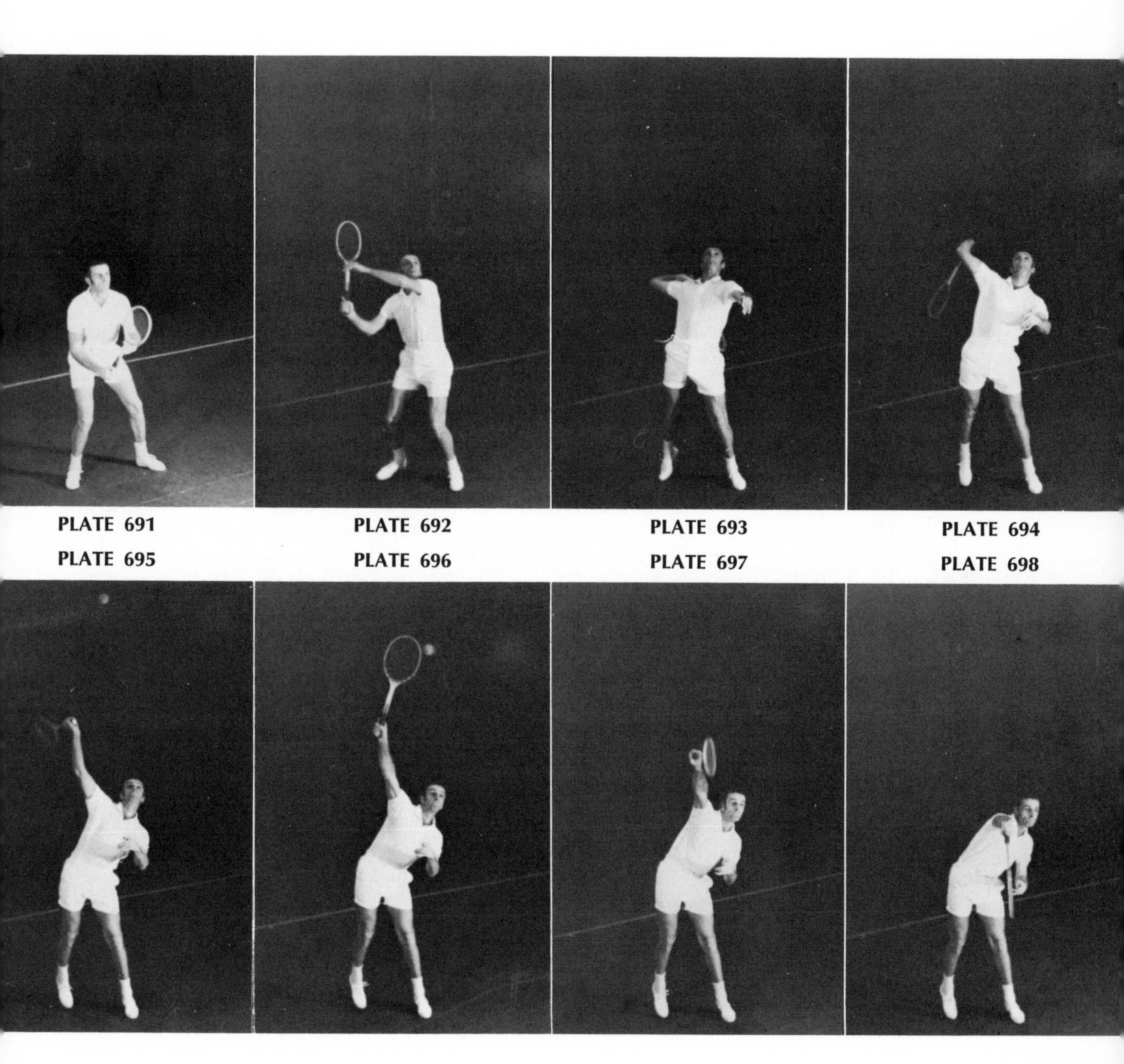

PLATE 691 **PLATE 692** **PLATE 693** **PLATE 694**

PLATE 695 **PLATE 696** **PLATE 697** **PLATE 698**

You should practice the overhead as much and as often as you possibly can. The ideal way, if you can manage it, is to use a ball-throwing machine. The machine can be set to give a reasonably good replica of a lob and it doesn't get tired or bored. The next best thing is to have a friend who is as eager to work on the overhead as you, so that you take turns tossing or hitting to each other. Do not underestimate the importance of spending hours and hours on your overhead, no matter how well you learn to play.

Now you should be ready to work on overheads which require you to move around on the court. As it is easiest to move to your right, your friend should first test you in that direction for a good while. You have to get sideways, of course, to go to your right; being sideways in transit, you should then have little trouble staying that way once you reach the ball. Beware of wasting time and effort by turning sideways to get to the ball, then facing the net to watch it, only to have to turn sideways again to hit it.

Next, try overheads that take you to the right and backwards. Turn your toes in the direction you intend to run, look over your shoulder at the ball as you go back, then stop at the appropriate place by planting your right leg and bending your knee. This will not only take up the shock of your stopping but also help you push off as you swing into the ball.

Moving to your left is still harder, and moving to your left and backwards is hardest of all. Whenever possible, run around a high lob so that you can play it with your regular overhead. A backhand overhead is next to impossible to hit with any power.

The fastest way to gain position is to pull your right foot back and then, putting one foot after the other, run toward the rear of the court. It is uncanny how a Rod Laver, Pancho Gonzales, Ken Rosewall, or Roy Emerson can cover ground in this way. Needless to say, you can't look where you're going, as you have to watch the ball. But at least you can proceed with the assurance that the court will not change its shape while you're running, nor will it probably contain any hills or valleys that will trip you. At first, it is no doubt best to try out this sort of running without any fielding problem at all. Next, have someone toss you balls to catch so you can perfect your footwork. Then, when your range to the left, rear portion of the court has improved, tackle an actual overhead stroke with your racket.

One of the best ways to get down to serious overhead practice in a game-like situation is the Emerson drill described on page 217.

Teaching the Overhead

The teaching procedure for the overhead can follow the same pattern that has just been outlined for self-teaching. Demonstrate the stroke; break the player in gently by having him catch lobs, nearby at first, then all over the court; then hit him simple lobs, gradually moving him farther afield, first to his right, then backwards to his right and finally to his left and backwards to his left. Keep a watch out for the problems described below.

Trouble Spots on the Overhead

1. *Bad Timing.* Probably the most common error in making overheads is the tendency to swing violently before the ball gets within hitting distance. The air is parted with a vicious swish and the ball drops gently by the side of the player who, if he has any presence of mind left, swings again at the ball after it bounces and play continues.

Why is the ball mistimed? Simply because the player could not wait and so he stopped watching the ball. First of all, a lob is in the air much longer than an ordinary shot. Second, it is not easy to hit a ball at just the right moment when its path is perpendicular to that of the player's stroke. Third, as the ball drops, it picks up speed, at the rate of gravity. The player's head has to be tilted back to watch the ball while it's in the air and a beginner is likely to relax his neck muscles too soon and thus take his eyes off the ball.

Another deterring factor, of course, is the sky. A beginner should always be allowed to start learning the overhead on whichever side of the court allows him to look away from the sun. It's a difficult enough stroke without having the sun as an extra handicap. For that matter, even a bright sky makes a pretty tough background to find a ball in. Some of the best players have been known to lose the ball in the sun when hitting overheads, and that is one of the reasons why the rules dictate changing courts on the odd game.

However, if a player is missing a fair number of overheads completely, he can be quite sure he is swinging too soon. The best way to perfect his stroke is to practice some simpler version of the problem: easy practice lobs that do not require moving, until the player can do ten or twenty in a row without a miss; or, going even farther back in his lesson, catching lobs with his hands.

2. *Bad Positioning.* A player may consistently place himself in such a way that he is too far ahead, to the right, to the left, or in back of, the point at

which he wants to meet the ball. Probably the most common tendency is for the player not to get in back of the ball. The result is that he meets the ball literally "overhead," or even behind him, and hits the opposite fence on the fly. The correct point of impact will vary with the player's depth on the court. If he is close to the net, the ball should be hit well out ahead of him; if the lob drives him back, it should be hit a little farther back. One of the best ways to control the positioning problem is for the player to sight the line of flight of the ball with his left hand—literally, point at it—and, after moving a little to the left of the ball, meet it well ahead of him.

Positioning difficulties can be a matter of lack of practice, poor physical conditioning, a consistent misreading of the ball's flight, or just plain laziness. In all these cases, the symptom is wildness on the overhead and the prescription is practice, practice, practice.

3. *Bad swing.* Any number of mistakes, in any number of combinations, are possible on an overhead swing, considering the problems of timing and footwork inherent in the stroke. It would be a moderately difficult swing even if the player were stationary and the ball suspended in midair.

One of the major problems possible is *grip*. The Western or semi-Western are the troublemakers, whereas the Eastern forehand is adequate and the Continental is desirable. With the Western grip, the racket faces too much to the right and the player constantly has to compensate, often by letting the ball drop too low and thus having to take a restricted swing.

If this is the case, it is best to correct the grip by degrees. Chances are, the problem also exists on the player's serve; he should work it out there before applying the solution to his overhead. See the section on grip problems on serve, page 189. Such a correction is best attempted under the guidance of an experienced teacher, but an intelligent player, heeding carefully our explanations of grip and studying the pictures shown here and perhaps films of himself as well, can work out the problem on his own.

The player may *abbreviate* his *swing,* that is, he may keep it in a very narrow arc, tucking his elbow in close to his body and gently tapping the ball. As long as he has some bend in his elbow, though, he is far better off than if there were none at all. Mainly, he should concentrate on freeing the upper part of his arm when the racket starts to move forward so that he can meet the ball at arm's length with *his* arm fully extended.

If there is *no elbow bend at all,* then the player's serve should be examined, either by studying films of himself or by an experienced teacher. He should study the serve action of the book, pages 149 through 205 and make the necessary changes in his motion before proceeding with the overhead. This may seem a long way around, but it will help his serve tremendously, as well as his overhead.

The Half Volley

With most good players, the stroke known as the half volley—a ground stroke hit just after the ball bounces—is so much a part of their game that the spectator rarely realizes it is an unusual stroke with its own peculiar problems. There is a special art to playing the ball right after its bounce and it requires good judgment and plenty of practice to know when to do it.

The half volley is risky because the ball, when met, retains a lot of its speed and upward motion. The latter, if not properly overcome, will cause the ball to jump wildly off the racket. The half volley must often be resorted to when one of an opponent's hardest-hit shots lands at a player's feet before he has time to do anything about it. And, it is often necessary for a player to half-volley on his way up to the net because it is the only way he is ever going to get there at all. But sometimes, and just as often, players will half-volley simply because they are too lazy either to move back and play the ball properly at the top of its bounce, or to move in and volley it as they should. The fact is that for a great many players the half volley is an excessively large part of the game.

To start learning the half volley, you should take up a position a little behind the service line and midway between the sidelines. Your faithful friend, partner-in-learning, and feeder should stand on his baseline and hit balls to you which bounce only about three or four feet in front of you. Use your regular forehand and backhand grips, since the pattern of swing is merely a much-shortened form of that used on the ground stroke. The backswing, particularly, is much shorter, and on the forehand, at least, it is not so essential that the player turn his feet sideways, provided he turns his shoulders.

The important thing in the swing is to tilt the racket face slightly forward so as to oppose the upward motion of the ball. How much tilt is a matter the player can only learn through experience and practice. The faster the ball and the higher its bounce, the more tilt is necessary. Naturally, since the ball is probably being played from below the top of the net, some of this upward motion is useful as it helps the half volley get over the net. Even in extreme cases, the forward tilt is not great; on the other hand, it is hardly ever absent from a well-made half volley, one that stays low as it goes over the net.

The forward motion of the stroke should be parallel to the ground, and, on the follow-through, the racket should move up just a little. The follow-through need not be long but it should always be present; a mere jab at the ball is not enough to guarantee control.

While one is more apt to half-volley in the forecourt, the shot can also be made in the backcourt. Indeed, when good players exchange ground strokes from backcourt they are often hitting what, for the ordinary mortal, would constitute half volleys. This is because their shots, if not hit on the half volley, would bounce so much farther back than the average player's. An advantage in rushing the shot is to hurry the opponent. It makes no sense, however, to half-volley from the backcourt out of laziness, since any steps saved are more than overshadowed by the riskiness of the shot itself.

To half-volley from the backcourt, the ordinary ground-stroke grips are used with as much of a swing as time permits. Generally speaking, however, the swing is more modest than that of a full ground stroke, and, as in the case of the half volley in the forecourt, the racket is tilted forward slightly to overcome the upward thrust of the ball. It is particularly important in all half-volleying that the weight be moving forward—under careful control.

Backcourt half-volleying is something to be used when necessary, to keep from being driven back too far, or as a means of launching an attack, but it must not be used as the lazy man's substitute for moving.

As you progress and show signs of becoming an adept player, your ability to half-volley will become more and more important. The player who can take the ball

HALF VOLLEY *swings show player bending his knees well, moving racket forward on a level plane, meeting ball just after its bounce.*

PLATE 699 **PLATE 700** **PLATE 701** **PLATE 702**

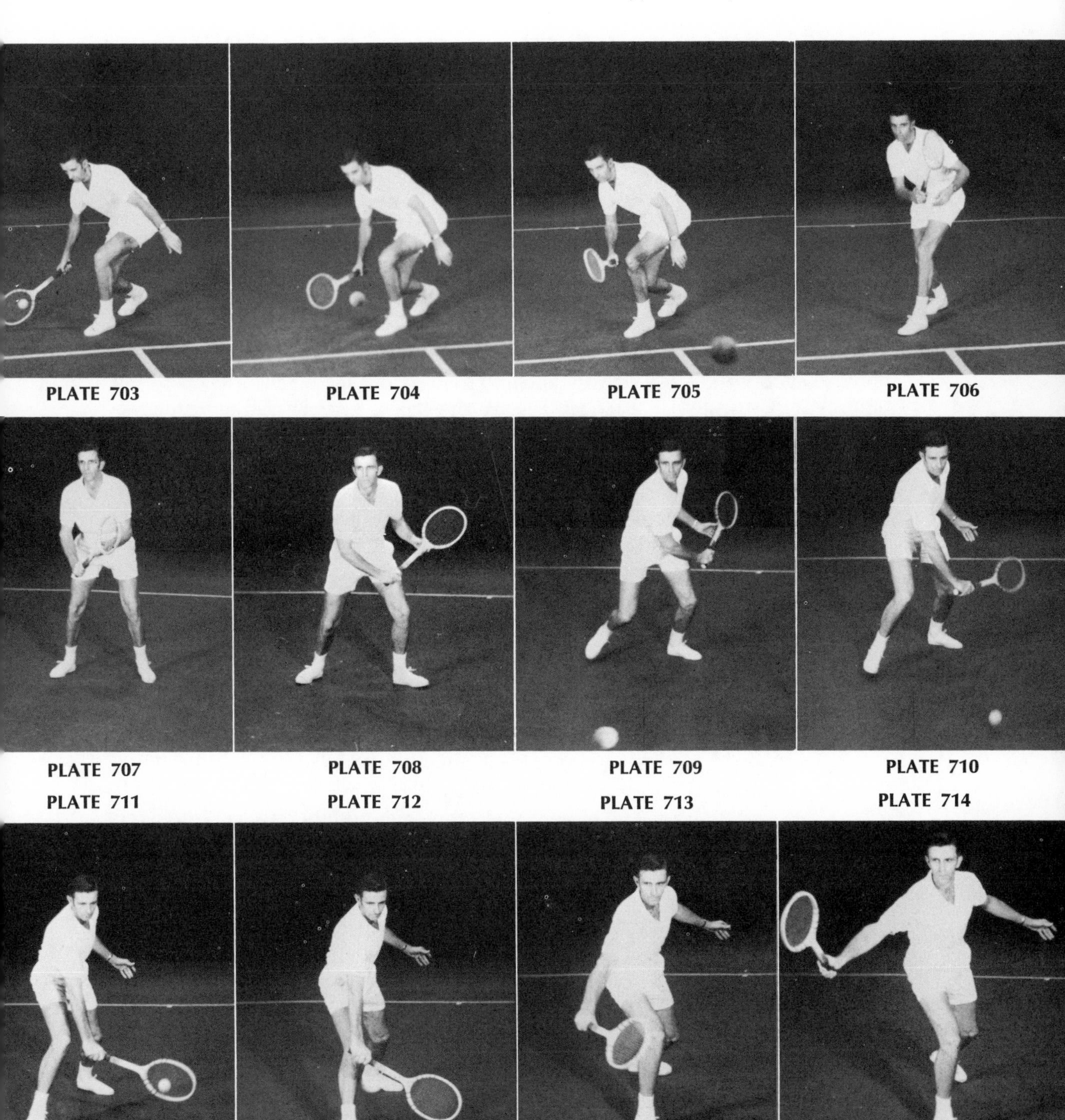

PLATE 703 PLATE 704 PLATE 705 PLATE 706

PLATE 707 PLATE 708 PLATE 709 PLATE 710

PLATE 711 PLATE 712 PLATE 713 PLATE 714

early will force his way to the net when others would despair of the chance. It is the half volley (or the ground stroke played on the rise) which is the opening wedge for the finishing volley or overhead.

Teaching the Half Volley

Demonstrate the half volley, explain its importance and the risks of overusing it, and then provide the player with practice shots of gradually increasing difficulty.

Half Volley Problems

1. *Grip.* The player will probably be able to get the right grip without too much difficulty, but he may not find it so easy to hold on to the racket at impact. This is understandable, since the ball is moving fast, is fighting its way upward, and the player has less time to react to any bad bounce. Moreover, the ball is apt to be hit off-center in a way that twists the racket. The player, therefore, should remember to grip tightly, and if that is not enough, he should take steps to strengthen his grip by regular exercises—swinging with the press on his racket, squeezing a tennis ball, or any other suitable ways.

2. *Swing.* The player may take too long a swing. If so, he must tone it down, principally by shortening his backswing while still trying to get the meat of the racket on the ball. He may drop his racket head in an effort to get down to the ball, instead of bending his knees and keeping the racket shaft parallel to the ground. The player may think that turning his racket slightly forward on the half-volley swing is the same as turning the racket face over the ball. It most certainly is not. The racket face should remain at the same slightly forward tilt throughout the swing.

3. *Foot Position.* The player should try to get both his feet and shoulders sideways for the half volley whenever possible, though time may not always permit. At the very least, he should attempt to turn his shoulders, since a good half volley can often be made, if somewhat awkwardly, from that position. He should also be sure his weight moves forward as he makes contact with the ball.

4. *Timing.* Timing is *the* most important aspect of a successful half volley; just as with an overhead, swinging too soon or too late is apt to be fatal. This is simply because the player is dealing with the ball when it is moving its fastest and its bounce (except off board surfaces, the best cement, and the new synthetics) is not always reliable. This stroke, then, like the overhead, needs regular, constant practice, even by the player who thinks he has mastered it.

Beginner Drill 7
The Lob

1. Take good supply of balls to baseline of court. Using Continental grip, make self-toss and lob ball using swing described on pp. 239–240. Lob at least 100 balls, striving for a height of about 20 to 25 feet and a target area of within 6 feet of opposite baseline.
2. Do same with backhand.
3. Have friend toss to forehand, gradually stepping up difficulty of tosses.
4. Do same with backhand.
5. Have friend hit balls to forehand from opposite side of net, gradually increasing difficulty of feeds.
6. Do same with backhand.
7. Rally; hit short shot to friend; he makes approach shot (somewhere near you, at first) and you lob; he practices his overhead.
8. Do Emerson drill (see p. 217), using lob at least half the time.
9. Do exercises 1 through 8, practicing topspin lob. See pictures on p. 235 for differences.

Lob Trouble Spots

Problem	Why it is a problem	What teacher should do	What player should do
1. Hand caught in regular ground-stroke grip.	Difficult to get necessary loft on ball. Nevertheless, player will have to make many lobs this way.	Have player be absolutely reliable about getting left hand back on racket throat after each shot to facilitate quick grip-change.	See left.
2. Stiffness at impact.	Ball goes too far.	Lob must often be used against hard-hit ball; thus player must develop feel for cushioning the	See left.

Problem	Why it is a problem	What teacher should do	What player should do
		impact of the ball so as to hit a high, soft shot. Explain need for being relaxed, yet controlled, while lobbing.	
3. Jabbing downward.	Finishing below ball may cause shot to rise and go too far.	Have player follow through with racket head finishing above the point of contact. Racket head should pass under ball, imparting backspin.	See left.
4. Turning racket face during swing.	Defeats whole purpose of lofting ball.	Have player keep racket face open and open it still farther on follow-through.	See left.
5. Excessive backswing.	Consumes too much time when it can't be spared.	Have player position racket in path of ball, using no more backswing than time allows.	See left.
6. Weight moving back while hitting.	Interferes with control of depth.	Often hard to avoid, since player is generally under greatest pressure when required to lob; quick preparation—getting set before the ball arrives—will help, however. Pushing racket through a little farther than normal will help compensate if player cannot avoid leaning back as he hits.	See left.

Beginner Drill 8
The Drop Shot

1. Standing near service line, bounce ball and hit forehand drop shot, trying to make ball land just over net. Hit twenty off forehand, twenty off backhand.
2. From same position, hit twenty forehand and twenty backhand drop shots on balls tossed by friend.
3. With you and friend standing at your respective baselines, have him hit short ball (to about your service line), on which you move in and make drop shot. Do it twenty times.
4. Move up with friend to respective service lines; rally, alternating between firm ground strokes and drop shots, striving to mask shots convincingly.
5. Rally with friend at full-court distance, starting with fairly deep shot and playing as if it were a real game point. Either player gaining advantage by eliciting short shot should move in and try drop shot.
6. Rally as above but move in to net behind deep approach shot and try to put ball away.
7. Again, rally, but use either drop shot or net attack, depending on which is more likely to work.

Drop Shot Trouble Spots

Problem	Why it is a problem	What teacher should do	What player should do
1. Chopping down on ball.	Sends ball too far.	Have player hit more gently, with more give, and slide racket under ball.	See left.

Problem	Why it is a problem	What teacher should do	What player should do
2. Attempting drop shot from too deep a position.	Gives opponent too much time to get to ball.	Explain to player drop shot should only be attempted as the launching of a net attack. (See p. 236 for further details.)	See left.

Beginner Drill 9

The Overhead

1. Take volleying position on court, minus racket, and have friend hit or throw lobs to you. Move under and catch them in front of and just to right of head. When first learning overhead, do this ten or fifteen minutes each time you practice.
2. Using forehand volleying grip, take net position and practice hitting overheads straight ahead deep on balls tossed or hit by friend. Friend's shots should come right to you at first, then increase, progressively, in difficulty.
3. Practice overhead during rallies.
4. Use Emerson drill (see p. 217).

Overhead Trouble Spots

Problem	Why it is a problem	What teacher should do	What player should do
1. Bad timing (swinging before ball arrives).	Point is almost certainly lost —and on a winning opportunity.	Have player practice extensively on easy lobs; at first, feed right to him, so he can take his time hitting, then gradually step up difficulty and pace.	Have friend provide lobbing practice suggested at left.
2. Bad timing (meeting ball too low).	Very likely, player will hit ball into net.	Same as above, but have player try to meet ball at higher point.	See left.
3. Bad positioning (usually, standing too far forward for given ball).	Causes loss of control of shot.	Have player try to meet ball farther ahead; feed easy lobs, then step up difficulty gradually.	See left.
4. Grip: Western or semi-Western	Aims ball too far to right, so that player must compensate awkwardly.	Have player move gradually to Eastern forehand, then Continental.	See left.
5. Absence of elbow bend.	Causes loss of power.	See if problem also occurs on serve; if so, correct it there, first. Show similarity of motion to baseball throw. Have player try it on easy, then progressively tougher, lobs.	Check films of your overhead —*and* of your serve. Rework serve, as shown in serve trouble-spots section, then use same motion.

Beginner Drill 10

The Half Volley

1. Stand at service line, friend at baseline; have him hit ball to your forehand so it bounces near you. With forehand grip, abbreviated backswing, and racket face tilted slightly forward, play ball "on the rise," twenty times on forehand, twenty on backhand.
2. At baseline, rally with friend and try to play balls on the rise. Use regular ground-stroke grips, but concentrate on hitting ball on the "short bounce" (just after it bounces). Do this for twenty rallies, resume playing ball normally for ten, then play on the rise again for twenty.

Half-Volley Trouble Spots

Problem	Why it is a problem	What teacher should do	What player should do
1. Grip: difficulty in holding on to racket.	Causes poor control; result of not meeting ball in center of racket.	Have player practice on slow enough shots so he consistently hits in center of racket. Have him do exercises to strengthen hand.	See left.
2. Excessive swing.	Racket not ready when ball arrives.	Have player shorten backswing. If necessary, have him hold racket in correct backswing position while you hit ball right to him.	Check film of yourself half-volleying; compare length of swing with that shown in photographs on pp. 248-49.

Problem	Why it is a problem	What teacher should do	What player should do
3. Poor positioning.	Puts racket out of control.	Have player be sure shoulders are sideways and he is not crowded by ball. If feet are also in position, so much the better.	See left.
4. Poor timing.	Sends ball out of control.	Have player practice half-volley frequently; Emerson drill (p. 217) will help.	See left.

14

Tactics For Rallies

One of the biggest problems of a young aspiring tennis player is to concentrate on improving his form and still win matches. He will pay close attention to form during practice, but when a match comes he may become either a hopeless pat-ball artist or a roaring tiger trying to hit every ball for a winner. In the first instance, he is apt to be overpowered, and, in the second, apt to be chopped down by someone more patient. His problem is to develop his game to the point where he can avoid both of these extremes.

He should by now be in possession of a forehand, a backhand, a serve, a volley, a lob, an overhead, a half volley, and perhaps even a drop shot. At least he has the fundamental knowledge of how to make these shots and can execute them some of the time. In that case, he is no longer a beginner but an intermediate. Assuming that he has already had the experience of playing practice sets with players of his own—or better—ability, there is no reason why he cannot begin playing competitively now, at least in his local club or park tournaments, or for his school team if he can make it. When he does, it will help if he has some idea of how to go about winning a tennis match.

The most valuable quality for a player to have when he first starts match play is consistency. He must realize that getting the ball in regularly is more important than hitting brilliant power-shots that go three feet out. This consistency at the expense of power will help his game in all its aspects, though, of course, eventually he must also develop his ability to hit hard.

Once a player understands the importance of acquiring consistency in all shots, the first stroke he should apply it to is the serve, for that is where the game of tennis begins. The player must condition himself to make an extra effort to win his own serve. The basic truism which a player cannot afford to forget is that to win a set he must hold his own service throughout and break his opponent's once. If he drops his own once, he will have to break his opponent's twice; if he drops his twice, he will have to take his opponent's three times, and so on.

The best way for an inexperienced player (or, for that matter, any player) to win his serve is to have a consistent, well-placed delivery. The foundations laid down in this book should help a player in this endeavor. If you will recall, our beginner was taught a spin service—one that combines topspin and sidespin. This type of serve makes a ball rotate forward on an axis which is about a 45° angle from the perpendicular. With such a serve, it is possible to hit the ball pretty briskly and still have it drop in the court, since the topspin draws the ball down. Furthermore, when the ball lands, it will take a nasty deep bounce, and if hit with sufficient spin will tend to glance off the opponent's racket.

If the player has learned only this delivery, he will be a lot better off than a player with only a flat serve, who is constantly risking double faults. Usually, a strong youngster with a heavy, flat serve will not maintain a very good percentage of successful first serves. His second ball, if he lacks the spinning serve, will probably be a gentle tap that invites punishment from the opposition. If it is not a gentle tap, it will probably be out. The big job for many young players with the ability to hit a spin serve is to trust it to bring the ball down into court.

Let's summarize briefly the formula for the spin serve. The service motion is like that of a well-executed overhead baseball throw, with—and this is of extreme importance—a pronounced elbow bend at the ultimate point on the backswing. The racket head then moves forward, up and over the upper right-hand portion of the ball, and finishes on the player's left side about shin height. It is the forward motion, up and over the ball, which gives it the combination of topspin and sidespin needed to drop earlier than a non-spinning ball and, therefore, stay in court.

The spin, of course, is vital protection against double faults. The player can swing hard and still keep the ball in court. And he has a greater margin of safety because he can aim higher over the net.

Another important point is that the player should make every effort to get his first serve in. Any server, however poor his delivery, is many times tougher if he gets his first ball in, since most beginners or intermediates are simply not used to having to return the first serve. They are so accustomed to waiting for a soft easy second serve that when a fairly easy first one lands in it comes as a distinct shock. On the other hand, the player who fails to get his first serve in will find his opponent moving in a step or two and gaining a real edge on his return. This means that the initiative on that point passes from the server to the receiver.

How does a player learn steadiness on his first serve? He must first be a hundred percent sure he appreciates its importance; if he looks around any tennis scene, he usually will find no shortage of unfortunates who lambaste their first serves and tap in their second. To gain consistency on his first serve, he should go out on a vacant court with a bucket of balls and practice the following routine: Serve one ball into the right court; if it is good, he should mentally score a point for himself. Then he should serve into the left court, and so on, alternating courts after only one service attempt. If he faults, he should score a point against himself. The object, of course, is to have the "ins" beat the "outs," but also to see how many consecutive "ins" he can chalk up.

To improve his chances of success in this type of drill, the player should strive for plenty of top and sidespin, rather than hitting the ball flat. He should aim about two feet above the net and swing just about as hard as for a flat serve. The spin will subtract from the speed but it will add accuracy and make the ball difficult for the receiver to handle. A medium speed ball which gets in most of the time will prove more disconcerting to an opponent than an occasionally successful flat serve.

The next problem the player faces is where to serve the ball. The spot to aim for will depend almost entirely on one's opponent and what position he tends to take to receive serve. If he leaves a great gap on his forehand side, the player should serve to that side to find out how good a serve it will take to avoid an aggressive return by his opponent. A wide serve, angled toward the sideline, even if returned well, will open up a shot at the opponent's backhand.

Another aspect of the opponent's position to note is whether he adjusts his position to compensate for any movement along the baseline made by the server. If he does not—and some otherwise intelligent players do not—then the player should move away from the center mark on the baseline and shoot for the opening his opponent has so graciously left.

To exploit these positional weaknesses and any stroking weaknesses the opponent may show, the player should practice serving to three main parts of the service court. These spots are: as close to the center service line and as deep as possible; deep in the opposite corner; and as short and close to the sideline as possible. Having practiced hitting these spots the player should then size up his opponent's ability to return each of the different serves.

This sizing up is done first by making a careful examination of both the opponent's form and his consistency in making ordinary ground strokes. Such examination should begin during the warm-up and be revised, if need be, while the match is in progress.

The player's object is to determine whether his opponent's backhand or forehand is the stronger stroke. The chances are that whichever one is weaker during rallies will be still weaker at returning service; that side, of course, should become the major target of the player's serve.

Before noting which side is weaker, the player should always remember to check automatically whether his opponent is right- or left-handed. It is surprising how often a fairly good club player will wander onto a court with a new opponent and sleepily aim his best shots to his opponent's left side only to wake up, too late, to the fact that his opponent is left-handed. "I wondered why he kept passing me," is the oft-heard lament.

Of course, a player's backhand will not always be his weaker side, and that is one very good reason why one must be able to serve equally well to all parts of the court. Even if the player's opponent has an obvious weakness on one side, not all the serves should be aimed in that direction. A player should switch off often enough to keep the opponent off balance and worried that he may have to go in any direction for the ball. Constant repetition of one type of serve to the exact same place every time will allow even the poorest players to get set and somehow figure out a way of getting the ball back. To repeat, it is often helpful first to serve wide to the stronger side for as an opponent moves to return serve, he opens up his weaker side to be exploited by the server's next shot.

So far, we have stressed learning a spin serve so as to be able to hit fairly hard while avoiding double faults; getting the first serve in; being able to serve to several separate spots on the court with some degree of accuracy; and serving either to the opponent's weaker side or wide to his strong side in order to expose the weak side.

The next problem for the player, obviously, is, what should he do after he has served?

If he is an intermediate—one who is just getting his bearings on the court—he should not go charging up to the net after serving, at least not if he is playing a match. (It's one thing in practice, since the only way to learn how to play the net is by trying it.) His object in a match is to play conservatively while still developing the weapons which will allow him to take chances later as his skill improves.

Since, for the time being, we are confining the player to the back of the court, we recommend that he learn a stroke which will help him both to keep his end of the rally going and to force errors from his opponent. This stroke, which flies neither as high as a lob nor as close to the net as a drive, could be called the standard rallying stroke. If hit from around the baseline, it should pass over the net by about three or four feet and should land within three feet of the opponent's baseline. Later on, it will be possible to bring the height down somewhat and still get the same depth by increasing the speed of the shot. This is the stroke that should be put into use as soon as the opponent has returned the player's service.

A great many young players aged ten to eighteen achieve success in tournaments and then never improve. Most of these are players who have mastered the standard rallying stroke—and nothing more. Unlike a good hard forehand or backhand drive, this stroke can be played with any kind of form, ranging from atrocious to excellent. It can be hit with excessive topspin or backspin or without much spin at all. If a player has no other weapon, he will beat players who are uncertain about their shots. But once those "uncertain" players get control, they will turn the tables on their previous tormentors. It is also true that if a young slugger lacks the standard rallying stroke, he may get farther than the "get every ball back" type of player, but he won't get to the top, either. All of us have seen outstanding young sluggers who were devastating until they met steady pluggers who returned most of their brilliant shots.

The way to combine these two qualities—ability to get most balls back and to hit them hard—is to execute the standard rallying stroke with correct form. This is the same form used to hit a drive, only with a less powerful swing and with just the slightest suggestion of a backward tilt to the racket face in order to keep the trajectory of the ball higher than on a drive. The player should use precisely the same grip, pattern of motion, footwork, weight control, and concentration that he would use on a drive. And, most essential on this medium-speed shot, he should follow through.

This is not a difficult stroke to make if the opponent hits an easy ball which takes a lazy, medium-high bounce. But suppose the opponent hits a very hard drive: What should the player do then? He should hit a well-controlled, soft return. Though such a shot is not the easiest to make off a hard drive, it is one of the most disconcerting to an opponent. With a really gifted player who has a keen natural sense of timing and a good eye, it will only be necessary to tell him to let up on his shot and slow the ball down. With the average pupil, however, some demonstration may be required first. One way to do this is for the teacher to rally with an assistant (or any available experienced player) and have his pupil watch while he deliberately slows down his assistant's hard shots, keeping the ball deep and keeping him away from the net. Failing an assistant, the teacher can give a one-man demonstration on a backboard, by hitting alternately a hard shot and a soft shot, taking special care not to neglect his follow-through. Then his pupil should take over and try to do the same thing. He will find the backboard an especially good place to learn to control and vary speed.

The standard rallying stroke is also difficult to make if a player has to run some distance and lunge for the ball. Control of balance and concentration are vital. Of course, if the player has been forced too far out of the court, it is wisest to lob, since this gives him time to recover and perhaps even draw an error from his opponent. If the player is desperate and his opponent has come to the net, he can try passing him there with a wide drive, brilliant if it succeeds, but risky.

Once the rally is under way, the player's objective should be to make his opponent move to get every shot and have to switch from forehand to backhand frequently. Such switching confounds even those who claim they don't change their grips at all. Furthermore, switching grips can easily upset an opponent's control of the angle of his racket face, to say nothing of the distraction caused by his having to readjust his footwork each time.

So far, we have stressed what might seem like a rather dim-witted style of play: keeping the ball in play while waiting for either an error by the opponent or an easy setup. Waiting for the other man to make the mistake seems dim-witted only because it is monotonous. Actually, especially among younger players, it is a very intelligent way to win.

There are, however, faster ways, one of which is to deliberately hit a short shot that will lure your opponent up to the net. The best time for a short shot is right after a deep one, and the best place is as far from your opponent as possible. It is not meant to be a drop shot that will win the point outright but neither should it be a setup. Ideally, it should take a low bounce so that your opponent has to play it from below the level of the net. Then, if he returns it, you have two choices: Either pass your opponent or lob over him. The former is riskier, but it's also more rewarding. The latter, however, has the virtue of tiring your opponent out and can, of course, be repeated several times during the same point. This is a particularly useful maneuver in women's tennis.

Drawing an opponent up to the net and either lobbing over him or passing him is probably the most labor-saving way of winning a match. But because a player may find this relaxation habit-forming, he had best be ready to abandon it the moment it stops working.

The other quick method of winning points, of course, is to force one's own way to the net, either with a strong serve or as soon thereafter as possible. While this is perhaps the hardest sequence to do well, most young players are partial to it since it gets quick, sensational, and crowd-pleasing results. Bang! goes the serve—stampede to the net—Smash! goes the putaway. The only trouble is, such a bang-bang game can be broken up if the player is too wedded to it.

A young player should beware of becoming "net happy." Certainly he must practice net play and use it during matches from time to time until it becomes a valuable part of his game. But he must also be cured early of the notion that net-rushing is the answer to all tennis problems. Few players have the endurance, the skill, and the consistency to play an entire match at the net without error of some kind. Any weakness displayed will eventually be exploited by an opponent, and woe be unto the player who has no other game to fall back on.

The intermediate player already has the general idea of how to mount a net attack as a result of his earlier training in volleying. At that time, someone rallied with him, hit him a short ball, he made his approach shot, and then attempted to put the ball away. As the player learns tactics, this sequence of shots should be practiced more intensively so that he can learn to be selective about the type of ball he should move in on. At first, he should not move in behind any ball bouncing deeper than his service line. Gradually, as he acquires control of his approach shot, he can attack from somewhat deeper shots. As he makes his approach shot, he must remember to take great care in controlling his body weight. As he comes to the place where he intends to hit the ball, he should all but stop, saving just a little bit of his momentum for the shot itself. If the ball is low, he must be sure to bend his knees and get down to the ball. As his weight moves into the ball, he should transfer it to his forward foot, absorbing his momentum by bending that knee. He must be sure not to straighten up during the shot or to bring his rear foot around until after he has hit the ball. In approaching the ball, he should pick a point two or three feet to the left or right of the line of the ball so that he will have swinging room. Many inexperienced players run right into a short ball and have no room to swing.

The player should direct his approach shot deep into his opponent's court, either to his weaker side, or straight ahead parallel to the sideline to cut down his opponent's angle for a passing shot. His volley should then go deep to the opposite side of the court. The player should stick to this routine until he has real possession of it before advancing from deeper shots, attacking with underspinning shots, or attempting wide-angled or stop volleys.

At this stage, the player is ready to try attacking the net behind the serve—so long as he confines such efforts to lessons and practice matches. The success of the net-rush behind serve depends almost *entirely* on the effectiveness of the serve. It must be hit deep and with plenty of spin so that it will give the net-rusher a little extra time to make his way forward. It is best, at first, for the player to restrict such serves to his opponent's backhand—that is, to the center service line if the opponent is right-handed, or to the sideline if he is left-handed. He should allow his momentum on the serve to carry him into the court, though his weight must not come through so soon as to throw his serve off line (an error common to many tournament players as well as intermediates).

The player should then move in as fast as his feet can carry him. By the time he nears his own service line, he should be able to see where his opponent's return is headed. He should then pause, depending on the circumstances, move the rest of the way in to volley, check a little to half-volley, or stop completely, to hit an overhead. He should practice this over and over against inferior opposition in practice matches before he ever tries it against players of his own ability, still more before he uses it in tournaments.

Thus far, we have talked about the serve and how to win a game in which the player is serving. Yet perhaps the most important and difficult stroke to execute well is the return of serve. Because the power serve—particularly the power serve with top and sidespin—is more widespread than ever, the serve is inherently more difficult to return than most strokes. Still, it is necessary to win the opponent's serve (or "break service," as it is known) at least once a set, or victory is impossible. The key stroke in this effort is the return of serve. A poor one loses the point immediately, a good one can put the receiver on even, or better, terms in the rally that follows.

The kind of return depends a lot on the opponent's serve—its speed, placement, spin, and particularly its depth. The first thing the player must do is to fix his eye on the ball while it is still in the opponent's tossing hand. Then he must watch it through the entire toss and hit, through its entire flight, through the bounce and right onto his own racket and off again, if he can. The player must do everything he can to condition himself to make good returns of serve. Leg training (rope skipping, running, etc.) is vital but eye-training is essential, and it is best provided by hours and hours of return of service drill.

Generally speaking, a flat first serve from an opponent can be effectively returned merely by blocking the ball, that is, pushing the racket forward without very much backswing. If the serve is slow or the player has very quick reflexes, he may be able to stroke the ball or even drive it. Sometimes, with a little bit of luck, it is possible to drive a serve back as hard as it was hit—but not on a steady basis except against a much inferior player.

If the opponent hits a spin service or an American twist (a high-kicking serve which bounces to the receiver's left), or, as is not uncommon among untutored players, a reverse twist, it is probably wise to chop the ball back in order to counteract the spin. In returning serve, the player should play the ball (early on the rise) so as not to let it play him, and be certain he gets his weight into the ball.

The next question is where to aim the return. A good safe place is deep to the opponent's backhand corner, assuming for the moment that he is not rushing the net. Why is this good? Partly because that is his weaker side, but primarily because he has just finished a violent motion (his serve), is momentarily off balance, and must recover and turn around in order to hit a ball on his backhand.

If the player uses this return seventy-five percent of the time and hits it to other parts of the court the rest of the time, he will not go too far wrong. Other strong returns include a drive to the forehand corner, a short chop (drawing the opponent in), or an occasional lob (even on a fairly easy serve, just as a surprise). Another effective return is one aimed right at the server if he gives any evidence of being slow on recovery. Naturally, the closer such a shot lands to the server's feet, the more likely he is to get tangled up in his own footwork.

If the opponent fails to get his first serve in and his second is short, the player can move in on the ball and attempt a wide-angled return toward either sideline. If his opponent stays back, he should simply hit a deep, forcing shot. If it is an outright winner, fine; if not, the next one, or the one after that, should be. If his opponent is also rushing the net, the return should be chopped low and to the side so that he will have to hit it up.

The mechanics of receiving the serve dictate that the player start his swing early and always move into the ball as he hits it, even if he is not swinging hard. Against a fast serve, he must cut down the length of his backswing, else he runs the risk of letting the ball play him.

If the player has returned the serve well, he can proceed as if he himself had served—either try to draw an error, lure the opponent up to the net and pass him or lob over him, or attack the net.

When playing against a big (i.e., powerful) serve, it is advisable to hit down the line—literally, down the sideline the receiver is nearest to. The reason is that most serves with real speed cause the receiver to hit late, so he can readily take advantage of the opportunity to "hit the ball where it was pitched." By hitting down the line, the receiver provides a tough shot for his opponent, even if the opposition knows exactly what he is doing.

Down the line should be the basic direction for the return of serve whether the server is moving in to the net or staying back. If the server is charging the net, however, it is highly important that the return be as low as possible so that the net-rusher will have to volley from below the net. The return of serve can either be a chip, that is, a shot with backspin, or a well-topped shot. The chip is the key to success in big-time tennis since it is the stroke that is most effective if the receiver is trying to take the net away from the server. Its great advantage is that it can be played early, on the rise, as the receiver moves in. Often, a bold, high-risk attack utilizing the chip shot is the only way for a receiver to break a big serve.

If the player has made a poor return of serve, he should scramble after every ball his opponent hits, attempting to hit a lob or make some sort of lucky stab for the ball to prolong the rally in hopes his opponent will make an error. Somehow or other, the player should try to turn the course of play in his favor, and as long as he keeps getting the ball back, he has a chance.

The player should learn how to handle an opponent who attacks the net on his serve. Until they get used to this type of attack, most players will be somewhat flustered by it. The player should get a good player (or teacher) to use this maneuver against him in practice so that he won't be rattled by it in competition. In this way, he can learn to watch the ball rather than his opponent and thus develop a much higher percentage of good returns. At first, he should ask his "opponent" to serve fairly easy balls and move in somewhat slowly. The player should then try to return the ball at medium height and wide enough so that the server has to move at least two steps to the right or left to play it. When the player begins to show some consistency in making such returns, he can attempt to make his returns skim the net so that the server will have to volley from a lower point. As his accuracy on this improves, the player should then try to play the ball earlier and hit it shorter, so that he cuts down on the time the server has to make his volley. Finally, he should try to make his down-the-line returns a little wider so that they go for outright passing shots.

When the player has some mastery over playing the ball early, keeping his returns low, and aiming them to different parts of the court, he can face up to stronger serves with varied speed, spin, and placement. If a young player is given a chance to get used to a net-rusher in practice, that monster will hold fewer terrors for him in actual matches. The drill suggested here will soon teach him that a low return, made early, to the net-rusher is much more effective, point in and point out, than an occasional brilliant down-the-line or cross-court passing shot.

Thus far, all our discussion on tactics has been on how to play a single rally under the two main governing conditions; the player's serve and his opponent's. But not all rallies are equally important, just as not all shots are equally important. The serve, we said, and the return of serve most affect the outcome of a rally. Next, we will consider which points, games, and sets a player should make a special effort to win.

15

Tactics for Games, Sets, and Matches

One of the oldest tennis maxims, as intelligent as it is unshakable, is "play to the score." Tennis scoring is such that a player does not have to go all out on every point. There are brief intervals when he can let up and conserve his strength. There are other moments when he must use every physical and mental resource he has. Only experience can help a player determine when these situations arise, but there are certain general guidelines he can learn in advance and safely follow.

It should be stated here that alternative systems to traditional tennis scoring have been advanced, the most prominent being VASSS, the Van Alen Simplified Scoring System. The idea is to get away from the awarding of points in multiples of five for a single rally, to cut down on the various units of scoring, and to get away from the deuce-advantage system both within a game and within a set. Tennis has always proved unwieldy for television, and one laudable aim of VASSS is to make a match of fairly predictable length so it can be programmed more easily. In the most commonly played version of the VASSS method, the player who first wins thirty-one points takes the match. The service changes hands every five points. Such a match requires both players to bear down the entire time. It is our opinion that this does not consider the human and strategic need to slow down slightly in the midst of a major effort and recoup one's forces. It makes no allowance for the player who is either temporarily bewildered by his opponent, or not properly warmed up, to get going in time.

Whatever the method of scoring, one inescapable obligation of the player is to know what the score is. Even if the beginner was carefully schooled in score-keeping and rules, he may now and then be absent-minded about keeping track of the score. He may even have to get into discussions with his opponent over how the points went and who won each of them, to arrive at the correct score. The player who keeps track of not just the score but of how the points were played and won, what mistakes and what winners he and his opponent each made, is in a position to plan his tactics with great care, for he will remember which shots worked and which failed.

In any game, whether the player serves or receives, he should go all out for the first point. Drawing first blood has psychological advantages which outweigh the mere fact of winning a point, since the other fellow is apt to play carefully just to get himself back even. The winner of the first point can thus gamble a little in putting the ball away, for it might reward him with the second point. For the server, a 30-love lead in any game should mean ultimate victory. If he is behind love-30, the initiative he holds with the serve should give him at least a fighting chance of coming back to win the game. A really great server like Pancho Gonzales is still a good bet to pull his serve out even if he is down love-40.

So far, then, the first point in a game is vital and the second somewhat less so for the winner of the first. For both players, the third point is extremely important. If the score is 30-love, it is the server's opportunity to put the game out of reach of his opponent. However, if it is love-30, the server must take chances. He must serve his first ball hard, and if he misses, even gamble by putting extra pace on his second so as to be able to command the offensive during the rally. The receiver also goes all out to win this point, but he can afford to be a little more cautious and need not attempt impossible shots for an outright winner. If the score is 15-all, the winner of the next point has a chance to tip the scales heavily in his favor.

The importance of the fourth point depends on the circumstances. If the score is 30-15, it is a great deal more important a point to the receiver than to the server. The server is two points away from winning the game, and that is where he will be even if he drops the 30-15 point. But if the receiver drops the 30-15 point, he has pretty well had it for that game. If the score is 15-30, it is vital that the server get back even, but if he is at all a respectable server, the odds favor his winning that particular point. If he loses it, all is not lost, but he is in trouble. From the receiver's point of view, winning the 15-30 point is a sizable feather in his cap and, though his job is not done, the odds turn well in his favor. He should go all out for that point.

If the score is 40-love, the server should serve and play conservatively, striving for depth rather than brilliance. His opponent, on the other hand, will have to take chances and try to get a foothold for the long uphill pull to deuce.

If the server is down love-40, he must gamble with the best serve he has, using depth and power. His opponent, since service breaks are hard to come by, will use a little caution, but he should be prepared to hit for a winner should the opportunity present itself.

On the fifth point, if the score is 40-15, the server should guard his lead with some caution but be quick to seize any opening presented by his opponent, who must continue to take chances in playing catch-up.

If the score is 30-all, the point is of equal importance to both players; he who wins it should eventually win the game.

With a score of 15-40, just as in love-30, the server should gamble with his best pitch; if that fails, he should serve a hard second ball for he has to take chances to win the point. The receiver operates with some caution but steps up the pressure he would exert at love-40.

At 40-30 (or "advantage in"), the server should hit hard but with care. The same applies to the receiver, for whom a little chance-taking might result in deuce, that is, only two points shy of a possible service break.

At 30-40 (or "advantage out"), the server should be the one to take risks while the receiver can play sound defensive tennis and concentrate on depth.

At deuce, it is a dog fight. The receiver, being in greater need of winning the game, should be willing to risk more to do it. The server, knowing his serve is a weapon in his favor, can afford to play a little more conservatively.

If, as we stated, it is important to draw first blood, and the server holds the edge since he is supposed to win his serve, it naturally follows that the player who wins the spin of the racket should choose to serve first. Despite the fact that topflight players may occasionally choose to receive, we recommend that a player should always serve first if he wins the spin. Why? Because if he holds his serve as he should, he will start the match off one game ahead and needs only to break his opponent's serve *once* each set to win the match. Obviously, if both players hold serve, the score will be tied. But even if the player loses his serve from a tie situation, he still has another chance to save matters by breaking his opponent's serve. Moreover, if the set goes an even number of games, he gets to serve first in the next set and renews his advantage. Since 6-1 and 6-3 are the only odd-numbered scores possible in an unextended set, chances are good that a player can retain first serves, at least through a three-set match, perhaps through a five-setter. If a player faces a notoriously weak server, or one who is likely to be slow warming up, it may add to his psychological edge to choose to receive first, if he is confident he can then win his own serve. His opponent, unnerved by having to display his frailty right at the start, could lose not *only* his serve but also his confidence, and the match, in short order.

Which games are the most important ones to go after in playing a match? The first two, since they set the psychological tone of the match and have a great deal to do with determining the eventual winner. Among good players, who can be depended on to hold their serves, it is a good idea to go all out to break the opponent's first serve. It is imperative, of course, that the player hold his own.

If, however, as should be the case, both players hold serve, there is little point in wasting valuable energy until and unless the opponent allows himself to get behind love-30 or 15-30. A little extra effort on service returns may well put him there; then, once again, all-out effort is called for as victory is in sight.

However, when the score gets up around 4-all, or when your opponent serves at 3-4, it is time to go all out again, since a service break now will very likely mean the set.

In a two-out-of-three-set match, for the player who has won the first set, no games in the entire match are more vital than the next two. He has established his lead, and in those next two games he can either consolidate it or let the whole match slip from his grasp. The tendency, here, is to let up, and it must be fought with every resource the player has. This is particularly true if he has been playing a little over his head while keeping his opponent from playing his best. That fellow, after losing a set, will instinctively work harder.

In this situation, if the player holds his serve, he will keep the pressure on his opponent. If he then manages to break his opponent's serve, he will take a commanding lead and force his opponent into all kinds of chance-taking in a desperate attempt to get back into the match. Gambling on shots, when you are not quite on your game, may well make things worse instead of better.

In a three-out-of-five-set match, the initiative in winning the second set is not quite so vital, since it is possible to drop a set and still regain one's form. This is not always easy, however, and if a player's momentum can carry him right through the second set, such a lead would put the odds tremendously in his favor.

Let us suppose the player now has that two-set lead. How hard should he go after the third set? A lot depends on how he feels. If he has won handily, at little cost in physical effort, naturally he should go all out for the third set. If he has really spent himself winning the first two, then he must size up his opponent carefully and see if he, too, has exhausted himself or is, in fact, coming on strong. The question to be decided, of course, is whether to let the set go and play for the fourth set following the usual ten-minute intermission, or to press on for immediate victory. Generally speaking, it is perilous for you to let your opponent regain his touch, for the complexion of the game can change completely and very often cost you the match. About the only safe generality is, if you are tired and ahead two sets to love, let your opponent take the third set. Keep pressure on him by serving hard and returning his serve hard. Go for winners most of the time so that the rallies end quickly, either for or against you. You will conserve energy and he will not be able to control his timing as easily as if you were playing steadily and cautiously.

If you won the first two sets and gave away the third, the time for your supreme effort is in the fourth. Further delay will probably only seal your doom, for if you let your opponent have the fourth, he will have two in a row, and the momentum now going his way.

If you won the first set, lost the second, and won the third, but are very fatigued, you will have to consider letting the fourth go. The same is true of losing the first and taking the next two, though when you are making uphill progress, it is best not to break your continuity.

Playing to the score is an aspect of tactics which is little affected by your opponent's strengths or weaknesses. Most of what has been said, so far, applies whether he is much better, the same, or much worse than you. Playing to the score is a constant, and once the player has grasped the strategy and can use it without severe lapses, he can move on to the critical business of sizing up his opponent and planning a match.

16
Match-Play Strategy

A cold and fishy stare at one's opponent's game is a real necessity for an intelligently planned match. In the ordinary team match (and in a good many tournament matches), a player sees his opponent for the first—and often, only—time the minute they step out on the court. This makes it necessary to size up the opponent in a very short period, namely, during the warm-up. Though the player may have to revise his calculations as the match unfolds, the more he finds out, and the sooner, the better able he will be to gain an edge in waging the match.

Let us assume, however, that the player is watching his future opponent play a match. His first question to himself should be: What can I do to beat this man? To find out, he must first know how well his player serves. A good look at him in action will tell a great deal. Does he win his serve regularly? Does he double fault much? Does he get his first serve in regularly? Is it hard to handle? Does he use spin? Does he have variety or only one spin? Does he serve to the same place all the time or does he vary the direction of his serves? Most important, does he serve short at any time, inviting punishment?

The scouting player should carefully measure his own ability to return his potential opponent's serve. He should look for some sign of routine in the opponent's serve that will give him a chance to be ready and waiting for it, so as to capitalize on it. Perhaps the opponent mixes up his direction very well, but always serves with the same speed and spin. Perhaps his second serve is too short. Anything about the opponent's serve that will allow the scouting player to risk a harder swing is to the good. He will have to break that serve at least twice to win a two-out-of-three-set match.

By closer examination, this player should look for some tip-off as to what the opponent intends with his serve. Two things are important to note here: Does he change his grip? (Forehand grip probably means a flat serve; Continental or backhand, a spin serve.) This is not always easy to detect, but some players can be very obvious about it. Secondly, where does he throw the ball? This can often be a giveaway on the kind of serve coming up. A right-handed player serving a slice will toss the ball slightly to his right. He will toss it back over his head and to the left if he is going to serve an American Twist. The player should mentally review the action the spin service takes—curving to the receiver's right and bouncing still farther to his right. The twist, on the other hand, curves to the receiver's right but bounces high and to his left. A ready recognition of these serves should be part of the mental equipment of any intermediate or advanced player, and he should have spent a great deal of time drilling on their correct reception, from both right- and left-handed servers.

A player should beware especially of servers with odd or sudden motions. Though his motion may be odd, the server may still be effective. He must be rated solely on the results he achieves, for if he fools his opponent, it makes no difference whether he serves underhanded or upside down.

After studying his prospective opponent's serve, the player should then study his return of serve, taking into consideration how demanding that serve is. The player should pay special attention to which serves are missed, or poorly handled, by his opponent-to-be. He should note whether they are mainly backhands or forehands, spinning serves or flat ones, hard serves or slow ones.

Our heavy emphasis on sizing up the opponent's serve and making plans for the use of one's own should not be unfamiliar to the reader: Remember, the effectiveness of the serve usually determines who will win the point and, likely, the match.

Once the question of relative serving strength has been explored, the next step is to size up the prospective opponent's other attributes. Is he a baseliner or a net-rusher, or can he play well from either quarter? As an experiment, the player should watch ten or twenty rallies, counting how many times his opponent comes to the net, and how many of those times he puts the ball away.

The opponent's ground strokes should then be examined closely for signs of exploitable weakness. If he puts heavy topspin on his shots, see whether he handles a high or a low ball better. Chances are, he will be more dangerous off a high shot. On the other hand, if he tends to chop most of his shots, he will probably be unhappy handling high-bouncers. If he uses the same side of the racket to hit backhand and forehand, he will undoubtedly have difficulty switching from one to the other. *He should be given every opportunity.* If he prefers to attack the net with a forehand approach shot, the scouting player will know to fire at his backhand, and vice versa.

The player should check on his opponent's volleying ability—especially on low balls and very hard-hit balls. His lob and his overhead should be scrutinized as well, particularly for signs that the overhead is erratic. Exploiting it may be the best way to break up his game.

The player should now have some ideas to work on and a tentative plan of attack to follow. He will get a much clearer picture of how well it will work as soon as he gets on the court with his opponent and begins to warm up. Now he can tell how it actually feels to be hitting against the player's shots, whether they are harder or easier to handle than he expected. During the warm-up the player should try each of the main strokes in his own repertoire, while making his opponent run through his, from different parts of the court at varying speeds and spins. The opponent should be tested on all kinds of volleys and overheads, and the player should insist that they both take their practice serves before the match begins. This is not only in accordance with the rules, but will give him a preview of his opponent's delivery.

The player should also, if possible, try to form some idea about his opponent's temperament. The opponent should be judged only on the basis of how well he is playing right now, not on the basis of his reputation. It makes no difference if he is big, tough, rude, strong, or has any of the other traits that might enable him to win a fistfight or a wrestling match. The only matter that counts is what he can do with a tennis racket. A small, slow-footed, soft-hitting but well-trained tennis player can pin back the ears of a man who is his physical superior in every other way. The player's attitude toward his opponent should be, "I don't care who you are, I'm going to beat you—and in a sportsmanlike manner." The opponent's temperament is only of importance in helping a player decide what kind of pressure he should apply to help him win the match. What kind of errors may the opponent be expected to make? How tough is he likely to be under fire? At what point in a set is he apt to relax and let down? And, how soon will his endurance give out? Otherwise, he should simply be a faceless racket-swinger.

Now the player is on his own. He should follow his plan as long as it works, revising it if need be, changing it entirely if it ceases to work. He should carefully note the progress of the match and every aspect of it. Then, whether he wins or loses, he should review it as painstakingly and objectively as he can. If his teacher was on hand, all the better, for the player can then compare notes with him afterward, exploring any weaknesses in the player's game that need drill.

Everything we have said so far about match play has been said to aid the player in his concentration. There is no more important attribute in a competitor. If he can concentrate, he can exercise the greatest courage in the clutch. The tennis competitor must concentrate on the ball—how he is going to control height, direction and depth. He must concentrate on the score of the game, the set, and the match, and play accordingly. Most important of all, he must keep in mind his "game plan," gained by his observations of his opponent before and during the match, and be alert to revise them as conditions warrant. By concentrating on the ball, the score, and his game plan, the player will be able to shut out distractions, external and internal, which plague many players. He will be so immersed in what he is doing that balls rolling across his court, crowd noise or movements, even a match on the next court, will not disturb him. Moreover, he will not start thinking about how tired he is, that his blister hurts, or what he is going to do that evening. By immersing himself in the match a player overcomes these adversities—and wins matches he was not expected to win.

17
Conclusion

The basic strokes, the supplementary strokes, and the fundamentals of tactics and strategy represent most of what passes between tennis teacher and pupil. We have not dwelled particularly on psychology and motivation. Motivation must come primarily from within the player—with help from a qualified teacher, where possible. For advanced tactics, we refer to the excellent books *The Game of Singles* and *The Game of Doubles,* by William F. Talbert and Bruce S. Old.

Our effort has been to put down in detail the kind of strokes a player should produce, the difficulties he will face in producing them, and how he can best overcome these difficulties so as to prevent them from becoming major handicaps. We believe ours is the most complete and detailed, yet practical and commonsense presentation of tennis teaching offered thus far. We have no illusions whatsoever that it is the final, or even the entire current word.

We have mentioned along the way certain areas where some serious research could tell us more about the game and the way people play it, as, for example, the problem of the back-pounding server. Scientifically-trained specialists should be able to help tennis teachers with this and similar complex coordination problems. Furthermore, scientists could help on the study of the role the eye plays in tennis, explaining why some people can follow a ball well while others have terrible difficulty—even if the former wears glasses and the latter has 20-20 vision. And finally, much remains to be done in the field of statistical analysis of the game.

As the reader has certainly noted, we have stressed a number of points not ordinarily emphasized in tennis books. We believe, for instance, that the advocates of group-teaching have gone overboard in their approach. They are quite right in stating that group-teaching is the only way the game can be spread rapidly, well, and on a large scale. It is also true that it is more fun than individual teaching for most of the participants, if done well. But sound as the group approach is in introducing the game, encouraging players, and giving them practice, it still is not as much help to the individual player with a really tough technical hurdle to overcome. Moreover, too many players slip through the group sieve, burdened with at least a few major technical weaknesses, to make it the be-all and end-all in instructional approach.

We have stressed the necessity of carefully analyzing a stroking problem, and of following a definite order of procedure to perfect the various strokes of tennis. On ground strokes, these include: grip, waiting position, footwork, pattern of swing, use of the left and right hands, racket-face angle, use of the wrist, elbow, and shoulders, type of spin obtained, and follow-through. On the serve, we have emphasized looking first at the foot position, next the toss, the coordination of the hands, the use of the serving arm, and, finally, the grip. We have recommended tackling specific problems in a specific order, so that the player and/or teacher making these observations can easily find out what is wrong and what to do about it.

We have shown many before-and-after sequence photographs showing the most recurrent errors, which players can cure by thorough understanding, steady practice, and accurate guidance. We have insisted that, even if the teacher or player thinks he knows exactly what is wrong, he should run through the entire checklist before he proceeds to correct it. Good doctors do this routinely and so should good tennis teachers and students.

We have underlined a number of seemingly small technical points which can make a player's progress much smoother. Item: It is important to detect quickly the use of the same side of the racket for forehand and backhand and training a player to use opposite sides saves many a headache later on. Item: It is important to learn the proper use of the left hand to steady the racket so grips can be changed by moving the right hand early in the backswing. Item: It is important to learn a continuous swing, to be sure the front foot is at a 45° angle so it can receive the transfer of weight, to be sure a player's backhand grip—particularly the heel of his hand—will allow him to get topspin when he wants it. Item: It is important on the serve to keep the forward foot in position throughout the swing, to make the hands work together, to toss accurately enough to be able to catch the ball without moving the left hand, and to have a full elbow bend to enhance both spin and power.

We have detailed the various ways of controlling each type of shot. On the ground strokes, control of height comes from the forward or backward tilt of the racket, control of direction by timing, and control of depth by hitting into the ball and using spin. All these controls apply to the volley, also, except that direction is controlled by setting the wrist at the correct angle. On the serve, we have pointed out how the grip affects control—the Eastern forehand grip being acceptable, the Continental more effective.

Perhaps our greatest emphasis, throughout the book, has been on practice and drill, drill and practice, especially on those shots which most challenge the eye and reflexes, namely, the overhead, the serve return, and the volley. These are the strokes which even the top players will grow rusty on if they lay off for a few days.

And finally, running through the book, the reader will find our cardinal piece of advice, the most essential rule for any tennis player—watch the ball.

APPENDIX

STYLES AND IDIOSYNCRASIES OF THE GREATS:

A Reminiscence by Ed Faulkner

Since the early thirties, when Ellsworth Vines was United States champion, there have been very few players whose style deviates markedly from what we recommend. It wasn't always so. The American Davis Cup team in the twenties had four players with different styles, as did the French Davis Cup team of that era. Moreover, these were all great tennis players.

Take Bill Tilden, for instance. He did all the things we advocate, *and* all the things we try to discourage. He used all types of strokes, topspin drives, chops, slices. He'd use a continuous swing and occasionally a straight swing. He would analyze an opponent's game and then decide what to use against him. Because of Tilden's extensive equipment, he could find a flaw in his opponents' game, and that's the shot he gave them, even if it took him a set or two to uncover the weakness.

On his forehand, Tilden nearly always used continuous motion for his drive. His grip was generally regarded as Eastern, though the heel of his hand was actually on the right vertical panel. It was characteristic of him to use the Continental grip on a low ball or to move towards the Western on a high one. Moreover, he developed quite a repertoire of head and shoulder fakes which made it look as if he was hitting in one direction when actually hitting in another.

WORLD TENNIS

PLATE 715

Bill Tilden

PLATE 717

René Lacoste

PLATE 716

Vinnie Richards

WORLD TENNIS

WORLD TENNIS

On his backhand, Tilden used nothing but slice at first, but then he switched to topspin, taking a winter off to practice it. He used the Eastern backhand grip, and the result was a beautiful shot.

One of Bill's idiosyncrasies was to make very little use of his left hand between strokes in changing from forehand to backhand, or vice versa. Use of the left hand is necessary for most people, but Tilden was a genius; he could volley with topspin or backspin, depending on the height of the ball. Nobody else could get away with this.

As part of his great ability to vary his game, Tilden was a master of spins. He made particular use of sidespin, whereas most of the best users of spin today, such as Rod Laver, stick mainly to topspin and backspin.

Tilden's serve was one of the fastest, a real cannonball. Few, if any, players have had a harder serve. The only contemporary in his class was Australia's Gerald Patterson, the rest of whose game did not measure up. Tilden could also serve with slice, the American Twist, and topspin. He would even throw in an occasional reverse twist, though never in an important match.

Tilden's teammate and rival, Billy Johnston, was "Big Bill's" complete opposite, both in build and in style. Much shorter and unusually slight, Johnston weighed around 125 pounds. His groundstrokes were completely Western—in fact, it would probably provoke very little argument to say that he carried the Western game further than anyone in the history of tennis. On his forehand, he brought the racket back over his head and whipped it around with tremendous speed, throwing the entire right side of his body into the ball. Consequently, he met the ball a lot earlier than most players would or should.

When Johnston switched to his backhand, he would flip the racket over, using the same face as for his forehand. He rotated his grip so far that it wound up fairly close to the Continental backhand, and as a result he always hit with backspin. This left his backhand somewhat weak, a flaw that Tilden (and later the French stars) exploited to some extent, though success against Johnston came principally from running him to exhaustion.

His serve, a spin serve of the type we teach, was a great serve, though not recognized as such. His service grip was Eastern backhand, surprising inasmuch as he did not use such a grip in any other part of his game. He got good spin on the ball, served deep, got a high percentage of first serves in, and rarely double-faulted.

While Johnston's volleying was not up to the rest of his game, he was nevertheless a good deal better net player than most other ranking players of his day, in spite of the fact that he had to spin the racket in his hand to change to the backhand grip.

It is interesting that the Western style reached its peak in Johnston and has rarely been seen since. The Kinsey brothers, who were only slightly younger than Johnston, and George Lott, whose peak came in the early thirties, are probably the only other topflight men to have used that style. It has held on a little longer in the women's game and, of course, is still widely seen in club and public parks level of play. Fewer and fewer players persist in it beyond the beginner stage, however. Why? Because there are more and better-informed teachers, as well as more knowledge available on the game and more written about it. By teaching beginners Eastern grips and a grip-change method that calls for just a slight movement of the racket hand, teachers can avoid the idiosyncrasies inherent in the Western style. Surprisingly few teachers and players, however, are able to recognize the problem when it does come up.

Davis Cup players Vinnie Richards and Dick Williams both were dedicated to playing the ball early, but with a fundamental difference in approach. Richards did so while on his way to the net. Williams played the ball right after the bounce, on the so-called short hop, but tended to stay in the backcourt. Because Richards used Continental grips on both forehand and backhand, his drives lacked power. His serve was not overpowering either, but since it possessed heavy sidespin it gave him time to get to the net. Once there, he could cover a tremendous range and put the ball away with any one of a variety of shots. Williams used Eastern grips and a continuous swing on both sides. More than most players, Dick Williams played for the sheer fun of it, and when he was on his game he could rise for brief periods to incredible heights.

These American players dominated the game from 1921 through 1926, turning back strong challenges by the French in 1925 and 1926. In 1927, however, the Four Musketeers of France, René Lacoste, Henri Cochet, Jean Borotra, and Jacques Brugnon, defeated the United States 3-2 and went on to hold the Cup for five more years. One might say that Cochet was a little like Williams—he played the ball early—and that Borotra was a little like Richards—he was a net rusher. Brugnon, though a valuable player, was not quite as good as his teammates. Of the four, Lacoste was the most interesting. He studied harder than anybody else, he planned, he drew diagrams of the court, and put down every shot. He planned his matches against Tilden this way, studying what Tilden would do in every position on the court. This gave him invaluable anticipation. Nevertheless, unlike most observers I don't think Lacoste had a great tennis mind. He was a great mechanical tennis player who planned his tactics and his strategy according to the person he was playing. But he didn't have Tilden's imagination. What Lacoste had to do mechanically, Tilden did naturally.

Lacoste's strokes were primarily defensive because he used the Continental grip on both sides. Basically, his game was sound and accurate. He would practice with me hitting balls within a six-inch range and wonder what was wrong whenever he missed. Nothing was wrong mechanically; it was just a matter of timing through concentration. He was fun to work with because he was such a perfectionist from the standpoint of control. Control is what he based his whole game on and what beat Tilden.

Lacoste had had some trouble with his backhand because he turned the face of his racket down on the backswing. I got him to put his left thumb on the front flat surface of the racket throat on his backswing and to keep it there to eliminate the tendency to turn. He actually exaggerated the grip and opened the face of his racket; as a result, his backhand improved tremendously, to the point where it was a great shot.

His serve was only average for a top tennis player. I would classify it as stronger than Ken Rosewall's but not quite as strong as Tom Okker's. As a volleyer he could do fairly well when he had to, but he generally stayed away from the net. His overhead was adequate but not terribly effective. As a court personality Lacoste didn't excite the crowd—he was all business.

Henri Cochet was a different breed of animal. He was a fiery, aggressive player who liked to play the ball early and do a lot with it. He had a good deal of imagination and put it to good use. On his groundstrokes, he hit with topspin off both sides. He volleyed well, but he did not have a big serve, perhaps due to a rather careless motion.

Cochet, however, could stir the crowds, as, even more so, could Jean Borotra. Borotra was a very competitive individual who wanted fiercely to win, and he would use the crowd to work for him. His determination and desire to win were amazing. He would try anything, even to disturbing his opponent's concentration by changing his shoes at a strategic moment. His style of play was based completely on the net attack. His groundstrokes were very individual, since, rather than hitting with topspin, he chopped. Using a short backswing, he just moved in and sought every chance to put the ball away. What was most amazing about his volleying ability was that he was a samesider. On his serve, he took an abbreviated backswing which prevented him from getting real power, but with this stroke he could make the ball slither away from an opponent.

PLATE 718 **Don Budge** WORLD TENNIS

Brugnon had the equipment of a doubles player—a good spin serve and volley. His groundstrokes, while adequate, were not at all spectacular.

After the great clash of these eight players, there was a lull until the next major figure emerged—Ellsworth Vines, a tall, slim Californian. He had a tremendous serve, one of the hardest of all time, and an equally strong forehand. His backhand was sliced and lacked the aggressiveness of the rest of his game, but he volleyed well and had a tremendous overhead.

Vines was the first player in a long time who combined a big serve and big groundstrokes with a relentless drive for the net. Tilden had had the serve and groundstrokes, Richards and Borotra the net attack, but Vines put them all together. He showed great power in his short amateur career, but he lacked variety and change of pace. It was not until he had toured for three years as a pro, playing mainly against Tilden, that he acquired the versatility that made him an all-around player. He had the equipment to be the greatest player of all time, but not the desire. Vines turned to golf in the middle thirties and while he became an excellent touring pro, he never made it to the top.

A close rival of Vines, and his conqueror at times, was England's Fred Perry. Perry, too, was an attacking player with a strong serve and powerful groundstrokes, as well as excellent volleying ability. His style looked very different from Vines's but it was actually quite similar. He used the Continental grip on both forehand and backhand, often facing the net on his forehand. He used continuous motion on both sides, and a full, flowing swing when time allowed.

Another California player with all-around equipment, J. Donald Budge, followed these two to the top. Budge was one of the great tennis players of all time. He had a powerful serve, an excellent forehand (once he'd unlearned the semi-Western grip), good volleying ability, and a phenomenal backhand. His grip on the backhand was Eastern; his racket on the backswing started low, rose about halfway through the backswing and then dropped, making a small loop before it came forward violently into the ball. It was an extraordinarily long swing with a tremendous, flowing follow-through, and with it, Budge could whistle the ball past an astonished opponent from way off the court. Budge, unlike Vines, had the desire to be the greatest of his era, and he was. Bobby Riggs finally managed to break up Don's play in post-war pro tours through a remarkable combination of all-court play, incredible retrieves, and needling of his opponent. Though Riggs took Budge's measure, Don was still a tough opponent for Jack Kramer and other fine players whose approach was more powerful but less complex than that of Riggs.

PLATE 719

Bobby Riggs

PLATE 720

Jack Kramer

WORLD TENNIS

PLATE 721

Pancho Gonzales

WORLD TENNIS

PLATE 722

Ken Rosewall

Riggs, a master gamesman, was also the master technician of every stroke. Lacking the power of other tennis greats, he developed textbook versions of forehand, backhand, serve, and volley. In his earlier days, he relied greatly on chops and spins, but as he gained stroking confidence (he never lacked *overall* confidence) he put more authority into his shots and became a successful attacking player.

Jack Kramer followed Riggs to the top, bringing with him one of the great forehands of the game. His grip was Eastern, his motion continuous, and his follow-through long. At first, he hit his backhand with slice but later, under the pressure of his pro tour with Riggs, he developed topspin. His serve was orthodox, save for one minor but startling idiosyncrasy—he tossed the ball up backhanded instead of palm up. His volleying was decisive and his overhead overpowering.

Kramer was succeeded on the throne by the only undisputed ruler since that time—Pancho Gonzales. Early in his career, Gonzales could do most of the things Kramer could, harder but with less accuracy. He developed his control and a variety of softer shots until he became a player equipped with everything. Now he must be rated as one of the greatest players of all time; the only question is whether as number one, two, three, or four.

The great parade of Australian stars began in 1951 when Frank Sedgman won Wimbledon and Forest Hills. The Aussies' style of play strongly emphasizes stroking fundamentals and the tremendous importance of physical conditioning. Of all the topflight Aussies, Ken Rosewall and Rod Laver have had the longest reigns. Both are lightning fast. While Laver has the stronger serve and greater power on groundstrokes, Rosewall may have an edge in his ability to control the ball when forced into a position that would elicit an error from anyone else. These two have shown an imagination and a flair which some of the lesser players, even the tremendously powerful Lew Hoad, have lacked.

From about 1960 until 1968, the relatively dull play of the more mediocre Australians and Americans reduced the allure of amateur tennis from the spectator's standpoint. This lull ended spectacularly and delightfully with the 1968 Open Wimbledon and the United States Open tournaments. There, the unprecedented confrontation of the world's top pros and amateurs made clear to all the fact that technical superiority and conditioning are not enough—one has to have brains and desire, too, and the pros have no monopoly in that department.

Two amateurs demonstrated this point during the first U.S. Open in 1968. Arthur Ashe and Tom Okker both had more going for them than just a serve and volley game, and more also than good groundstrokes. Each was capable of taking

WORLD TENNIS ED FERNBERGER

PLATE 723

Rod Laver

PLATE 725

Arthur Ashe

PLATE 724

Tom Okker

PETER TROSTORFF

speed off the ball and moving his opponent around the court. Okker used his wits as well as speed and strokes to defeat all-time greats Gonzales and Rosewall and enter the final. Ashe's judicious use of the lob against Clark Graebner in the semifinal turned a close match into a decisive victory. Ashe and Okker then put on a corking five-set final in which Okker tried everything he knew to overcome the advantage of Ashe's tremendous serve, and nearly did so. What a show those two put on.

These players as well as those coming along further behind, like Stan Smith and Bob Lutz, are learning the varied game which calls for excellence in all departments, particularly in strategy and tactics. And the use of new surfaces slower than grass in key outdoor matches will accentuate this trend. A reduction in the speed of the surface is enough to keep the server in the backcourt nearly two-thirds of the time, and if the server stays back a rally can ensue. The fans should get to see much more tennis and the game itself should reach new heights.

FOR YOUR CONVENIENCE IN ORDERING ADDITIONAL COPIES OF ED FAULKNER'S TENNIS

Please send ______ ED FAULKNER'S TENNIS @ $7.95
copies

If you include your check for $7.95 The Dial Press will pay handling and postage charges. Please add tax where applicable.

☐ please bill.

name ____

address ____

city ____________________ **state** ________________ **zip** __________

Please send ______ ED FAULKNER'S TENNIS @ $7.95
copies

If you include your check for $7.95 The Dial Press will pay handling and postage charges. Please add tax where applicable.

☐ please bill.

name ____

address ____

city ____________________ **state** ________________ **zip** __________

Please send ______ ED FAULKNER'S TENNIS @ $7.95
copies

If you include your check for $7.95 The Dial Press will pay handling and postage charges. Please add tax where applicable.

☐ please bill.

name ____

address ____

city ____________________ **state** ________________ **zip** __________

BUSINESS REPLY MAIL
No Postage Stamp Necessary if Mailed in the United States

FIRST CLASS
PERMIT NO. 2317
NEW YORK, N.Y.

THE DIAL PRESS
750 Third Avenue
New York, New York 10017

TRADE SALES DEPT.

BUSINESS REPLY MAIL
No Postage Stamp Necessary if Mailed in the United States

FIRST CLASS
PERMIT NO. 2317
NEW YORK, N.Y.

THE DIAL PRESS
750 Third Avenue
New York, New York 10017

TRADE SALES DEPT.

BUSINESS REPLY MAIL
No Postage Stamp Necessary if Mailed in the United States

FIRST CLASS
PERMIT NO. 2317
NEW YORK, N.Y.

THE DIAL PRESS
750 Third Avenue
New York, New York 10017

TRADE SALES DEPT.

FOR YOUR CONVENIENCE IN ORDERING ADDITIONAL COPIES OF
ED FAULKNER'S TENNIS

Please send ______ ED FAULKNER'S TENNIS @ $7.95
copies

If you include your check for $7.95 The Dial Press will pay handling and postage charges. Please add tax where applicable.

☐ please bill.

name ______________________

address ______________________

city __________ **state** __________ **zip** __________

Please send ______ ED FAULKNER'S TENNIS @ $7.95
copies

If you include your check for $7.95 The Dial Press will pay handling and postage charges. Please add tax where applicable.

☐ please bill.

name ______________________

address ______________________

city __________ **state** __________ **zip** __________

Please send ______ ED FAULKNER'S TENNIS @ $7.95
copies

If you include your check for $7.95 The Dial Press will pay handling and postage charges. Please add tax where applicable.

☐ please bill.

name ______________________

address ______________________

city __________ **state** __________ **zip** __________

BUSINESS REPLY MAIL
No Postage Stamp Necessary if Mailed in the United States

FIRST CLASS
PERMIT NO. 2317
NEW YORK, N.Y.

THE DIAL PRESS
750 Third Avenue
New York, New York 10017

TRADE SALES DEPT.

BUSINESS REPLY MAIL
No Postage Stamp Necessary if Mailed in the United States

FIRST CLASS
PERMIT NO. 2317
NEW YORK, N.Y.

THE DIAL PRESS
750 Third Avenue
New York, New York 10017

TRADE SALES DEPT.

BUSINESS REPLY MAIL
No Postage Stamp Necessary if Mailed in the United States

FIRST CLASS
PERMIT NO. 2317
NEW YORK, N.Y.

THE DIAL PRESS
750 Third Avenue
New York, New York 10017

TRADE SALES DEPT.